MW01629294

Second Grade Thinking Skills and Key Concepts

TEACHER'S MANUAL

Thinking Skills and Key Concepts products available in print or eBook form.

• Kindergarten • First Grade • Second Grade

Written by

Sandra Parks
Howard Black

Graphic Design by
Howard Black

© 2016
THE CRITICAL THINKING CO.™
www.CriticalThinking.com
Phone: 800-458-4849 • Fax: 541-756-1758
1991 Sherman Ave., Suite 200 • North Bend • OR 97459
ISBN 978-1-60144-845-3

MIX
Paper from responsible sources
FSC www.fsc.org FSC® C011935

Reproduction of This Copyrighted Material
The intellectual material in this product is the copyrighted property of The Critical Thinking Co.™ The individual or entity who initially purchased this product from The Critical Thinking Co.™ or one of its authorized resellers is licensed to reproduce (print or duplicate on paper) each page of this product for use within one home or one classroom. Our copyright and this limited reproduction permission (user) agreement strictly prohibit the sale of any of the copyrighted material in this product. Any reproduction beyond these expressed limits is strictly prohibited without the written permission of The Critical Thinking Co.™ Please visit http://www.criticalthinking.com/copyright for more information. The Critical Thinking Co.™ retains full intellectual property rights on all its products (eBooks, books, and software).
Printed in the United States of America by McNaughton & Gunn, Inc., Saline, MI (Mar. 2016)

Table of Contents

© 2016 The Critical Thinking Co.™ • www.CriticalThinking.com • 800-458-4849

© 2016 The Critical Thinking Co.™ • www.CriticalThinking.com • 800-458-4849

THINKING SKILLS AND KEY CONCEPTS

GOALS/STUDENT OUTCOMES

- Improve young students' vocabulary development and observation skills
- Clarify thinking processes required for concept learning (identifying similarities and differences, sequencing, classifying, and recognizing analogy)
- Improve students' understanding of mathematics, social studies, and science concepts
- Improve students' listening, speaking, and writing skills

THINKING SKILLS INSTRUCTION

FIGURAL SKILLS

Describing Shapes
Naming shapes, finding shapes to match a description, and describing characteristics of a shape

Figural Similarities and Differences
Matching shapes, drawing equal parts

Figural Sequences
Recognizing and producing the next figure in a sequence

Figural Classification
Classifying by shape and/or color, forming classes

Figural Analogies
Completing analogies about size, color, and rotation

Describing Things
Matching a picture to a description, describing people or objects shown in pictures, describing parts of a whole

Verbal Similarities and Differences
Comparing and contrasting occupations, animals, and geographical features

Verbal Classifications
Explaining characteristics of a class, exceptions, and sorting objects or people into classes

Verbal Analogies
Completing analogies about important characteristics

Observation Skills
Identifying significant details in pictures that show examples of key concepts

CONTENT OBJECTIVES

MATHEMATICS OBJECTIVES

Properties of Polygons & Solids
Describing angles, parallel sides, polygons, and solids; drawing common polygons

Reading and Writing Mathematical Terms
Recognizing and using geometry terms, ordinal numbers, and positional words

Pattern Recognition
Recognizing sequential patterns, rotation, and analogies

Fractions
Identifying and drawing halves, thirds, fourths

SOCIAL STUDIES CONCEPTS

Geographical Features
Land forms, bodies of water, latitude, longitude, directions, locations on maps

Occupations
Consumer/ producer, goods/ services, kinds of workers (health, government, construction, sales)

Communities
Families, jobs, buildings, transportation, government Native American, and colonial communities

Economics
Wants/needs; making, saving, spending money

SCIENCE CONCEPTS

Matter, Water, and Weather

Animals
Living/non-living things, plants/ animals, type of animal (fish, bird, mammal, amphibian, reptile, insect), habitat, live birth/eggs, life cycle, protection, food

METHODS TO IMPROVE THINKING AND LEARNING

Direct Instruction
Prior knowledge, objective, practice, metacognition, application

Developmental Forms
Concrete (pictures and picture books), semi-concrete (student book), abstract (discussion)

Cooperative Learning
Paired problem-solving, think/pair/share

Graphic Organizers
Show thinking (description, compare and/or contrast, order, class relationships)

Whole Sentence Responding
Instructions and activities use complete sentences

Mental Models
Graphics show key characteristics of mathematics, social studies, science concepts

Language Integration
Activities promoting vocabulary acquisition include drawing activities, discussing picture books, writing paragraphs to explain key concepts

PROGRAM EVALUATION

- Student performance on language proficiency and cognitive abilities tests
- Student performance on normed- or criterion-referenced achievement tests
- Improved student writing
- Number of students placed in advanced academic classes, including gifted programs, and subsequent successful performance in such classes

Introduction

PROGRAM DESIGN

Rationale

Thinking Skills and Key Concepts is a program is designed to:

- Improve students' observation and description skills
- Develop academic vocabulary
- Develop thinking processes that underlie content learning (describing/defining, identifying similarities/differences, sequencing, classifying, and analogy)
- Improve students' understanding of important mathematics, social studies, and science concepts taught in second grade
- Improve students' listening, speaking, and writing skills.

In *Second Grade Thinking Skills and Key Concepts* lessons, students describe the properties of polygons and solids, matter, water, weather, geographical features, occupations, communities, and animals.

Thinking Skills

The thinking skills developed in this program include describing, finding similarities and differences, sequencing, and classifying. These processes were selected because of their prevalence in academic disciplines, particularly mathematics and science instruction. Students must be proficient in these thinking skills because most state standards, particularly those based on the Common Core State Standards, emphasize concept development and reading comprehension.

These thinking processes are commonly featured on achievement and cognitive abilities tests. Since improved school performance is an important goal of thinking skills instruction, activities provide many variations of each thinking skill.

Within each chapter, thinking skills are sequenced in the order in which a child develops intellectually. A student first observes and describes objects, recognizes their characteristics, distinguishes similarities and differences, puts objects or events in order, and groups objects by class.

To transfer thinking skills to other contexts, students must remember the steps in their own thinking. They practice metacognition of the thinking skill in each lesson. In each chapter, lessons feature the same thinking processes, giving students many transfer examples. This repetition builds students' confidence and competence as thinkers and learners.

Academic Vocabulary Development

Students discuss detailed photographs in order to develop key terms associated with mathematics, science, and social studies. Through peer discussion students with limited vocabulary hear and express the properties of key academic concepts. Since most state standards promote increased use of non-fiction books to improve reading comprehension, most lessons are introduced by discussing picture books that feature details to improve students' background about concepts in science and social studies.

Second Grade Thinking Skills and Key Concepts features numerous activities for listening, speaking, and writing. Thinking skills lessons emphasize writing as a technique for improved content learning. Lessons include writing structured sentences to express the thinking skills taught in that chapter.

INSTRUCTIONAL METHODS

Direct Instruction

Each chapter features direct instruction for each thinking process. When introducing a skill, the teacher identifies a school-related or non-academic example

© 2016 The Critical Thinking Co.™ • www.CriticalThinking.com • 800-458-4849

in which the student has used that thinking process, cueing the student that he or she already has some experience and competence with that skill. Stating the lesson objective clarifies both the content and the thinking skill.

The "Thinking About Thinking" section of each lesson reminds students of the thinking process practiced in the lesson. Research on thinking process instruction indicates that, without metacognition, subsequent transfer is less likely. Metacognition is fostered by peer and class discussion. The student then identifies other contexts in which he or she has used this skill. This association with past personal experience increases the student's confidence in his or her thinking and encourages transfer of the skill.

Developmental Forms

Students clarify their thinking by peer and class discussion of richly detailed photographs. Colored drawings, photographs, and picture books depict the significant details that illustrate examples of key concepts. Peer and class discussion clarify concepts and promote vocabulary.

Listening and speaking employ different learning styles, allowing students to recognize different ways to describe an object. Discussion reinforces the student's memory of the thinking process, promotes transfer to similar tasks, and enhances his or her confidence and willingness to participate in class.

Cooperative Learning

Peer discussion significantly enhances language acquisition, particularly for second-language students. Through conversations, students hear and express both the thinking process and the content. Before students learn to read (an in-put process), they first listen (a more basic in-put process). Before students write (an out-put process), they first speak (a more basic out-put process).

Many students of poverty have limited experience listening or speaking for a sustained period. Peer discussion promotes the quality and accuracy of students' responses. Evaluation of thinking skills instruction shows that young children, particularly bilingual students, gain confidence and willingness to participate in class discussion when they have had an opportunity to "rehearse" their comments with a partner.

Whole-Sentence Responding

In *Thinking Skills and Key Concepts* lessons and activities, students and teachers respond in whole sentences. Teachers who have used this technique report that this practice is so significant in promoting students' language proficiency, that it should be considered an essential element of instruction.

Mental Models

A mental model is a framework that features the key characteristics that a student must know to understand a concept. A mental model helps a student to:

- Predict what one needs to know to understand a new concept
- Remember characteristics
- State clear definitions or adequate descriptions
- Explain a concept to someone else

By the end of each chapter, second grade students should know the significant characteristics of each of the following concepts. Teachers should use picture books or actual objects, when possible, to illustrate the key characteristics shown below.

CONCEPT	KEY CHARACTERISTICS
Polygon	Lines (curved or straight, parallel or intersecting), sides (equal or unequal), number of sides, size of angle
Solids	Number of faces, what shape is seen from each side
Patterns	Describing color, size, shape, and color/size/shape sequences

Fractions	Halves, thirds, fourths
Matter	Solid, liquid, gas
Water	Properties, water cycle
Weather	Precipitation (rain, snow, hail, fog), instruments to measure
Land Forms/ Water Forms	Size, shape, height/depth, fresh/ salt, relationship to land or bodies of water
Living/Non-living things	Growth, food, reproduction, plants/ animals
Animals	Type (mammals, birds, fish, reptiles, insects, amphibians), live birth/hatch from eggs, vertebrate/ non-vertebrate, appearance, habitat, life cycle, behavior, protection
Needs and	Food, shelter, health care, safety, transportation
Jobs	Types of jobs (goods/services, government workers, health care workers, food workers, sales), what they do, equipment (clothing, vehicles, tools) where they work
Communities	Families, workers (producers/ services), government, transportation, buildings, finding community locations on a map
Country	Cardinal directions, geographical features, (equator, latitude, longitude), climate, Native Americans and Colonial communities

Language Integration Activities

Language acquisition research suggests several strategies to help young children develop and express new or partially-conceived concepts. *Thinking Skills and Key Concepts* lesson plans include drawing activities, storytelling, and writing exercises.

- **Drawing Activities -** Students depict details of concepts explored in the *Thinking Skills and Key Concepts* program (jobs, buildings, weather, animals, Native Americans and colonial communities).
- **Storytelling** - Personal narratives and imaginative stories extend concept development in the *Thinking Skills and Key Concepts* program.
- **Writing** - Students create sentences, definitions, descriptions, and paragraphs, and full stories about concepts featured in the *Thinking Skills and Key Concepts* lessons.
- **Picture Book Extension** - Fiction and nonfiction books for second grade students depict and explain important concepts. Curriculum guidelines based on Common Core State Standards emphasize using non-fiction books to promote reading comprehension and to teach science and social studies objectives. Consult your school librarian to identify appropriate books that show multicultural diversity.

EVALUATING THINKING SKILLS INSTRUCTION

Thinking skills instruction has been evaluated using many assessment procedures:

- Student performance on cognitive abilities tests
- Student performance on normed-referenced achievement tests
- Student performance on criterion-referenced achievement tests
- Student performance on language proficiency tests
- Number of students placed in heterogeneous grouped classes or advanced academic programs, as well as students' subsequent successful performance in gifted or academic excellence classes

Cognitive Abilities Tests

The figural and verbal subtests of cognitive abilities tests are closely correlated to *Thinking Skills and Key Concepts* goals and activities.

The following cognitive abilities tests have been used in program effectiveness

© 2016 The Critical Thinking Co.™ • www.CriticalThinking.com • 800-458-4849

evaluation of thinking instruction using the *Thinking Skills and Key Concepts* series:

- Cognitive Abilities Test (Woodcock-Johnson)
  Riverside Publishing Company
  425 Spring Lake Dr.
  Itasa, IL 60143
  800-323-9540 • 312-693-0325 (fax)
- Test of Cognitive Skills
  CTB-McGraw Hill
  P.O. Box 150
  Monterey, CA 93942-0150
  800-538-9547 • 800-282-0266 (fax)

Norm-Referenced Achievement Tests

Composite scores on norm-referenced achievement tests are generally poor indicators of improved thinking skills. Some subtests do reflect the thinking skills addressed in *Thinking Skills and Key Concepts* instruction. Program evaluation using this series has indicated substantial gains in subtests which measure reading comprehension and mathematics concepts. If achievement test information is used to report the effectiveness of *Thinking Skills and Key Concepts* instruction, only those subtests should be monitored.

Language Proficiency Tests

Program evaluation of *Thinking Skills and Key Concepts* shows substantial gains in vocabulary, reading comprehension, and mathematics. Most districts have not developed science and social studies assessments. Anecdotal data and students' drawings show unusual conceptualization of primary science and social studies concepts. Students using *Thinking Skills and Key Concepts* are found to be well prepared for third grade instruction in science and social studies which is commonly measured by state and local assessments.

Because one goal of the *Thinking Skills and Key Concepts* program is language development, increased vocabulary can be shown on a variety of language tests.

Tests commonly used to evaluate the effect of thinking instruction on language development include the following:

- Peabody Picture Vocabulary Test
- ESOL proficiency tests

Inclusion and Performance in Mainstream or Advanced Academic Classes

The *Thinking Skills and Key Concepts* series is commonly used to promote access to academic excellence programs or to prepare special education students to be successful in mainstream classes. This program has been successful in Title 1 classes, bilingual programs, ESOL classes, special education classes, and remedial programs. School districts evaluate this goal by the number of students who gain access to more advanced programs, the speed with which the transition is accomplished, and the students' level of achievement when included in general or advanced classes.

© 2016 The Critical Thinking Co.™ • www.CriticalThinking.com • 800-458-4849

INSTRUCTIONAL RECOMMENDATIONS

- **Schedule *Thinking Skills and Key Concepts* lessons.** Conduct thinking skills instruction to correlate with the content objective specified in local district's curriculum plan or pacing guide. Chapters that do not correlate closely may be taught at any time during the school year.
- **Teach thinking lessons consecutively.** Thinking skills lessons within each chapter are carefully sequenced to prepare students for classification and analogy skills. While the topic of each chapter can be scheduled to fit curriculum guides, once instruction has begun in each thinking skill chapter, lessons should be taught consecutively to complete the entire sequence.
- **Encourage peer discussion.** The quality of student responses and their attentiveness significantly improve when peers discuss their answers before class discussion. Peer discussion is particularly effective in special education, bilingual, and Title I classes.
- **Conduct short exercises.** Each page usually takes one 20-30 minute session in order to have time for the "Thinking About Thinking" and "Personal Application." Discuss a few exercises with ample time for students to explain their thinking, rather than conducting additional lessons.
- **Identify and use students' background knowledge.** Use these lessons diagnose students' prior knowledge. Remember the language that students use in their descriptions. Use the same words to remind students of the thinking processes in subsequent social studies and science lessons.
- **Use *Thinking Skills and Key Concepts* lessons before or after social studies or science activities.** Possible responses in each lesson plan exceed the answers commonly expected from students in second grade. Continue accepting students' comments until key characteristics have been mentioned. Jot down unusual responses in the lessons for future use.
- **Teach other mathematics, science, and social studies concepts using the same thinking processes.** Use correct terms for the thinking process to cue students to transfer the thinking process to other contexts. Use the same methods (peer and class discussion, observation of pictures or objects, etc.) in other lessons.
- **Insist that students use complete sentences when responding.** Students whose language proficiency is underdeveloped are inclined to answer in single words or phrases. To realize the language acquisition benefits of these lessons, students should answer in complete sentences, expressing whole thoughts that are grammatically correct.
- **Lessons should not be given as homework assignments or as an independent activities.** The lessons in *Thinking Skills and Key Concepts* are designed to enhance cognitive development through discussion and observation. Exercises from the student book should not be used as a substitute for class discussion.
- **Use non-fiction picture books to introduce concepts.** Before each lesson, read non-fiction picture books about animals, jobs, buildings, communities, Native Americans and Colonial communities that are featured in the lesson.
- **Check students' understanding of mental models.** At the end of each chapter discuss an example of weather, animals, jobs, buildings, or communities not featured in the lesson. Check whether students have internalized the mental model sufficiently so that they can identify the key characteristics without prompting.

© 2016 The Critical Thinking Co.™ • www.CriticalThinking.com • 800-458-4849

VOCABULARY AND SYNONYMS

Reinforce the language of thinking in thinking skills activities and in other lessons. The following list includes terms that teachers and students can use in *Thinking Skills and Key Concepts* lessons, content lessons, and personal applications. Students may create a "thinking thesaurus" of the words and idioms that they use to describe their thinking. Encourage them to express their thinking using the terms below.

WORD	SYNONYMS
Arrange	place, assemble, organize, put together, gather, build
Category	class, group, kind, type
Class	group, category, kind, type
Classify	arrange, group
Compare	match, find similarities
Contrasts	differs, is unlike
Decrease	lessen, shrink, become smaller
Definition	meaning, explanation, description
Describe	explain, give details
Detail	part, piece
Differences	unlike, contrasts, not like
Discuss	talk about, describe, explain
Eliminate	remove, take out, erase, end
Equal	same, matching, same size
Examine	find the details, look at
Explain	make sure, show, tell
False	not true, not real, untrue, unreal
Figural	drawn, geometric
Figure	shape, diagram, drawing
Geometric	figural, having shape
Identify	find, recognize, pick out, show
Locate	identify, place, find
Location	place, position
Matching	equal, making an equal pair
Member	belongs to a group or class
Observe	pay attention to, examine, look at carefully
Order	rank, sequence
Part	piece, detail
Pattern	arrangement, design
Prepare	produce, create, ready, plan
Produce	make, create, assemble
Recognize	identify, be familiar with
Relationship	connection, how related or similar
Select	pick out, identify, locate, decide
Sequence	steps, order, rank, change
Shape	figure, pattern, drawing
Significant	important, basic
Similarity	likeness, sameness
Sort	group, classify, organize
True	real, correct, accurate
Verbal	spoken, said in words
Whole	entire, complete, total

GUIDE TO USING THE LESSON PLANS

CHAPTER TITLE

CURRICULUM APPLICATIONS

Lists content objectives which feature the thinking skill or require it as a prerequisite.

TEACHING SUGGESTIONS

Alerts the teacher to special vocabulary or concepts in the lesson. Identifies materials or special concerns when conducting the lessons.

LESSON

Introduction

Indicates to the student when he or she has seen or used a similar kind of learning.

Stating the Objective

Teacher Comment: Explains to the student what he or she will learn in the lesson.

Conducting the Lesson

Teacher Comment: **Bold type shows suggested dialogue for teachers.**

Student Response: Sample student answers.

Thinking About Thinking

Helps the student clarify and verbalize the thinking process: metacognition.

Personal Application

Relates the skill to the student's experience and cues the student when to use the thinking skill.

© 2016 The Critical Thinking Co.™ • www.CriticalThinking.com • 800-458-4849

CHAPTER ONE – DESCRIBING SHAPES (Pages 1-26)
GENERAL INTRODUCTION

CURRICULUM APPLICATIONS
Language Arts: Use visual discrimination for reading readiness.
Mathematics: Name geometric shapes.
Science: Recognize shapes of leaves, insects, or shells.
Social Studies: Recognize geographic features on maps.
Enrichment Areas: Recognize shapes of road signs; describing patterns in art.

TEACHING SUGGESTIONS
- Ask students to discuss and explain their answers in complete sentences. When asked, "How many sides does a square have?" a student may correctly answer "four." If the student responds, "A square has four sides," he or she has named the shape and its characteristics, imprinting the term for its shape and properties. This practice seems artificial at first, but it promotes vocabulary development for young children, especially second-language learners.
- Integrate these shape terms into your language arts program by discussing picture books which emphasize shape.
- In many of these lessons the teacher directions to students include language that shows order (first ..., next...., last; first ..., second ..., third ...., last). Many young students may not understand or use these terms. Repeating of these sequences and hearing them in student responses models the language patterns that students will need in primary grades writing tasks.
- Ask students to cut out pictures of objects that are good examples of the shapes discussed in this chapter. Organize their pictures into a bulletin board display, grouping and labeling the objects by shape.

Page 2: DESCRIBING LINES

LESSON

Introduction
Teacher Comment: **Lines are thin marks that can be any color. Some lines are straight. Some lines are curved. Some curved lines are open and some are closed.**

Explaining the Objective
Teacher Comment: **In this lesson you will identify lines and color them.**

Conducting the Lesson
Teacher Comment: **Look at the box at the top of the page. Some of the lines are straight and some are curved. Color the straight lines red; color the curved lines blue.**

- Check students' work.

Teacher Comment: **Look at the curves in the second box. Some of the curves are open and some are closed. Color the open curves green. Color the closed curves purple.**

© 2016 The Critical Thinking Co.™ • www.CriticalThinking.com • 800-458-4849

• Check students' work.

Teacher Comment: **Look at the pictures in the third box. Notice that some of the curves are open and some are closed. Circle the pictures that show open curves green. Circle the pictures that show closed curves purple.**

• Check students' work.

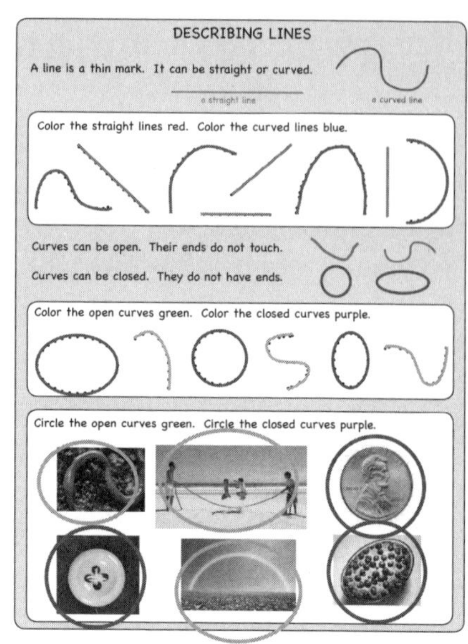

Thinking About Thinking

Teacher Comment: **What did you think about when you colored the curved or straight lines?**

Student Response:

1. I looked for straight lines and curved lines. I decided whether they were open or closed curves.
2. I checked how the lines looked and how it felt to draw a straight or a curved line.

Personal Application

Teacher Comment: **When do you need to draw straight or curved lines?**

Student Response: I need to draw straight or curved lines when I write letters or draw pictures.

Page 3: FINDING AND DRAWING CIRCLES AND OVALS

LESSON

Introduction

• Hold up a circle.

Teacher Comment: **A circle is a closed curve. (Run a finger around the circle to show that it is closed.) It has no beginning or end and looks the same from any side. (Rotate the circle to show that its appearance does not change.) What objects are shaped like a circle?**

• Answers will vary.

• Hold up an oval.

Teacher Comment: **An oval is also a closed curve. (Run a finger around the oval.) It looks like a flattened circle. (Rotate the oval to a vertical position.) In one position it looks tall. (Rotate the oval to a horizontal position.) Now it looks short.**

Explaining the Objective

Teacher Comment: **In this lesson you will trace and color circles and ovals.**

Conducting the Lesson

Teacher Comment: **Look at the first box. Name the objects that are circles.**

Student Response: The pictures of the watch, the bicycle, and the plate have circles.

Teacher Comment: **Draw a red line around each circle.**

• Check students' work.

© 2016 The Critical Thinking Co.™ • www.CriticalThinking.com • 800-458-4849

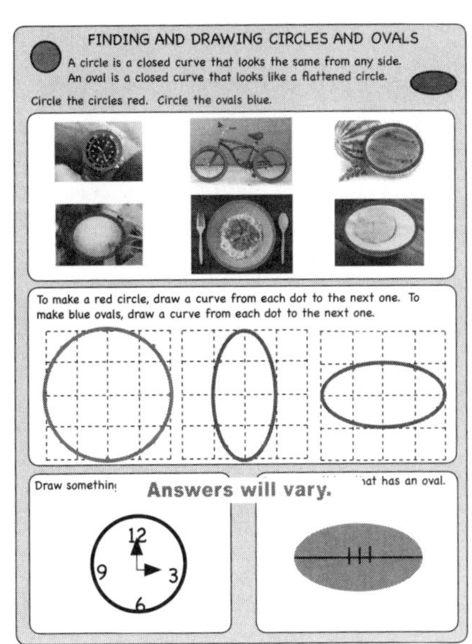
FINDING AND DRAWING CIRCLES AND OVALS

A circle is a closed curve that looks the same from any side.
An oval is a closed curve that looks like a flattened circle.

Circle the circles red. Circle the ovals blue.

To make a red circle, draw a curve from each dot to the next one. To make blue ovals, draw a curve from each dot to the next one.

Answers will vary.

Teacher Comment: **Name the pictures that have ovals.**
Student Response: The pictures of the watermelon, the lemon, and the egg have ovals.
Teacher Comment: **Draw a blue line around each oval.**

- Check students' work.

Teacher Comment: **Look at the second box. Draw a curve from one dot to another. Draw a red circle. Draw two blue ovals.**

- Check students' work.

Teacher Comment: **In the bottom boxes draw something that has a circle and something that has an oval.**

- Check students' work. Answers will vary.

Thinking About Thinking

Teacher Comment: **What did you think about when you traced circles and ovals?**
Student Response:
1. I looked for a curved line that looked like an "O" from all sides.
2. I looked for a curved line that looked like a flat "O" that looks tall or short from different sides.
3. I paid attention to how it felt to color and trace a circle, and how it felt different to trace and color an oval.

Personal Application

Teacher Comment: **When do you need to find or draw circles and ovals?**
Student Response: I need to find or draw circles when I'm making pictures or finding shapes.

Page 4: DESCRIBING LINES

LESSON

Introduction

Teacher Comment: **Sometimes straight lines cross and sometimes they do not. If they do not cross, they are parallel lines. They are always the same distance apart.**

Explaining the Objective

Teacher Comment: **In this lesson you will find parallel lines and lines that touch to make angles.**

Conducting the Lesson

Teacher Comment: **Look at the first box. Trace the parallel lines blue. Trace the lines that are not parallel green.**

- Check students' work.

- Use a folding ruler to make the angles and shapes in this lesson. Fold the ruler to make an acute angle like the green one. Hold up the acute angle and run a finger along the two sides to show the angle.

  Teacher Comment: **When straight lines touch, they form an angle. Sometimes the angle makes a sharp point like the green angle.**
- Open the ruler to make the top line completely vertical, making a right angle. Run a finger along the two sides to show the angle.

  Teacher Comment: **When the top line is straight up, it makes a square corner. A little red square is shown inside it. This square corner is called a right angle.**

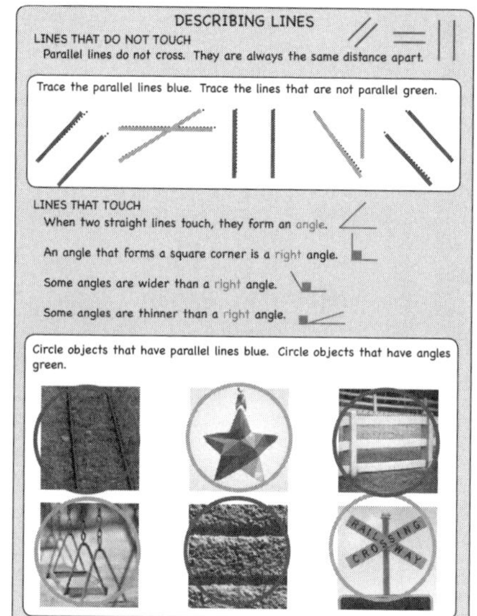
DESCRIBING LINES

LINES THAT DO NOT TOUCH

Parallel lines do not cross. They are always the same distance apart.

Trace the parallel lines blue. Trace the lines that are not parallel green.

LINES THAT TOUCH

When two straight lines touch, they form an angle.

An angle that forms a square corner is a right angle.

Some angles are wider than a right angle.

Some angles are thinner than a right angle.

Circle objects that have parallel lines blue. Circle objects that have angles green.

- Open the ruler wider to make an obtuse angle. Run a finger along the two sides to show the angle.

  Teacher Comment: **Sometimes an angle is wider than a right angle. Notice that the top angle is wider than the little red square.**
- Close the ruler to make a sharp angle. Run a finger along the two sides to show the angle.

  Teacher Comment: **Sometimes an angle is thinner than a right angle. Notice that the angle is much sharper than the little red square.**

  Teacher Comment: **Whether the angle is sharp, square, or wide, when two lines touch, they make an angle.**
- Identify some examples of sharp, right, or wide angles in objects in the classroom.

  Teacher Comment: **Name the objects in the bottom box.**

  Student Response: The objects are railroad tracks, a colored star, a fence, the side of a swing, lines in a brick wall, and a railway crossing sign.

  Teacher Comment: **Circle the objects that have parallel lines blue. Circle the objects that have angles green.**

- Check students' work.

Thinking About Thinking

Teacher Comment: **What did you think about when you showed which lines were parallel and which made angles?**

Student Response:

1. I looked for lines that did not cross; they were parallel.
2. I looked for lines that cross; they made angles.
3. I picked the colors to show whether the lines were parallel or made angles.

Personal Application

Teacher Comment: **When do you need to find parallel lines or angles?**

Student Response: I need to find parallel lines or angles when I draw most objects.

© 2016 The Critical Thinking Co.™ • www.CriticalThinking.com • 800-458-4849

Page 5: DESCRIBING POLYGONS

LESSON

Introduction

Teacher Comment: **When the ends of three or more lines touch, they form shapes called polygons.**

Explaining the Objective

In this lesson you will identify polygons and color them.

Conducting the Lesson

Teacher Comment: **Look at the drawings in the first box. Some of these designs are closed shapes. They are polygons. Some of these designs are not closed. They are not polygons. Color the polygons red. Mark an "X" through the designs that are not polygons.**

- Use a folding ruler to make an equilateral triangle.

Teacher Comment: **There are many kinds of polygons, depending on the number of their sides. When straight lines touch on three corners, they become a triangle. A triangle is a polygon with three sides and three angles.**

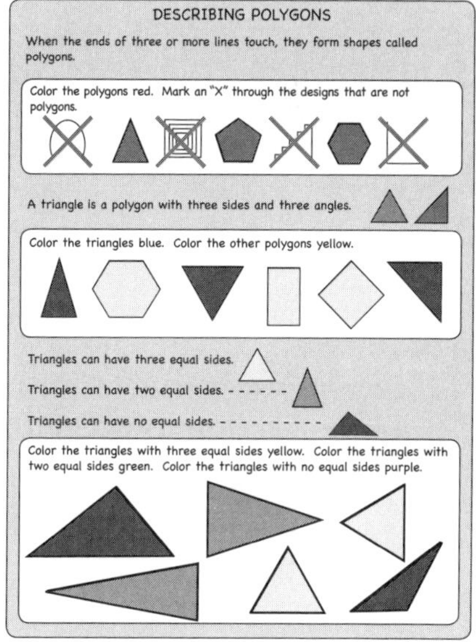
DESCRIBING POLYGONS

When the ends of three or more lines touch, they form shapes called polygons.

Color the polygons red. Mark an "X" through the designs that are not polygons.

A triangle is a polygon with three sides and three angles.

Color the triangles blue. Color the other polygons yellow.

Triangles can have three equal sides.

Triangles can have two equal sides.

Triangles can have no equal sides.

Color the triangles with three equal sides yellow. Color the triangles with two equal sides green. Color the triangles with no equal sides purple.

- Hold up the triangle and run your finger along all three sides, counting as you touch each side.

Teacher Comment: **Color the triangles blue. Color the other shapes yellow.**

- Hold up the triangle.

Teacher Comment: **Triangles can have three equal sides.**

- Fold the ruler to make two sides much longer in order to form a tall, sharp isosceles triangle.

Teacher Comment: **Sometimes the triangle can be very sharp like this one. It has two equal sides.**

- Fold the ruler to make an acute triangle with three uneven sides.

Teacher Comment: **Sometimes none of the sides are the same length.**

- Fold the ruler to make an obtuse triangle with three uneven sides.

Teacher Comment: **Sometimes the triangle looks slanted and none of the sides are the same length. It doesn't matter how long the sides are or how sharp the angles are. If the shape has only three sides, it is a triangle.**

- Identify some examples of triangles in objects in the classroom.

Teacher Comment: **In the third box, color the triangles with three equal sides yellow.**

- Check students' work.

Teacher Comment: **Color the triangles with two equal sides green.**

- Check students' work.

© 2016 The Critical Thinking Co.™ • www.CriticalThinking.com • 800-458-4849

Teacher Comment: **Color the triangles with no equal sides purple.**

• Check students' work.

Thinking About Thinking

Teacher Comment: **What did you think about when you showed which shapes were triangles?**

Student Response:

1. I checked whether the polygon had just three sides.
2. I checked the length of each side to tell whether the triangle had three equal sides, had only two equal sides, or had no equal sides.
3. I paid attention to how it felt different to color different kinds of triangles.

Personal Application

Teacher Comment: **When do you need to find triangles?**

Student response: I need to find triangles when I draw objects such as roofs, bridges, mountains, signs, etc.

Page 6: DESCRIBING TRIANGLES

LESSON

Introduction

Teacher Comment: **If a triangle has three equal sides, it also has three equal angles. If a triangle has two equal sides, it has two equal angles. If a triangle has no equal sides, it has no equal angles.**

Explaining the Objective

In this lesson you will identify how many equal angles a triangle may have.

Conducting the Lesson

Teacher Comment: **In the first box color the triangles with three equal angles yellow.**

• Check students' work.

Teacher Comment: **Color the triangles with two equal angles green.**

• Check students' work.

Teacher Comment: **Color the triangles with no equal angles purple.**

• Check students' work.

Teacher Comment: **In the second box find the triangles in the pictures and trace them blue.**

• Check students' work.

© 2016 The Critical Thinking Co.™ • www.CriticalThinking.com • 800-458-4849

Teacher Comment: **In the third box draw triangles by connecting the dots with straight lines.**

- Check students' work.

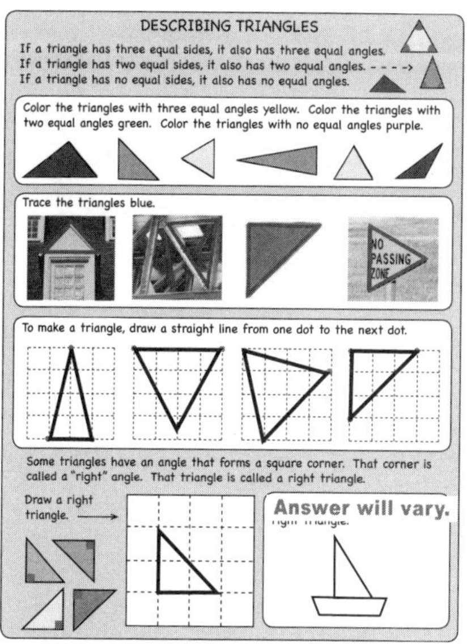

Teacher Comment: **Some triangles have an angle that forms a square corner. That corner is called a "right" angle. That triangle is called a right triangle. Look at the bottom boxes. Draw a right triangle in the box with lines.**

- Check students' work.

Teacher Comment: **In the empty box draw something that has a right angle.**

- Check students' work.

Thinking About Thinking

Teacher Comment: **What did you think about when you showed which triangles had equal angles?**

Student Response:

1. I knew that the number of equal angles was the same as the number of equal sides.
2. I checked whether three sides, two sides, or no sides were equal.
3. I picked the colors to show whether the shape was a triangle with three equal angles, two equal angles, or no angles equal.
4. I paid attention to how it felt to trace and color triangles with different sides and angles.

Personal Application

Teacher Comment: **When do you need to find triangles with equal angles?**

Student response: I need to find triangles when I draw objects such as tents, roofs, bridges, hats, and signs.

Page 7: DESCRIBING QUADRILATERALS

LESSON

Introduction

Teacher Comment: **A quadrilateral is a polygon with four sides and four angles. Some quadrilaterals, such as the green one, have no equal sides. Some quadrilaterals, such as the yellow one, have two equal sides–its tilted sides are equal. Some quadrilaterals, such as the blue square, have four equal sides.**

Explaining the Objective

In this lesson you will trace and draw quadrilaterals.

© 2016 The Critical Thinking Co.™ • www.CriticalThinking.com • 800-458-4849

Conducting the Lesson

Teacher Comment: **In the second box color the quadrilaterals orange. Color the other shapes purple.**

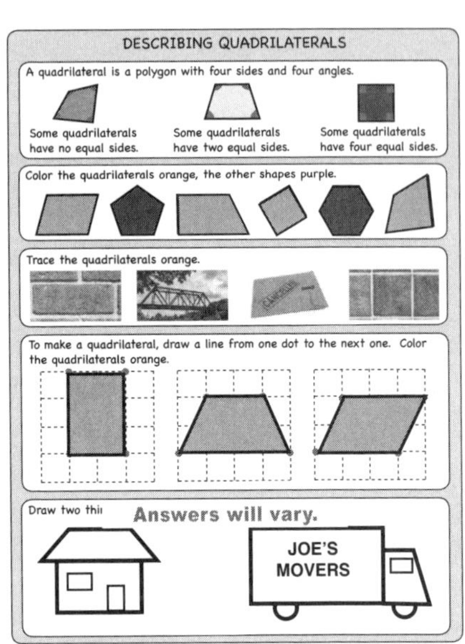

• Check students' work.

Teacher Comment: **In the third box find the quadrilaterals in the pictures and trace them orange.**

• Check students' work.

Teacher Comment: **In the fourth box draw quadrilaterals by connecting the dots with straight lines.**

• Check students' work.

Teacher Comment: **Look at the bottom box, draw two things that have quadrilaterals.**

• Check students' work.

Thinking About Thinking

Teacher Comment: **What did you think about when you showed which shapes were quadrilaterals?**

Student Response:

1. I checked whether the shape had four sides.
2. I picked the colors to show whether or not the shape was a quadrilateral.
3. I paid attention to how it felt to draw a quadrilateral.

Personal Application

Teacher Comment: **When do you need to draw quadrilaterals?**

Student response: I need to draw quadrilaterals when I draw boxes, doors, windows, money, signs, etc.

Page 8: DESCRIBING TRAPEZOIDS AND PARALLELOGRAMS

LESSON

Introduction

Teacher Comment: **Some quadrilaterals have one pair of parallel sides. That quadrilateral is a trapezoid. It looks like a triangle with its top cut off.**

• Use a folding ruler to make a trapezoid. Hold up the trapezoid.

Teacher Comment: **This shape is a trapezoid. It looks like a triangle with its top cut off.**

• Use your finger to trace where the top of that triangle would be.

Teacher Comment: **Notice that the trapezoid has four sides.**

• Run your finger along all four sides, counting as you touch each side.

© 2016 The Critical Thinking Co.™ • www.CriticalThinking.com • 800-458-4849

Teacher Comment: **Notice that the trapezoid is different from a rectangle because two of its sides are slanted.**

- Adjust the folding ruler to make a parallelogram.

Teacher Comment: **Some quadrilaterals have two pairs of parallel sides. One pair is the top and bottom of the shape.**

- Run your finger along the top and bottom.

Teacher Comment: **The other pair of parallel sides is the sides of the shape. That quadrilateral is a parallelogram.**

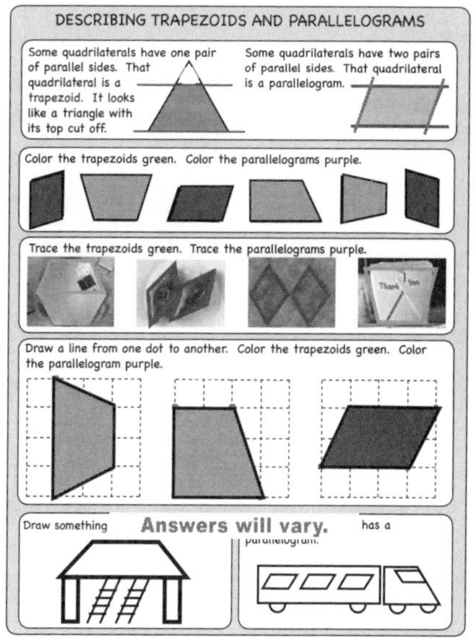
DESCRIBING TRAPEZOIDS AND PARALLELOGRAMS

Some quadrilaterals have one pair of parallel sides. That quadrilateral is a trapezoid. It looks like a triangle with its top cut off.

Some quadrilaterals have two pairs of parallel sides. That quadrilateral is a parallelogram.

Color the trapezoids green. Color the parallelograms purple.

Trace the trapezoids green. Trace the parallelograms purple.

Draw a line from one dot to another. Color the trapezoids green. Color the parallelogram purple.

Draw something Answers will vary. has a

Explaining the Objective

In this lesson you will identify, trace, and draw trapezoids and parallelograms.

Conducting the Lesson

Teacher Comment: **In the second box color the trapezoids green. Color the parallelograms purple.**

- Check students' work.

Teacher Comment: **In the third box find the trapezoids and parallelograms in the photographs. Trace the trapezoids green. Trace the parallelograms purple.**

- Check students' work.

Teacher Comment: **In the fourth box draw two trapezoids and a parallelogram by connecting the dots with straight lines.**

- Check students' work.

Teacher Comment: **Look at the bottom boxes. In one box draw something that has a trapezoid. In the other box draw something that has a parallelogram.**

- Check students' work.

Thinking About Thinking

Teacher Comment: **What did you think about when you showed which shapes were trapezoids or parallelograms?**

Student Response:

1. I checked whether the shape had one or two pairs of parallel lines.
2. I paid attention to how it felt to draw and color trapezoids and parallelograms.

Personal Application

Teacher Comment: **When do you need to find trapezoids or parallelograms?**

Student response: I need to find trapezoids or parallelograms to draw objects such as trains, boats, roofs, or things that have those shapes.

Page 9: DESCRIBING RECTANGLES AND SQUARES

LESSON

Introduction

Teacher Comment: **In the last lesson we learned about parallelograms. A rectangle is a parallelogram with four sides and four right angles. A square is a rectangle with equal sides.**

Explaining the Objective

In this lesson you will trace and draw rectangles and squares.

Conducting the Lesson

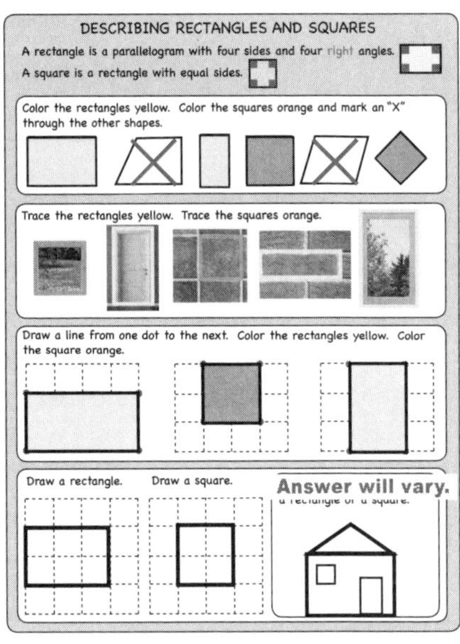

Teacher Comment: **In the first box color the rectangles yellow. Color the squares orange.**

• Check students' work.

Teacher Comment: **In the first box mark the shapes that are not rectangles or squares with an "X."**

• Check students' work.

Teacher Comment: **In the second box are pictures of rectangles and squares. Trace the rectangles yellow. Trace the squares orange.**

• Check students' work.

Teacher Comment: **In the third box draw two rectangles and a square by connecting the dots with straight lines. Color the rectangles yellow and the square orange.**

• Check students' work.

Teacher Comment: **On the dotted lines draw a rectangle and a square.**

• Check students' work.

Teacher Comment: **In the empty box draw something that has either a rectangle or a square.**

Thinking About Thinking

Teacher Comment: **What did you think about when you showed which shapes were rectangles and which were squares?**

Student Response:

1. I checked whether all four sides were equal or whether two sides were longer.
2. I picked the colors to show whether the shape was a rectangle or square.
3. I paid attention to how it felt different to trace and color a rectangle or a square.

 © 2016 The Critical Thinking Co.™ • www.CriticalThinking.com • 800-458-4849

Personal Application

Teacher Comment: **When do you need to find rectangles and squares?**

Student response: I need to find rectangles and squares when I draw objects such as boxes, doors, windows, boats, trains, etc.

Page 10: DESCRIBING PENTAGONS AND HEXAGONS

LESSON

Introduction

Teacher Comment: **A polygon with five sides and five angles is a pentagon. A polygon with six sides and six angles is a hexagon.**

Explaining the Objective

Teacher Comment: **In this lesson you will trace and draw pentagons and hexagons.**

Conducting the Lesson

Teacher Comment: **In the first box color the pentagons green. Color the hexagons purple. Mark the other shapes with an "X."**

- Check students' work.

Teacher Comment: **In the second box, which objects are pentagons?**

Student response: The home plate and the traffic sign are pentagons.

Teacher Comment: **Trace those pentagons green.**

- Check students' work.

Teacher Comment: **In the second box, which objects are hexagons?**

Student response: The table, the bolt nuts, and the honey comb are hexagons.

Teacher Comment: **Trace those hexagons purple.**

- Check students' work.

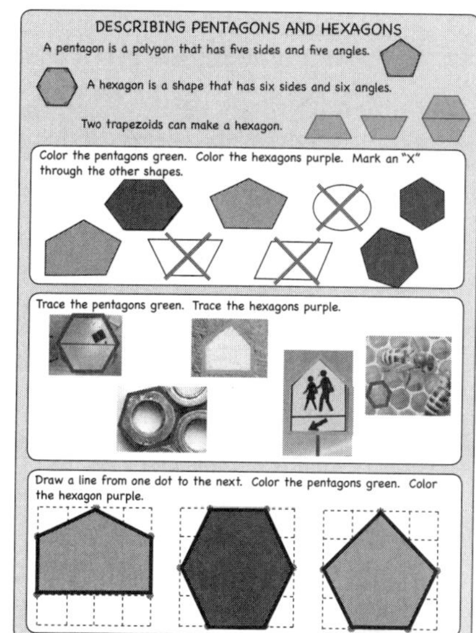

Teacher Comment: **In the third box draw a line from one dot to the next.**

- Check students' work.

Teacher Comment: **Color the pentagons green. Color the hexagon purple.**

- Check students' work.

Thinking About Thinking

Teacher Comment: **What did you think about when you showed which shapes were pentagons or hexagons?**

Student Response:

1. I checked whether the shape had five or six sides.
2. I picked the colors to show that the shape was a pentagon or hexagon.
3. I paid attention to how it felt to trace and color a pentagon or hexagon.

Personal Application

Teacher Comment: **When do you need to find pentagons or hexagons?**

Student Response: I need to find pentagons or hexagons when I draw objects that have them.

Page 11: FINDING POLYGONS IN A DESIGN

LESSON

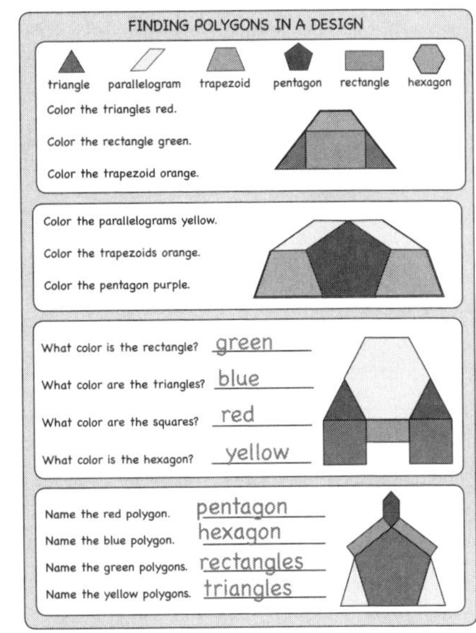

Introduction

Teacher Comment: **We have drawn different polygons.**

Explaining the Objective

Teacher Comment: **In this lesson you will find and color different polygons in designs.**

Conducting the Lesson

Teacher Comment: **In the top box color the triangles red. Color the rectangle green. Color the trapezoid orange.**

Teacher Comment: **In the second box color the parallelograms yellow. Color the trapezoids orange. Color the pentagon purple.**

Teacher Comment: **In the third box write the color of each kind of polygon.**

Teacher Comment: **In the bottom box write the name of the polygon that is colored.**

Thinking About Thinking

Teacher Comment: **What did you think about to find and color polygons in a design?**

Student Response:

1. I matched each polygon to its color.
2. I colored each polygon to match its color.
3. I named the shape or color of each polygon.

Personal Application

Teacher Comment: **When do you need to find or color polygons in a design?**

Student Response: I need to find or color polygons to draw pictures that contain different shapes.

© 2016 The Critical Thinking Co.™ • www.CriticalThinking.com • 800-458-4849

Page 12: MATCHING SHAPE AND PICTURE

LESSON

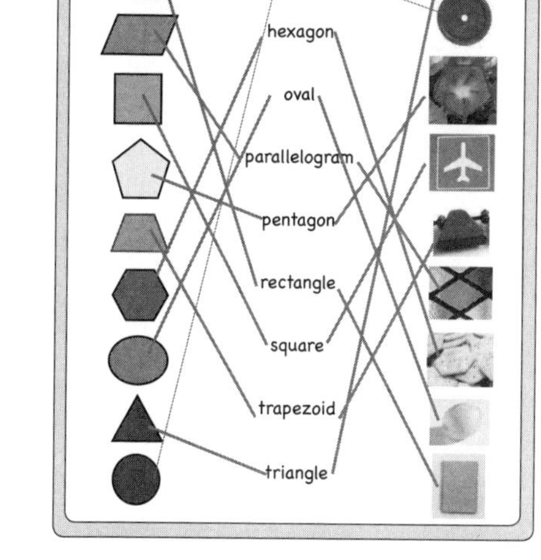

Introduction

Teacher Comment: **We have studied different shapes.**

Explaining the Objective

Teacher Comment: **In this lesson you will match drawings and pictures of shapes to their names.**

Conducting the Lesson

Teacher Comment: **The second word on the list is "hexagon." Draw a line from the word "hexagon" to the drawing of a hexagon. Draw a line from the word "hexagon"to the picture of an object that is a hexagon.**

- Check students' work. If students correctly and confidently match the name to the drawings of the remaining polygons, direct them to complete the rest of the exercise. If not repeat this dialog for the whole lesson.

Thinking About Thinking

Teacher Comment: **What did you think about when you matched shape words to drawings and pictures?**

Student Response:

1. I read the word for each shape.
2. I found the drawing that matches then I found the picture that shows that shape.

Personal Application

Teacher Comment: **When do you need to find a shape in a picture?**

Student response: I need to find a shape in a picture to draw or describe it.

Pages 13: DESCRIBING SHAPES

LESSON

Introduction

Teacher Comment: **We have matched shape names to drawings and pictures.**

Explaining the Objective

Teacher Comment: **In this lesson you will use words from a WORD BOX to name and describe the angles and sides of polygons.**

Conducting the Lesson

Teacher Comment: **Name the shape in the first box.**

Student Response: The first shape is a triangle.

Teacher Comment: **How many sides and angles does a triangle have?**

© 2016 The Critical Thinking Co.™ • www.CriticalThinking.com • 800-458-4849

Student Response: A triangle has three sides and three angles.

Teacher Comment: **Write those words on the blanks in the first box.**

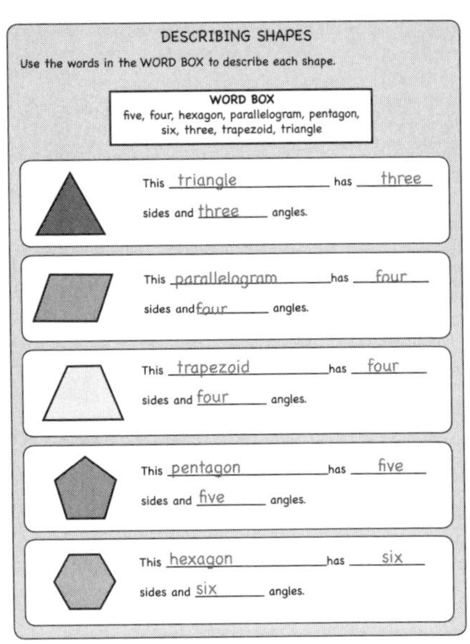

- Check students' work. Continue this dialog to discuss students' answers.

Thinking About Thinking

Teacher Comment: **What did you think about when you named each shape and described its sides and angles?**

Student Response:

1. I remembered the name of the shape.
2. I found the word for its name and wrote it.
3. I then found the word for its number of sides and angles and wrote it.

Personal Application

Teacher Comment: **When do you need to name and describe polygons?**

Student Response: I need to tell the name and describe polygons when I am asked to describe or write about them.

Page 14: DESCRIBING QUADRILATERALS

LESSON

Introduction

Teacher Comment: **We have learned the names of polygons and have counted their sides and angles.**

Explaining the Objective

Teacher Comment: **In this lesson you will use words from a WORD BOX to name quadrilaterals and describe their sides.**

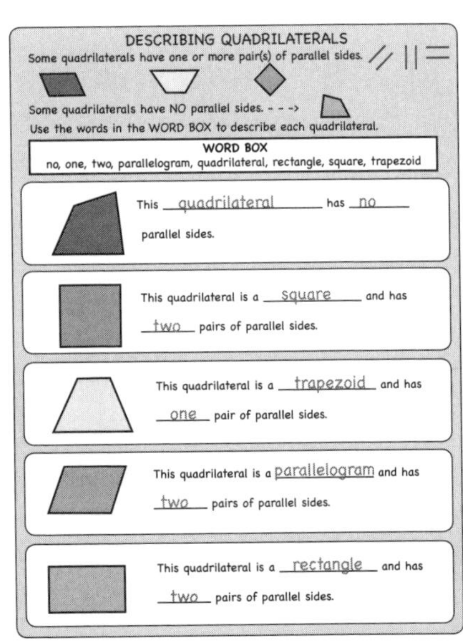

Conducting the Lesson

Teacher Comment: **The drawings at the top of the page show that quadrilaterals can have no parallel sides, one pair, or two pairs of parallel sides. Describe the number of parallel sides you see in the red shape in the top box.**

Student Response: The red shape is a quadrilateral with no parallel sides.

Teacher Comment: **Write those words on the blanks in the first box.**

- Check students' work. Continue this dialog to discuss students' answers.

© 2016 The Critical Thinking Co.™ • www.CriticalThinking.com • 800-458-4849

Thinking About Thinking

Teacher Comment: **What did you think about when you wrote a description of a shape?**

Student Response:

1. I named the shape and then counted its pairs of parallel sides.
2. I found the word for the shape and copied it.

Personal Application

Teacher Comment: **When do you need to write about a shape?**

Student Response: I need to write about shapes when I write about objects.

Page 15: DESCRIBING QUADRILATERALS

LESSON

Introduction

Teacher Comment: **We have learned the names of quadrilaterals and have counted their pairs of parallel sides.**

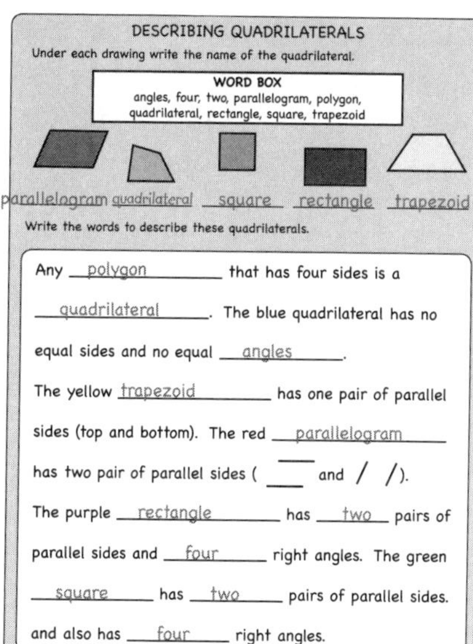
DESCRIBING QUADRILATERALS

Under each drawing write the name of the quadrilateral.

WORD BOX
angles, four, two, parallelogram, polygon, quadrilateral, rectangle, square, trapezoid

parallelogram quadrilateral square rectangle trapezoid

Write the words to describe these quadrilaterals.

Any polygon that has four sides is a quadrilateral. The blue quadrilateral has no equal sides and no equal angles. The yellow trapezoid has one pair of parallel sides (top and bottom). The red parallelogram has two pair of parallel sides (— and / /). The purple rectangle has two pairs of parallel sides and four right angles. The green square has two pairs of parallel sides. and also has four right angles.

Explaining the Objective

Teacher Comment: **In this lesson you will use words from a WORD BOX to name quadrilaterals and describe their parallel sides.**

Conducting the Lesson

Teacher Comment: **The drawings at the top of the page show five quadrilaterals. Write their names on the lines beneath each drawing.**

- Check students' work.

Teacher Comment: **Use the words from the WORD BOX to complete the paragraph.**

- Check students' work.

Thinking About Thinking

Teacher Comment: **What did you think about when you wrote a description of a shape?**

Student Response:

1. I named the shape and then counted its pairs of parallel sides.
2. I found the word for the shape and copied it.

Personal Application

Teacher Comment: **When do you need to write about or describe a shape?**

Student Response: I need to write about or describe shapes when I write about or describe objects.

© 2016 The Critical Thinking Co.™ • www.CriticalThinking.com • 800-458-4849

Page 16: DESCRIBING POLYGONS

LESSON

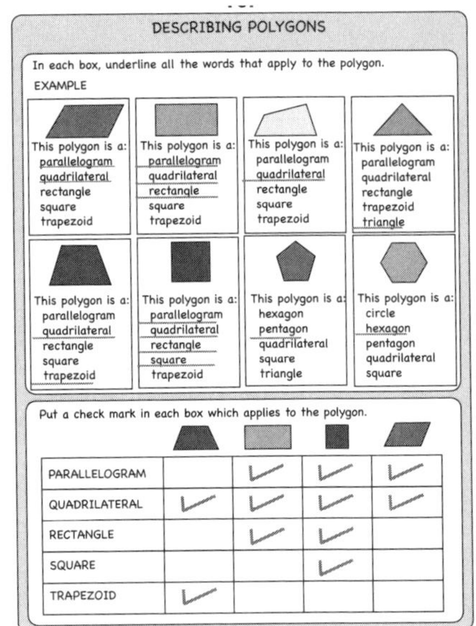

DESCRIBING POLYGONS

In each box, underline all the words that apply to the polygon.

EXAMPLE

This polygon is a: parallelogram quadrilateral rectangle square trapezoid

This polygon is a: parallelogram quadrilateral rectangle square trapezoid

This polygon is a: parallelogram quadrilateral rectangle square trapezoid

This polygon is a: parallelogram quadrilateral rectangle trapezoid triangle

This polygon is a: parallelogram quadrilateral rectangle square trapezoid

This polygon is a: parallelogram quadrilateral rectangle square trapezoid

This polygon is a: hexagon pentagon quadrilateral square triangle

This polygon is a: circle hexagon pentagon quadrilateral square

Put a check mark in each box which applies to the polygon.

PARALLELOGRAM		✓	✓	✓
QUADRILATERAL	✓	✓	✓	✓
RECTANGLE		✓	✓	
SQUARE			✓	
TRAPEZOID	✓			

Introduction

Teacher Comment: **We have learned the names of quadrilaterals and have counted their pairs of parallel sides.**

Explaining the Objective

Teacher Comment: **In this lesson you will identify the words that apply to a polygon.**

Conducting the Lesson

Teacher Comment: **The red polygon is a quadrilateral that is a parallelogram. Both these words are underlined in the example. Name the orange polygon.**

Student Response: The orange polygon is a rectangle.

Teacher Comment: **What other words apply to a rectangle?**

Student Response: The rectangle is quadrilateral and a parallelogram.

Teacher Comment: **Underline "parallelogram," "quadrilateral," and "rectangle."**

• Check students' work. Continue this dialog to discuss students' answers.

Teacher Comment: **In the lower box, put a check mark by each word that fits the polygon.**

Thinking About Thinking

Teacher Comment: **What did you think about when you identified the words that apply to a polygon?**

Student Response:

1. I checked whether each word fit the shape above that box.
2. I realized many words would describe the same shape.

Personal Application

Teacher Comment: **When do you need to identify words that apply to a polygon?**

Student Response: I need to write about shapes when I write a description of what I see.

Page 17: DRAWING EQUAL SHAPES

LESSON

Introduction

Teacher Comment: **We have studied and described polygons.**

Explaining the Objective

Teacher Comment: **In this lesson you will draw a polygon that is the identical size and shape.**

© 2016 The Critical Thinking Co.™ • www.CriticalThinking.com • 800-458-4849

Conducting the Lesson

Teacher Comment: **The blue rectangle is three spaces wide and four spaces high. To draw an equal shape, count spaces, not dots. Name the polygon you see in the second box. Tell how wide and how high it is.**

Student Response: The trapezoid is four spaces wide and three spaces high.

Teacher Comment: **On the dot grid draw a trapezoid that is four spaces wide and three spaces high.**

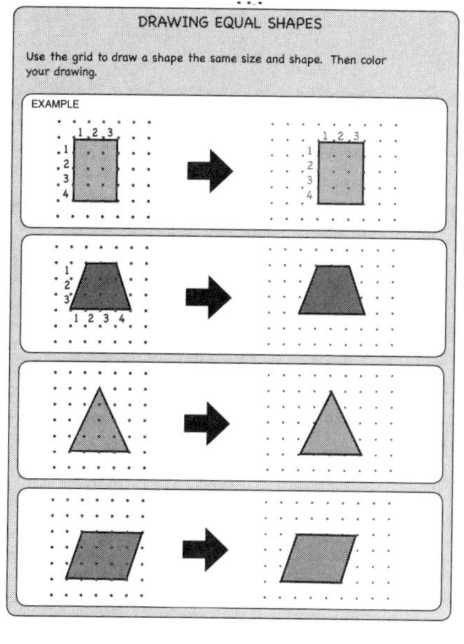

- Check students' work. Continue this dialog to discuss students' answers.

Thinking About Thinking

Teacher Comment: **What did you think about when you drew equal shapes?**

Student Response:

1. I counted the number of spaces that the shape was wide and high.
2. I used the dots to find where to draw the angles.
3. I paid attention to how it felt to draw and color equal polygons.

Personal Application

Teacher Comment: **When do you need to draw equal shapes?**

Student Response: I need to draw equal shapes when I copy a picture.

Page 18: DRAWING SHAPES

LESSON

Introduction

Teacher Comment: **We have learned to draw equal shapes.**

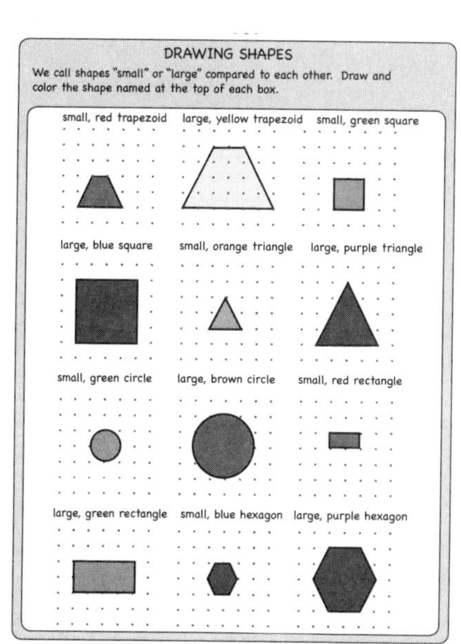

Explaining the Objective

Teacher Comment: **In this lesson you will draw and color polygons to fit a description.**

Conducting the Lesson

Teacher Comment: **The drawings are examples of a small and a large trapezoid. How wide and how high is the small, red trapezoid?**

Student Response: The small, red trapezoid is three spaces wide and two spaces high.

Teacher Comment: **How wide and how high is the large, yellow trapezoid?**

Student Response: The large, yellow trapezoid is six spaces wide and four spaces high.

© 2016 The Critical Thinking Co.™ • www.CriticalThinking.com • 800-458-4849

Teacher Comment: **Draw and color a small, green square on the grid at the right.**

- Check students' work. If students can read the descriptions, allow them to draw and color the remaining shapes. If not, continue this dialog to direct students' drawings.

Thinking About Thinking

Teacher Comment: **What did you think about when you drew small or large shapes?**

Student Response:

1. I decided how large or small a shape should be by counting spaces.
2. I checked the color that I should pick.
3. I used the dots to draw the right shape and the right size.

Personal Application

Teacher Comment: **When do you need to draw shapes to fit a description?**

Student Response: I need to draw shapes that follow the directions given.

Page 19: FINDING SHAPES

LESSON

Introduction

Teacher Comment: **We have learned to draw shapes.**

Explaining the Objective

Teacher Comment: **In this lesson you will show which shapes make a design.**

Conducting the Lesson.

Teacher Comment: **Name the yellow shape.**

Student Response: The yellow shape is a square.

Teacher Comment: **The yellow square is made of two parts. At the right are four rectangles. Look at the sizes of the shapes on the right. Circle the two that make the square figure on the left.**

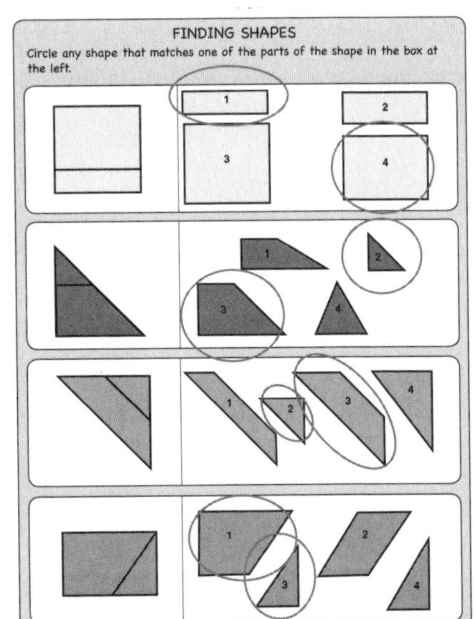

- Check students' work.

Teacher Comment: **Shapes one and four should be circled. Why were shapes two and three not circled?**

Student Response: Shapes two and three are each too tall.

- Check students' work. Continue this dialog to discuss students' answers.

 © 2016 The Critical Thinking Co.™ • www.CriticalThinking.com • 800-458-4849

Thinking About Thinking

Teacher Comment: **What did you think about when you found the parts that made a larger shape?**

Student Response:

1. I looked at the size of the parts of the large shape.
2. I found the shape parts that were exactly the same size.
3. I checked that the other shapes were not the right size.

Personal Application

Teacher Comment: **When do you need to find parts that make a larger shape?**

Student Response: I need to find parts of a large shape to put a puzzle together.

Page 20: FINDING SHAPES THAT COMPLETE A SQUARE

LESSON

Introduction

Teacher Comment: **We have learned to identify the parts that make a large shape.**

Explaining the Objective

Teacher Comment: **In this lesson you will find the part that completes the large square.**

Conducting the Lesson

Teacher Comment: **The dashed line shows the shape of the missing part. Which of the rectangles is the right size and shape to complete the purple square?**

Student Response: The first rectangle completes the purple square.

Teacher Comment: **Why do the other shapes not complete the square?**

Student Response: The second rectangle is too wide to fit. The third and fourth rectangles are too short.

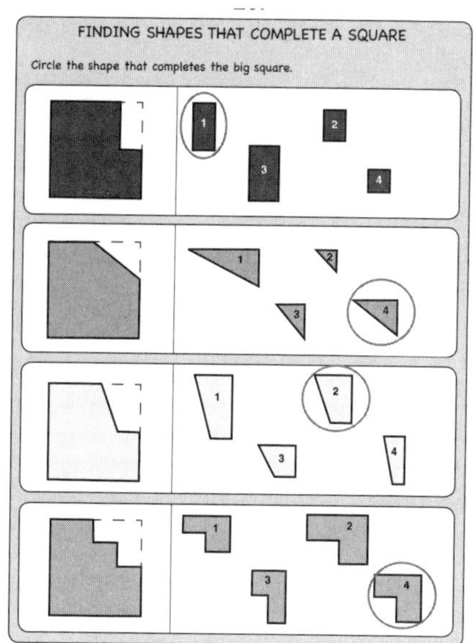

- Check students' work. Continue this dialog to discuss students' answers.

Thinking About Thinking

Teacher Comment: **What did you think about when you completed a square?**

Student Response:

1. I looked at the missing corner to decide the size and shape of the missing piece.
2. I found the shape that fit the same size and shape.
3. I checked that the others did not fit as well.

Personal Application

Teacher Comment: **When do you need to find a missing piece?**

Student Response: I need to find a missing piece to put together a puzzle.

© 2016 The Critical Thinking Co.™ • www.CriticalThinking.com • 800-458-4849

Page 21: COMBINING SHAPES

LESSON

Introduction

Teacher Comment: **We have learned to identify the shape that completed a square.**

Explaining the Objective

Teacher Comment: **In this lesson you cross out the figures that cannot be formed by joining the two shapes in the box.**

Conducting the Lesson

Teacher Comment: **There are a red square and a red rectangle in the first box. Mark out any of the figures on the right that cannot be made with that square and that rectangle.**

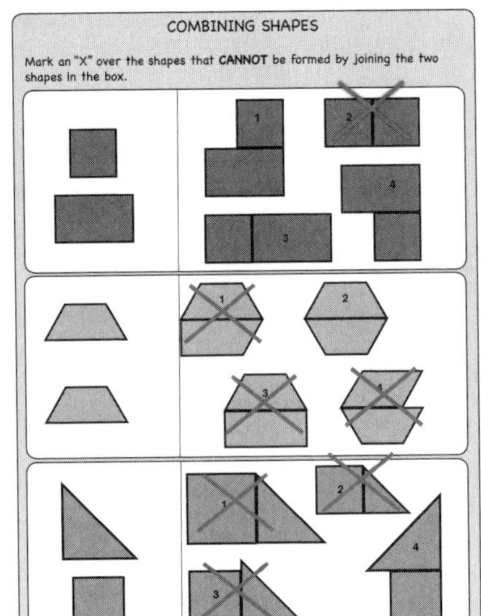

• Check students' work.

Teacher Comment: **Why should shape number two be crossed out?**

Student Response: Shape two is made from two squares instead of a square and a rectangle.

• Check students' work. Continue this dialog to discuss students' answers.

Thinking About Thinking

Teacher Comment: **What did you think about when you combined shapes?**

Student Response:

1. I looked at the size and shape of the two shapes.
2. I looked for the matching pieces in the combined shapes.
3. I checked that the other combined shapes did not match.

Personal Application

Teacher Comment: **When do you need to combine shapes?**

Student Response: I need to combine shapes to help me draw an object.

© 2016 The Critical Thinking Co.™ • www.CriticalThinking.com • 800-458-4849

Page 22: DRAWING PICTURES BY COMBINING SHAPES

LESSON

Introduction

Teacher Comment: **We have learned to combine shapes and draw many polygons.**

Explaining the Objective

Teacher Comment: **In this lesson you will combine shapes to make a new drawing.**

Conducting the Lesson

Teacher Comment: **In the top box draw a truck using circles and rectangles.**

- Check students' work.

Teacher Comment: **In the second box use a trapezoid and triangles to draw a sailboat.**

- Check students' work.

Teacher Comment: **In the third box draw a house by combining a triangle and rectangles.**

- Check students' work.

DRAWING PICTURES BY COMBINING SHAPES

Combine circles and rectangles to draw a truck.

Combine a trapezoid and triangles to draw a sailboat.

Combine a triangle and rectangles to draw a house.

Thinking About Thinking

Teacher Comment: **What did you think about when you combined shapes that produced a drawing?**

Student Response:

1. I thought about the object I was to draw.
2. I remembered where the shapes fit in the object.
3. I drew the object to show the shapes.

Personal Application

Teacher Comment: **When do you need to combine shapes to produce a drawing?**

Student Response: I need to combine shapes to help me draw an object that has different shapes in it.

© 2016 The Critical Thinking Co.™ • www.CriticalThinking.com • 800-458-4849

Page 23: DESCRIBING SOLIDS

LESSON

Introduction

Teacher Comment: **In the last lessons all the shapes are drawn on a flat piece of paper. If the paper is folded correctly, it may form different solids. A solid is an object that you can hold in your hand. It has height, width, and thickness.**

Explaining the Objective

Teacher Comment: **In this lesson you will learn the names of three solids.**

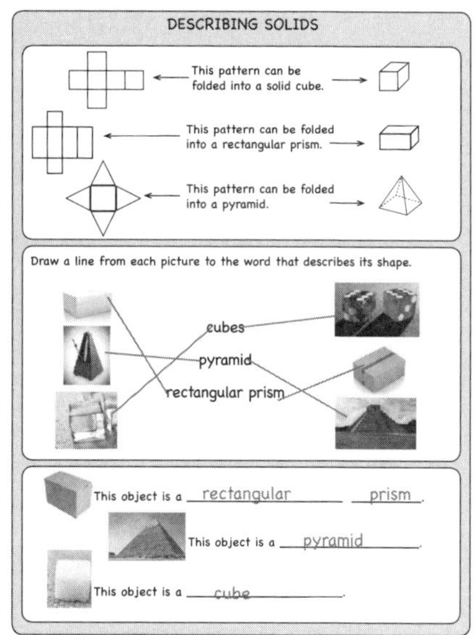

Conducting the Lesson

- Use the patterns in the appendix to prepare completed solids. Use a second copy of the pattern to fold.
- Hold up a pattern for a cube.

  Teacher Comment: **On this piece of paper, all the squares are flat. When I fold the piece of paper correctly, the flat paper becomes a solid. This solid is a cube. Let's count the number of squares.**
- Point to each square as you count.

- Hold up a pattern for a rectangular prism. (See the photocopy masters in the appendix.)

  Teacher Comment: **On this piece of paper all the rectangles and squares are flat. When I fold the piece of paper correctly, the flat paper becomes a solid. This solid is a rectangular prism. Count the number of rectangles and squares in the pattern.**

  Student Response: There are four rectangles and two squares in the pattern.

  Teacher Comment: **The rectangles form the sides of the prism and the squares form the ends.**

- Hold up a pattern for a pyramid. (See the photocopy masters in the appendix.)

  Teacher Comment: **On this piece of paper all the triangles and the squares are flat. When I fold the piece of paper correctly, the flat paper becomes a solid. This solid is a pyramid. Count the number of triangles and squares in the pattern.**

  Student Response: There are four triangles and one square in the pattern.

  Teacher Comment: **The triangles form the sides of the pyramid and the square forms the base (bottom).**

  Teacher Comment: **Look at the second box. Draw a line from each picture to the word that describes that solid.**

- Check students' work.

© 2016 The Critical Thinking Co.™ • www.CriticalThinking.com • 800-458-4849

Teacher Comment: **In the bottom box write the names of the three solids shown.**

- Check students' work.

Thinking About Thinking

Teacher Comment: **What did you think about when you named a solid?**

Student Response:

1. I looked at the picture to see what the sides looked like.
2. If it looked like a square from any direction, I knew that it was a cube.
3. If it looked like a rectangle from some directions and a square from another direction, I knew it was a rectangular prism.
4. If it looked like a triangle from four directions and a square at the bottom, I knew it was a pyramid.

Personal Application

Teacher Comment: **When do you need to describe a solid?**

Student Response: I describe a solid when I write about an object.

Page 24: DESCRIBING SOLIDS

LESSON

Introduction

Teacher Comment: **In the last lessons we described some solids: cubes, pyramids, and prisms.**

Explaining the Objective

Teacher Comment: **In this lesson you will learn about three other solids: cones, cylinders and spheres.**

Conducting the Lesson

- Hold up a flat piece of paper and squeeze it into a ball and hold it up.

Teacher Comment: **What shape do you see?**

Student Response: I see a circle.

Teacher Comment: Rotate the ball. **What does the ball look like from all directions?**

Student Response: The ball looks like a circle from any direction.

Teacher Comment: **This ball is a solid that is called a "sphere."**

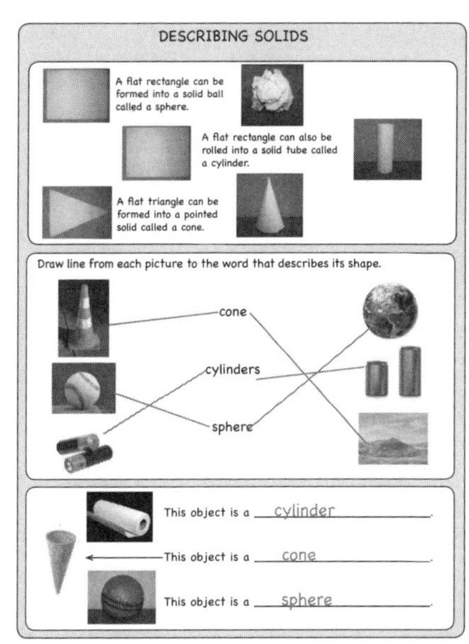

DESCRIBING SOLIDS

A flat rectangle can be formed into a solid ball called a sphere.

A flat rectangle can also be rolled into a solid tube called a cylinder.

A flat triangle can be formed into a pointed solid called a cone.

Draw line from each picture to the word that describes its shape.

cone

cylinders

sphere

This object is a cylinder.

This object is a cone.

This object is a sphere.

- Hold up a flat piece of paper.

Teacher Comment: **This piece of paper is flat.**

- Roll the paper into a cylinder. Hold the cylinder so that you and the class see through it.

© 2016 The Critical Thinking Co.™ • www.CriticalThinking.com • 800-458-4849

Teacher Comment: **What shape do you see?**

Student Response: I see a circle.

• Hold the cylinder so that you and the class see it from its side.

Teacher Comment: **What shape do you see?**

Student Response: I see a rectangle.

Teacher Comment: **A solid that looks like a circle from one direction** (show the circle) **and a rectangle from the other** (show the rectangle) **is called a "cylinder."**

• Twist a piece of colored paper into a cone. Cut the base so that it is flat to create a pattern for a cone.

Teacher Comment: **This piece of paper is flat.**

• Hold up the flat pattern for the cone.

Teacher Comment: **When I roll it into a solid, it becomes a cone. When you look at it from the side, what shape do you see?**

Student Response: I see a triangle.

• Point the base toward the class.

Teacher Comment: **When you look at the bottom, what shape so you see?**

Student Response: The bottom is a circle.

Teacher Comment: **A solid that looks like a triangle from the side and a circle from the bottom is called a "cone."**

Teacher Comment: **Look at each object in the second box. Draw a line from each picture to the word that describes that solid.**

Teacher Comment: **Look at each object in the bottom box. On each line write its name (cone, cylinder, or sphere).**

• Check students' work.

Thinking About Thinking

Teacher Comment: **What did you think about when you matched the word for the solid to the picture?**

Student Response:

1. I looked at the picture to see what the sides looked like.
2. If it looked like a circle from all sides side, I knew that it was a sphere.
3. If it looked like a triangle from the side and a circle on the bottom, I knew that it was a cone.
4. If it looked like a rectangle from one side and a circle on the ends, I knew it was a cylinder.

Personal Application

Teacher Comment: **When do you need to know the words for different kinds of solids?**

Student Response: I need to know the words for solids in order to tell about them.

© 2016 The Critical Thinking Co.™ • www.CriticalThinking.com • 800-458-4849

Page 25: DESCRIBING SOLIDS

LESSON

Introduction

Teacher Comment: **We have learned to describe solids that make an object.**

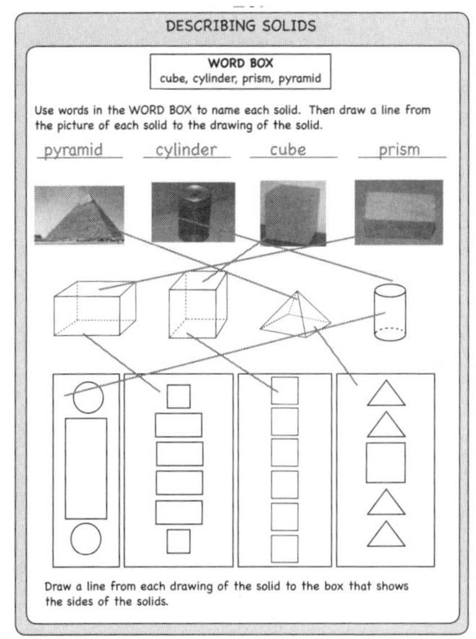

DESCRIBING SOLIDS

WORD BOX
cube, cylinder, prism, pyramid

Use words in the WORD BOX to name each solid. Then draw a line from the picture of each solid to the drawing of the solid.

pyramid cylinder cube prism

Draw a line from each drawing of the solid to the box that shows the sides of the solids.

Explaining the Objective

Teacher Comment: **In this lesson you will identify the shapes that make the sides of the solid.**

Conducting the Lesson

Teacher Comment: **On the lines above each picture write the name of the solid.**

Student Response: The solids are a pyramid, a cylinder, a cube, and a prism.

• Check students' work.

Teacher Comment: **Draw a line from the picture of each solid to the drawing of the solid.**

• Check students' work.

Teacher Comment: **Look at the drawings of the solids. Draw a line from each drawing to the box at the bottom of the page that shows the sides of the solid.**

• Check students' work.

Thinking About Thinking

Teacher Comment: **What did you think about when you described the patterns of solids?**

Student Response:

1. I looked at the shape and number of sides.
2. I found the drawing that matched each side.

Personal Application

Teacher Comment: **When do you need to see what the sides of solids look like?**

Student Response: I need to see what the sides of solids look like in order to build the solid.

© 2016 The Critical Thinking Co.™ • www.CriticalThinking.com • 800-458-4849

Page 26: COMBINING SOLIDS

LESSON

Introduction

Teacher Comment: **We have learned to identify solids.**

Explaining the Objective

Teacher Comment: **In this lesson you will identify more than one solid in some objects.**

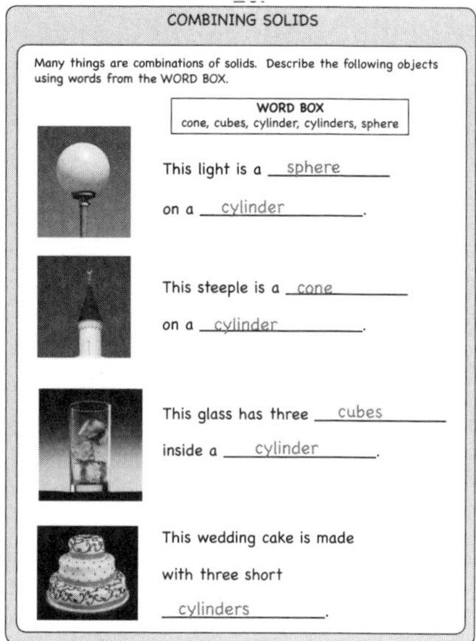
COMBINING SOLIDS

Many things are combinations of solids. Describe the following objects using words from the WORD BOX.

WORD BOX
cone, cubes, cylinder, cylinders, sphere

This light is a sphere on a cylinder.

This steeple is a cone on a cylinder.

This glass has three cubes inside a cylinder.

This wedding cake is made with three short cylinders.

Conducting the Lesson

Teacher Comment: **Look at the picture of the street light. What two solids do you see?**

Student Response: I see a sphere on top of a cylinder.

Teacher Comment: **Write "sphere" on the first line and "cylinder" on the second.**

- Check students' work. Continue this dialog to discuss students' answers.

Thinking About Thinking

Teacher Comment: **What did you think about when you described solids in objects?**

Student Response:

1. I looked for the solids.
2. I told their position in the object.

Personal Application

Teacher Comment: **When do you need to describe solids in objects?**

Student Response: I need to describe solids in objects to tell how to make them or what they look like.

© 2016 The Critical Thinking Co.™ • www.CriticalThinking.com • 800-458-4849

CHAPTER TWO – THINKING ABOUT POSITION (Pages 27-32)

GENERAL INTRODUCTION

CURRICULUM APPLICATIONS

Language Arts: Identify and correctly use words that describe location (above/below, inside/outside, front/behind, between, beside). Describe location of objects or buildings from written directions or when discussing picture books. Write sentences that describe position.
Social Studies: Identify location on maps. Identify locations of buildings: residences, government or recreational buildings, and stores. Identify the location of various parts of buildings.
Science: Identify and correctly express the location of parts of organisms, objects, and structures. Follow directions in science activities.
Art: Identify the location of parts of paintings, sculpture, and other artworks. Follow directions in art activities.
Physical Education: Follow directions in physical exercises and sports activities.

TEACHING SUGGESTIONS

- Drawing: Ask students to draw a picture of objects that show given locations or positions. Students may write or tell short stories in which position or location is important.
- Introduce these lessons by reading picture books in which location or position is important to the story.

Page 28: DESCRIBING POSITION – FIRST, MIDDLE, LAST

LESSON

Introduction

- Introduce this lesson by asking three students to come to the front of the class and line up as they would to walk down the hall.
  Teacher Comment: **Who is first in line?**
  Student Responses will vary.
  Teacher Comment: **Who is last in line?**
  Student Responses will vary.
  Teacher Comment: **Who is in the middle?**
  Student Responses will vary.
- Ask the three students to turn and face the class.
  Teacher Comment: **These students are still in the same position:** (pointing) **first,** (pointing) **middle,** (pointing) **last.**
  Teacher Comment: **We use "first," "middle," and "last" to tell where something is compared to others.**

Explaining the Objective

Teacher Comment: **In this lesson you will learn to find shapes that show "first," "middle," and "last" position.**

Conducting the Lesson

Teacher Comment: **In the top row, what shape is red?**
Student Response: The circle is red.

Teacher Comment: **Write "circle" on the first line.**

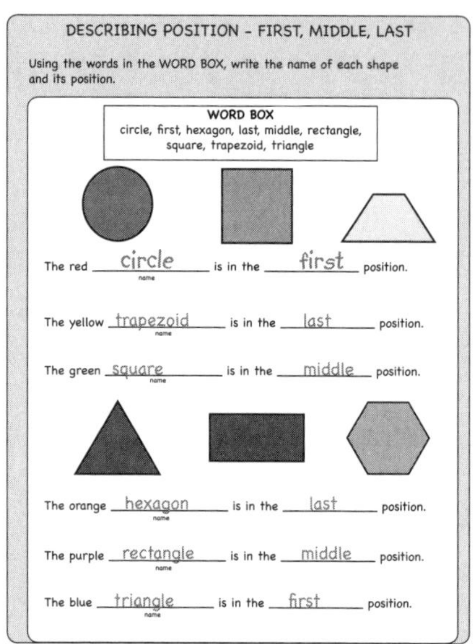

Teacher Comment: **What is the position of the red circle?**
Student Response: The red circle is in the first position.
Teacher Comment: **Write "first" on the next line.**

- You may want to explain that there is another way to tell position. "The first shape is a red circle."

- Check students' work. Continue this dialog to discuss students' answers.

Thinking About Thinking

Teacher Comment: **What did you think about when you decided which shapes were in first, middle, or last position.**
Student Response:
1. I looked at the first and the last ones.
2. I decided which shape was between them.
3. I named the shapes that were first, middle, and last.

Personal Application

Teacher Comment: **When is it important to describe first, middle, or last position?**
Student Response: I describe position to give directions or tell about the location of people or things in a story.

Page 29: DESCRIBING POSITION – FIRST, SECOND, THIRD, FOURTH

LESSON

Introduction

Teacher Comment: **We have described position as "first," "middle," and "last." Another way to describe position is to count each position from left to right.**

- Introduce this lesson by asking four students to come to the front of the class and line up as they would to walk down the hall.

Teacher Comment: **Who is first in line?**
Student Responses will vary.
Teacher Comment: **Who is second in line?**
Student Responses will vary.
Teacher Comment: **Who is third in line?**
Student Responses will vary.
Teacher Comment: **Who is fourth in line?**
Student Responses will vary.

- Ask the four students to turn and face the class.

© 2016 The Critical Thinking Co.™ • www.CriticalThinking.com • 800-458-4849

Teacher Comment: **These students are still in the same position:** (pointing) **first,** (pointing) **second,** (pointing) **third, and** (pointing) **fourth.**

Teacher Comment: **We have shown that "first," "second," "third," and "fourth" tell where something is, counting from left to right, compared to others.**

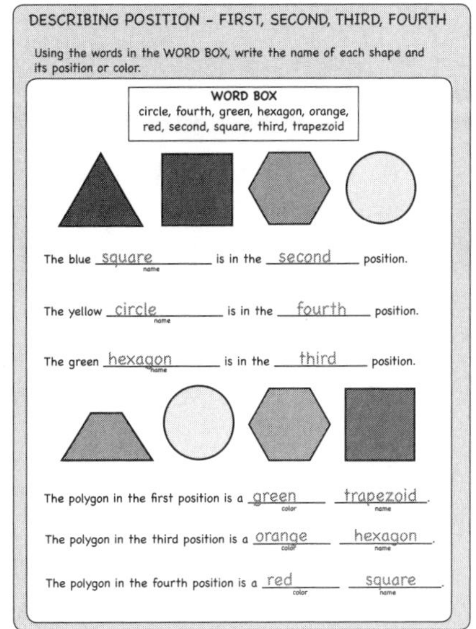

DESCRIBING POSITION - FIRST, SECOND, THIRD, FOURTH

Using the words in the WORD BOX, write the name of each shape and its position or color.

WORD BOX
circle, fourth, green, hexagon, orange, red, second, square, third, trapezoid

The blue square (name) is in the second position.

The yellow circle (name) is in the fourth position.

The green hexagon (name) is in the third position.

The polygon in the first position is a green (color) trapezoid (name).

The polygon in the third position is a orange (color) hexagon (name).

The polygon in the fourth position is a red (color) square (name).

Explaining the Objective to Students:

Teacher Comment: **In this lesson you will describe position by counting whether the shape is in first, second, third, or fourth position.**

Conducting the Lesson

Teacher Comment: **In the top row, name the blue polygon.**

Student Response: The blue polygon is a square.

Teacher Comment: **Write "square" on the first line.**

Teacher Comment: **What is the position the blue square?**

Student Response: The blue square is in the second position.

Teacher Comment: **Write "second" on the next line.**

Teacher Comment: **Read the sentence.**

• Check students' work. Continue this dialog to discuss students' answers.

Teacher Comment: **There is another way to describe first, second, third, and fourth position. In the bottom row which polygon is green?**

Student Response: The trapezoid is green.

Teacher Comment: **Write "trapezoid" on the first line.**

Teacher Comment: **What is the position the green trapezoid?**

Student Response: The green trapezoid is in the first position.

Teacher Comment: **Write "first" on the second line.**

Teacher Comment: **Read the sentence.**

Thinking About Thinking

Teacher Comment: **What did you think about when you decided which shapes were in first, second, third, or fourth position?**

Student Response:

1. I counted the shapes.
2. I named the first shape.
3. I named the shape for the number of each position.

Personal Application

Teacher Comment: **When is it important to describe things by telling its position?**

Student Response: I describe things by telling its position to give directions or tell about the location of people or things in a story.

© 2016 The Critical Thinking Co.™ • www.CriticalThinking.com • 800-458-4849

Page 30: SHOWING POSITION – LEFT, CENTER, RIGHT

LESSON

Introduction

Teacher Comment: **We have described positions by counting from left to right.**

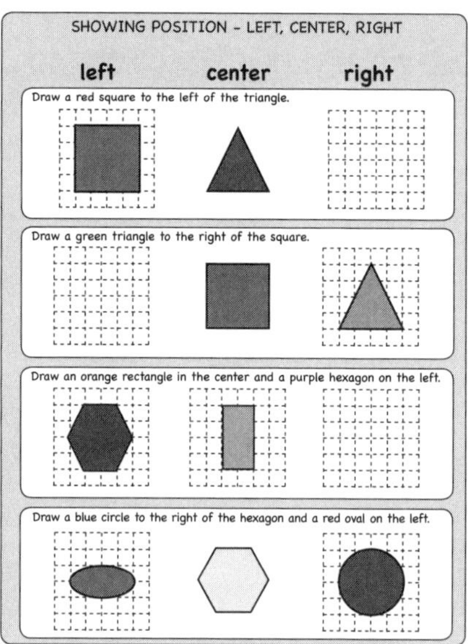

- Ask three students to come to the front of the class and to face away from the class. Ask the class to raise their left hands and to name the student who is on the left. Repeat these instructions to name the student on the right.

Explaining the Objective

Teacher Comment: **In this lesson you will draw shapes that are to the left or the right side.**

Conducting the Lesson

Teacher Comment: **Look at the first box. Point to the grid to the left of the blue triangle. The center shape is a blue triangle. Point to the grid to the right side of the blue triangle. Draw a square on the grid to the left of the blue triangle. Color it red.**

- Check students' work.

Teacher Comment: **In the second box draw a green triangle on the grid to the right of the red square.**

- Check students' work. Continue this dialog to discuss students' answers.

Thinking About Thinking

Teacher Comment: **What did you think about when you decided which shapes were in left, center, or right position?**

Student Response:

1. I found the shape described in the sentence.
2. I read the position where I should draw.
3. I decided which direction was left or right.
4. I drew and colored the shape in the position the sentence described.

Personal Application

Teacher Comment: **When is it important to know which position is left, center, or right?**

Student Response: I need to know left or right positions in order to follow or to give directions or to tell about the location of people or things in a story.

© 2016 The Critical Thinking Co.™ • www.CriticalThinking.com • 800-458-4849

Page 31: SHOWING POSITION – ABOVE, BELOW

LESSON

Introduction

Teacher Comment: **We have learned to describe positions that are in a row.**

Explaining the Objective to Students

Teacher Comment: **In this lesson you describe positions that are above or below each other.**

Conducting the Lesson

Teacher Comment: **Look at the first box. Draw a blue square on the grid above the yellow circle.**

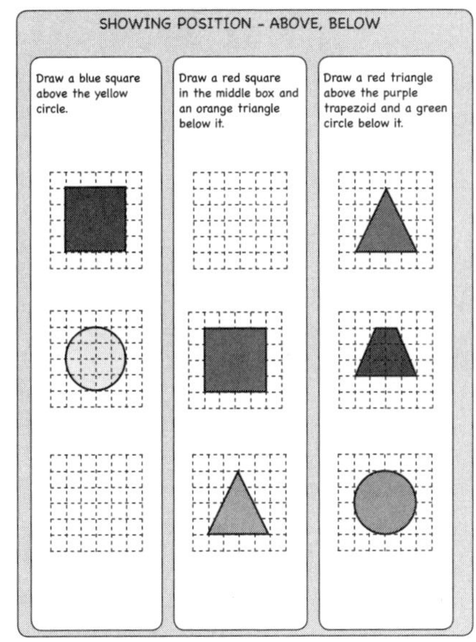

- Check students' work. Continue this dialog to discuss students' answers.

Thinking About Thinking

Teacher Comment: **What did you think about when you decided which shapes were above or below the others?**

Student Response:

1. I looked at the middle one.
2. I decided which direction was above or below.
3. I decided the color and shape that fit that position.

Personal Application

Teacher Comment: **When is it important to describe above or below positions?**

Student Response: I describe above or below positions to give directions or tell about the location of people or things in a story.

© 2016 The Critical Thinking Co.™ • www.CriticalThinking.com • 800-458-4849

PAGE 32: WRITING POSITION WORDS

LESSON

Introduction

Teacher Comment: **We have learned to describe above and below positions.**

Explaining the Objective

Teacher Comment: **In this lesson you will write about positions.**

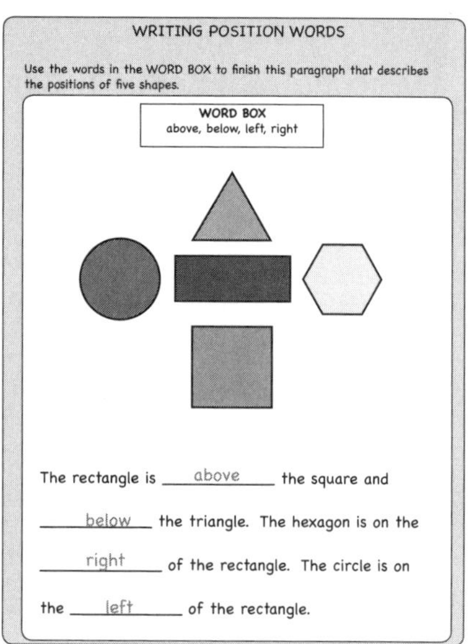

Conducting the Lesson

Teacher Comment: **Use the words in the WORD BOX to complete the paragraph that describes the positions of five shapes.**

- Check students' work.

Thinking About Thinking

Teacher Comment: **What did you think about when you decided which shapes were above, below, left, or right of the another?**

Student Response

1. I found the first shape in the sentence.
2. I decided the position of the next shape compared to the first one.
3. I checked each position of each shape compared to the first one.

Personal Application

Teacher Comment: **When is it important to describe which shape is above, below, left, or right of the other?**

Student Response: I describe above, below, left, or right positions to give directions or tell about the location of people or things in a story.

© 2016 The Critical Thinking Co.™ • www.CriticalThinking.com • 800-458-4849

CHAPTER THREE – SIMILARITIES AND DIFFERENCES—SHAPES (Pages 33-43)

GENERAL INTRODUCTION

CURRICULUM APPLICATIONS

Language Arts: Visual discrimination for reading readiness, writing sentences that describe size, shape, and position.
Mathematics: Identify similar figures. Write numerals in the correct direction (5, 7, etc.).
Science: Recognize similarly shaped leaves, insects, or shells.
Social Studies: Read maps.
Enrichment Areas: Recognize shapes of road signs. Discern patterns in art.

TEACHING SUGGESTIONS

- Ask students to name the polygons and their properties as they explain their answers.
- Integrate these geometry concepts into your language arts program by discussing picture books.
- Model using the sentence structure of comparison (both ... and) and contrast (...but .... or ... next). Encourage students to speak and write using those terms and patterns.

Page 34: FINDING EQUAL SHAPES

LESSON

Introduction

Teacher Comment: **We have learned about polygons and solids. In these lessons you will describe similarities and differences in various shapes.**

Explaining the Objective

Teacher Comment: **If the sides and the angles of two shapes are exactly alike, the shapes are equal. An equal shape may be turned to a different position. In a group of shapes you will cross out any shape that is not equal to the first one.**

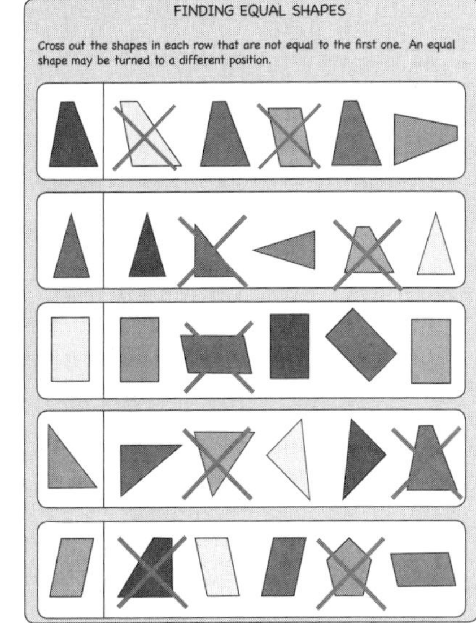

Conducting the Lesson

Teacher Comment: **Name the blue shape in the first box.**
Student Response: The blue polygon is a trapezoid.
Teacher Comment: **Which shapes are exactly the same shape as the blue trapezoid?**
Student Response: The red, purple, and green trapezoids are exactly like the blue trapezoid.
Teacher Comment: **Why is the yellow trapezoid not equal?**

Student Response: The yellow trapezoid is not equal because it is tilted. Its angles are not the same as the blue trapezoid.

Teacher Comment: **Why is the orange polygon not equal?**

Student Response: The orange polygon is not equal because it is a parallelogram, not a trapezoid.

• Check students' work. Continue this dialog to discuss students' answers.

Thinking About Thinking

Teacher Comment: **What did you pay attention to when you found the shapes that were equal?**

Student Response:

1. I checked whether the sides were equal.
2. I checked whether the angles were equal.
3. I decided why some shapes did not match.

Personal Application

Teacher Comment: **When might you have to find equal shapes?**

Student Response: I have to find equal shapes when I put away toys or match building blocks.

Page 35: COMPARING SHAPES

LESSON

Introduction

Teacher Comment: **We have found shapes that are equal and shapes that are not.**

Explaining the Objective

Teacher Comment: **In this lesson you will decide how two shapes are alike or different.**

Conducting the Lesson

Teacher Comment: **Look at the two shapes and decide how they are alike and how they are different. In the example the shapes are both yellow. They have the same color. Notice the "S" next to color. One shape is a circle and the other is a hexagon. Notice that the "D" tells that the shape is different. Both shapes are large and there is an "S" next to size.**

Teacher Comment: **Write "S" for "Same" and "D" for "Different" for color, shape, and size.**

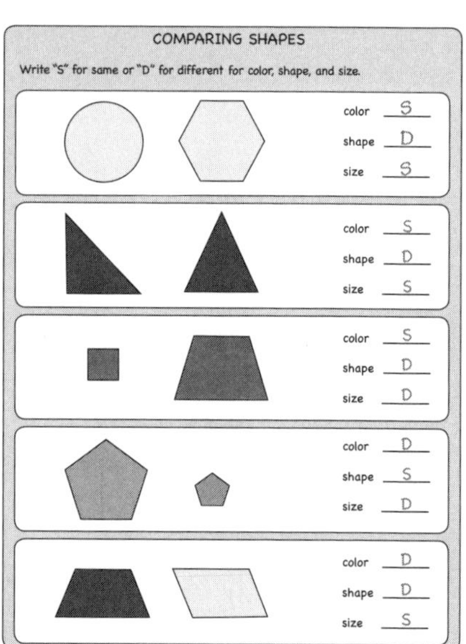

• Check students' work. Continue this dialog to discuss students' answers.

 © 2016 The Critical Thinking Co.™ • www.CriticalThinking.com • 800-458-4849

Thinking About Thinking

Teacher Comment: **What did you pay attention to when you wrote how shapes were alike and different?**

Student Response:

1. I looked to see whether the shapes were different colors.
2. I looked to see whether the pair were a different shape.
3. I looked to see whether the pair were a different size.

Personal Application

Teacher Comment: **When do you need to tell if shapes are different?**

Student Response: I need to tell if shapes are different when I make requests or match blocks.

Page 36: COMPARING SHAPES

LESSON

Introduction

Teacher Comment: **We have compared polygons for shape, size, and color.**

Explaining the Objective

Teacher Comment: **In this lesson you will describe how shapes are alike and different.**

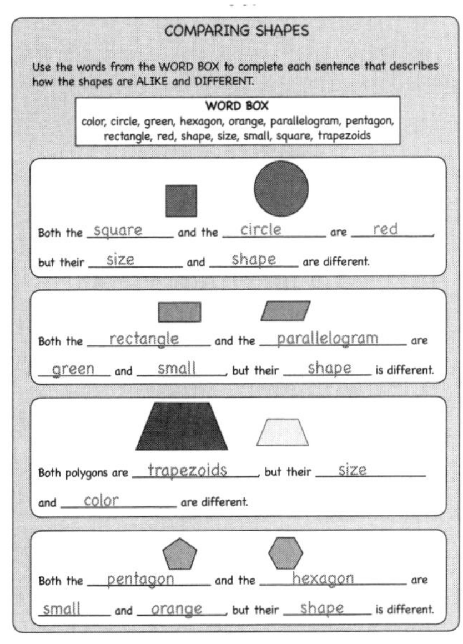

Conducting the Lesson

Teacher Comment: **Look at the first pair of shapes. Use the words in the WORD BOX to complete a sentence to describe how the shapes are alike and different.**

- Check students' work. Continue this dialog to discuss students' answers.
- Model the sentence pattern for describing shape and color. Encourage students to speak in whole sentences using this pattern with other polygons and objects.

Thinking About Thinking

Teacher Comment: **What did you pay attention to when you wrote a description of the shapes?**

Student Response:

1. I looked at their shapes, their size, and their color.
2. I found the words for their shapes, their size, and their color and copied the words.

Personal Application

Teacher Comment: **When do you need to write about a shape?**

Student Response: I need to write about shapes when I write a description of what I see.

© 2016 The Critical Thinking Co.™ • www.CriticalThinking.com • 800-458-4849

Page 37: DRAWING A DIFFERENT SHAPE

LESSON

Introduction

Teacher Comment: **We recognized how shapes are alike or different.**

Explaining the Objective

Teacher Comment: **In this lesson you will draw a polygon that is different from the first one.**

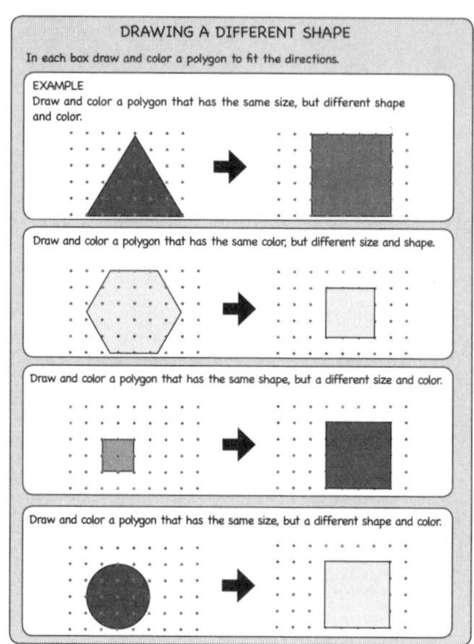

Conducting the Lesson

Teacher Comment: **The instructions say to draw and color a polygon that is the same size, but different color and shape. The square is a different shape and color, but the same size as the triangle. The red square is not the only possible answer. What other answer would also be correct?**

Student Response: Students' answers will vary.

Teacher Comment: **In the second box draw and color a polygon that has the same color, but different size and shape.**

- Check students' work. Continue this dialog to discuss students' answers. Note that many responses are possible.

Thinking About Thinking

Teacher Comment: **What did you pay attention to when you drew a different shape according to instructions?**

Student Response:

1. I decided how my drawing should be the same as the first one.
2. I decided what shape would fit the instructions to be different.
3. I drew and colored the shape.
4. I checked that I had drawn a shape that fit the directions.

Personal Application

Teacher Comment: **When do you need to draw shapes that are the same or different?**

Student Response: I need to draw shapes that are the same or different to make a picture larger or smaller or to make it a different color.

© 2016 The Critical Thinking Co.™ • www.CriticalThinking.com • 800-458-4849

Page 38: COMPARING QUADRILATERALS

LESSON

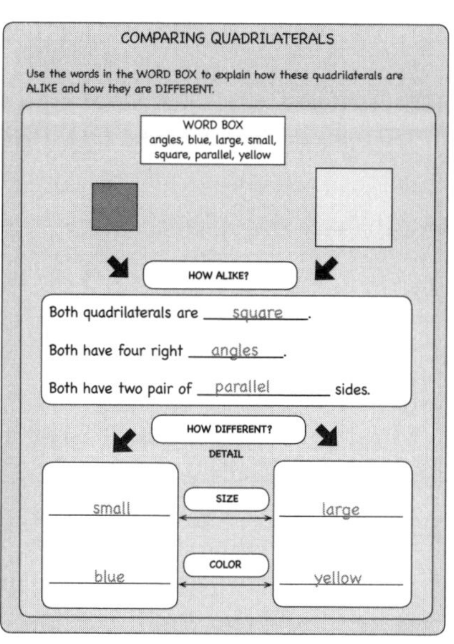

Introduction

Teacher Comment: **We have learned to describe and draw how shapes are alike and different.**

Explaining the Objective

Teacher Comment: **In this lesson you will compare and contrast two shapes. When you tell how they are alike, you compare them. When you tell how they are different, you contrast them.**

Conducting the Lesson

Teacher Comment: **On the first line in the "HOW ALIKE" box, what word in the WORD BOX tells what kind of quadrilaterals these are?**

Student Response: Both quadrilaterals are square.

Teacher Comment: **Write the word that completes each of the sentences.**

Teacher Comment: **Use words from the WORD BOX to write how these squares are different.**

• Check students' work.

Thinking About Thinking

Teacher Comment: **What did you think about when you compared and contrasted two shapes?**

Student Response:

1. I thought about how the two shapes were alike.
2. I wrote how they were alike.
3. I thought about how the two shapes were different.
4. I wrote how they were different.

Personal Application

Teacher Comment: **When do you need to compare and contrast shapes?**

Student Response: I need to compare and contrast shapes to describe them to someone else.

© 2016 The Critical Thinking Co.™ • www.CriticalThinking.com • 800-458-4849

Page 39: DIVIDING SHAPES INTO TWO EQUAL PARTS

LESSON

Introduction

Teacher Comment: **We have described how shapes are alike and different.**

Explaining the Objective

Teacher Comment: **In this lesson you will divide shapes into two equal parts.**

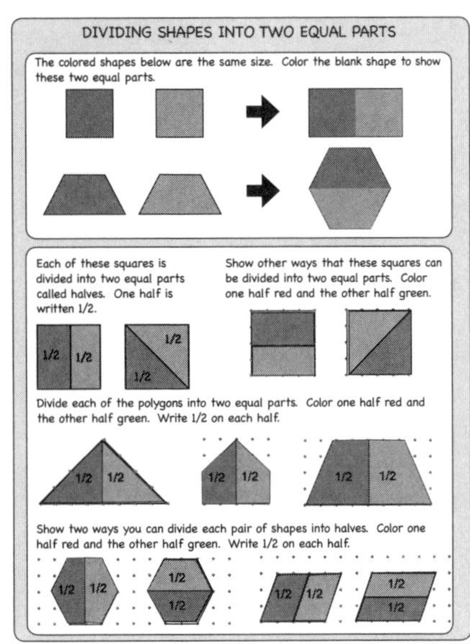
DIVIDING SHAPES INTO TWO EQUAL PARTS

The colored shapes below are the same size. Color the blank shape to show these two equal parts.

Each of these squares is divided into two equal parts called halves. One half is written 1/2.

Show other ways that these squares can be divided into two equal parts. Color one half red and the other half green.

Divide each of the polygons into two equal parts. Color one half red and the other half green. Write 1/2 on each half.

Show two ways you can divide each pair of shapes into halves. Color one half red and the other half green. Write 1/2 on each half.

Conducting the Lesson

Teacher Comment: **Look at the pairs of shapes. Color the rectangle and the hexagon to show these equal parts.**

• Check students' work.

Teacher Comment: **In the second box, each of two squares is divided into two equal parts. On the blank squares, show other ways that squares can be divided into two equal parts. Color one half red and one half green. When each part is one of two equal parts, we call the fraction "one-half" and write it "1/2."**

• Check students' work.

Teacher Comment: **In the last two rows divide each polygon into two equal parts. Color one half red and the other half green. Write 1/2 on each half.**

• Check students' work.

Teacher Comment: **Notice that it doesn't matter which direction you draw the line. Whenever you divide a square equally you divided a square into halves.**

Thinking About Thinking

Teacher Comment: **What did you pay attention to when you divided shapes into two equal parts?**

Student Response:

1. I looked to see if the two parts were exactly the same size and shape.
2. I remembered that a shape was divided into two equal parts.
3. I wrote the fraction to show that each half was one of two parts.

Personal Application

Teacher Comment: **When do you need to divide shapes into equal parts?**

Student Response: I need to divide things into halves when I must divide food equally or draw just one-half of something.

© 2016 The Critical Thinking Co.™ • www.CriticalThinking.com • 800-458-4849

Page 40: DIVIDING SHAPES INTO THREE EQUAL PARTS

LESSON

Introduction

Teacher Comment: **We have divided shapes into equal parts. Those equal parts are called fractions.**

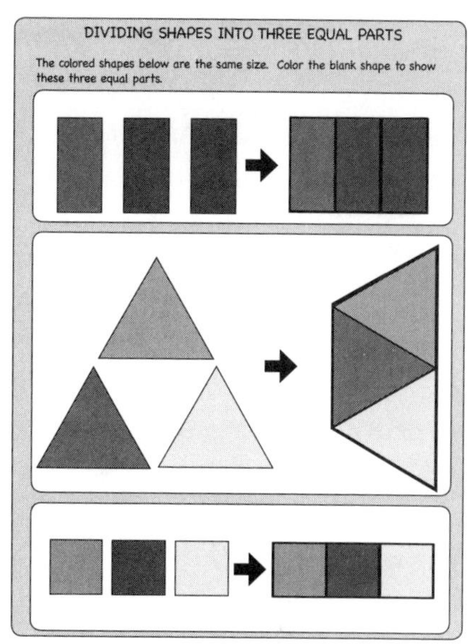

Explaining the Objective

Teacher Comment: **In this lesson you will color each of three equal parts of a shape.**

Conducting the Lesson

Teacher Comment: **When you show three equal parts of a shape, you are dividing it into thirds. We write the fraction as 1/3. Look at the blank rectangle on the right. Color each third red, blue, or purple.**

- Check students' work. Continue this dialog to discuss students' answers.

Thinking About Thinking

Teacher Comment: **What did you pay attention to when you divided a shape into thirds?**

Student Response:

1. I looked to see how the three fit into the blank shape.
2. I drew and colored the shape to show thirds.

Personal Application

Teacher Comment: **When do you need to divide things into thirds?**

Student Response: I need to divide things into thirds when I must divide food or objects equally.

Page 41: DIVIDING SHAPES INTO THREE EQUAL PARTS

LESSON

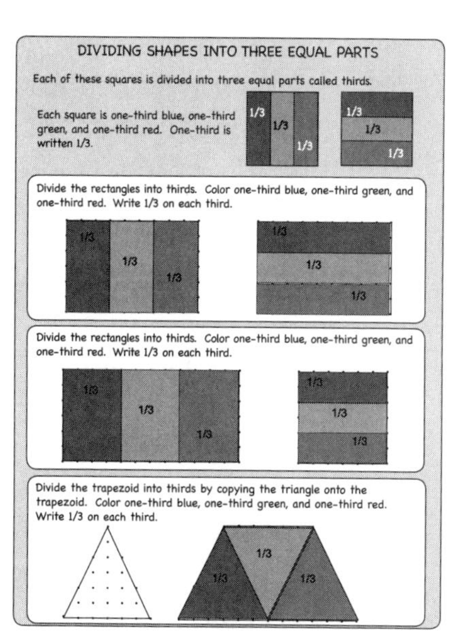

Introduction

Teacher Comment: **We have seen how three equal parts make up a whole shape.**

Explaining the Objective

Teacher Comment: **In this lesson you will divide shapes into three equal parts called thirds.**

Conducting the Lesson

Teacher Comment: **Each of the top squares is divided into three equal parts called thirds. Each square is one-third blue, one-third green, and one-third red. Divide the rectangles in the first box into thirds. Color them one-third blue, one-third green, and one-third red. Write 1/3 on each third.**

- Check students' work. Continue this dialog to discuss students' answers.

Thinking About Thinking

Teacher Comment: **What did you pay attention to when you divided a square into thirds?**

Student Response:

1. I looked to see whether the three parts were exactly the same size and shape.
2. I remembered that the shape was divided into three parts.
3. I wrote the fraction to show that each third was one of three parts.

Personal Application

Teacher Comment: **When do you need to divide things into thirds?**

Student Response: I need to divide things into thirds when I must divide food or objects equally.

Page 42: DIVIDING SHAPES INTO FOUR EQUAL PARTS

LESSON

Introduction

Teacher Comment: **We have divided shapes into parts to show halves and thirds.**

Explaining the Objective

Teacher Comment: **In this lesson you will divide a shape into four equal parts called fourths.**

Conducting the Lesson

Teacher Comment: **When you draw lines to show four equal parts of a shape, you are dividing it into fourths. We write each fourth as the fraction "1/4." In the first box divide the rectangles into fourths. Color one-fourth red, one-fourth orange, one-fourth yellow, and one-fourth green. Write 1/4 on each fourth.**

- Check students' work. Continue this dialog to discuss students' answers.

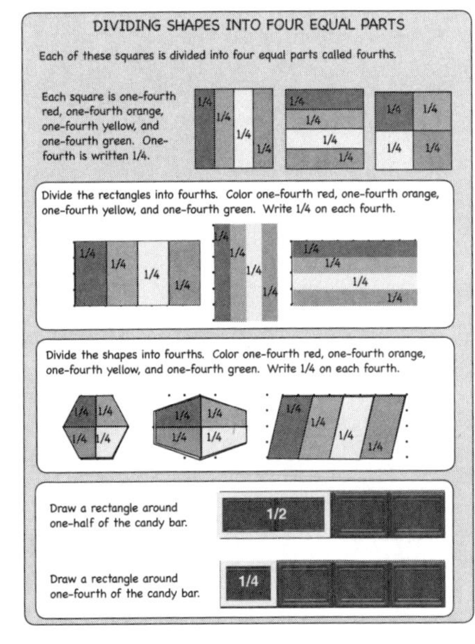

Thinking About Thinking

Teacher Comment: **What did you pay attention to when you divided each shape into fourths?**

Student Response:

1. I looked to see whether the four parts were exactly the same size and shape.
2. I wrote the fraction that showed one-fourth.

© 2016 The Critical Thinking Co.™ • www.CriticalThinking.com • 800-458-4849

Personal Application

Teacher Comment: **When do you need to divide things into fourths?**

Student Response: I need to divide things into fourths when I must divide food or objects equally.

Page 43: COUNTING PARTS OF A RECTANGLE

LESSON

Introduction

Teacher Comment: **We have learned to divide shapes into halves, thirds, and fourths.**

Explaining the Objective

Teacher Comment: **In this lesson you will count the squares in equal parts of a polygon.**

Conducting the Lesson

Teacher Comment: **In the top box trace eight small, equal squares. Color one-half of them red and one-half of them green.**

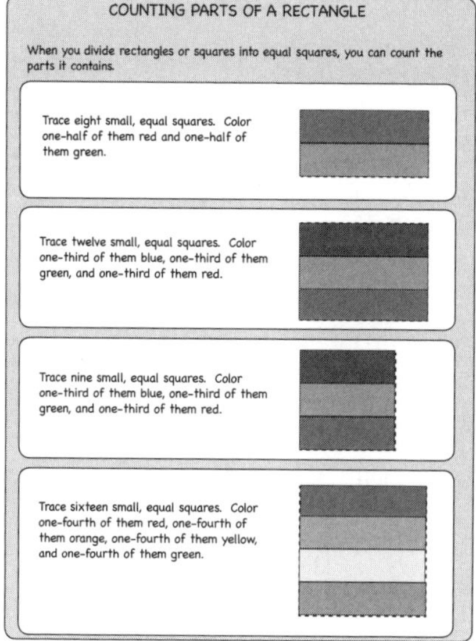

- Check students' work

Teacher Comment: **How many squares make up each half of the rectangle?**

Student Response: Four squares make up each half.

- Continue this dialog to discuss students' answers.
- Note that other designs are possible.

Thinking About Thinking

Teacher Comment: **What did you pay attention to when you counted how many squares equal parts contain?**

Student Response:

1. I counted the squares in the whole rectangle.
2. I counted the squares in a fraction of the whole rectangle.
3. I colored each fraction that showed the rectangle is divided equally.

Personal Application

Teacher Comment: **When do you need to count how many pieces make equal parts?**

Student Response: I need to know how many pieces make up equal parts when I must divide food or objects equally.

CHAPTER FOUR – RECOGNIZING PATTERNS (Pages 44-55)
GENERAL INTRODUCTION

CURRICULUM APPLICATIONS

Language Arts: Identify letter patterns in decoding unfamiliar words. Write sentences that describe size, shape, and sequence.
Mathematics: Identify repeating geometric patterns and simple bar graphs.
Science: Identify repeating patterns in leaves, shells, and life cycles.
Social Studies: Identify latitude and longitude.
Enrichment Areas: Use art exercises involving patterns. Repeat patterns in written music.

TEACHING SUGGESTION

• Check that students "read" the sequence of shapes from left to right.

Page 45: WHAT COMES NEXT?

LESSON

Introduction

Teacher Comment: **When the same shape or color is repeated, it becomes a sequence. When sequences are repeated many times, they make a pattern. Patterns are all around us in nature and in man-made things. Where in this room can you see examples of sequences?**

Student Response: Examples may include fabric in clothing, brick or cement block walls, floor tiles, ceiling tiles, window blinds, leaf arrangements on plants, etc.

Explaining the Objective

Teacher Comment: **In this lesson you will continue each sequence.**

Conducting the Lesson

Teacher Comment: **Say the color sequence that you see in the top row.**

Student Response: The sequence is red, red, yellow, yellow, red, red, yellow, blank.

Teacher Comment: **What color should the last square be?**

Student Response: The last square should be yellow because the pattern is two red squares followed by two yellow squares.

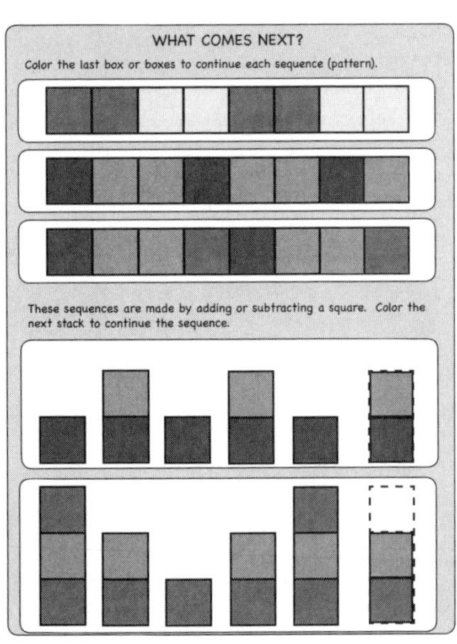

• Check students' work. Continue this dialog to discuss students' answers.

Teacher Comment: **In the second part of this lesson the sequences are made by adding or subtracting a square at a time. Color the blank stack to continue the sequence.**

© 2016 The Critical Thinking Co.™ • www.CriticalThinking.com • 800-458-4849

Thinking About Thinking

Teacher Comment: **What did you pay attention to when you decided which color came next?**

Student Response:

1. I looked carefully at the colors of the squares.
2. I looked for a sequence of colors.
3. I figured out what the next color would be.

Personal Application

Teacher Comment: **When do you need to finish a sequence?**

Student Response: I need to finish a sequence when I draw or describe brick walls, leaves, floor or ceiling tiles, etc.

Page 46: WHAT COMES NEXT?

LESSON

Introduction

Teacher Comment: **In the last lesson you colored a stack of squares to continue a sequence.**

Explaining the Objective

Teacher Comment: **In this exercise you will find the shape that completes the sequence and circle or draw it.**

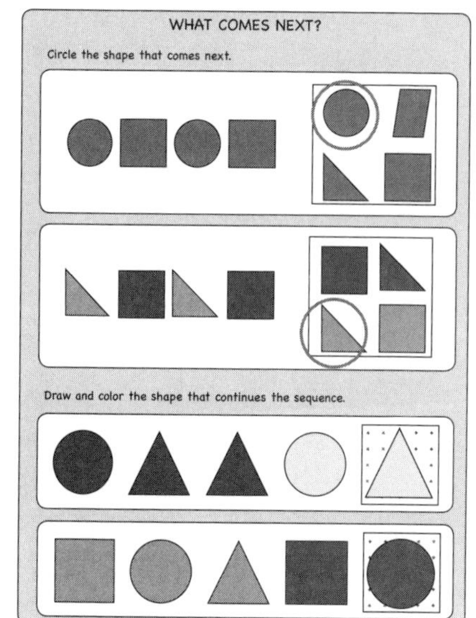

Conducting the Lesson

Teacher Comment: **What is the sequence of the shapes in the first box?**

Student Response: The sequence is red circle, red square, red circle, red square.

Teacher Comment: **What shape comes next?**

Student Response: The next shape should be a red circle.

Teacher Comment: **Draw a circle around the red circle.**

Teacher Comment: **What is the sequence of the shapes in the second box?**

Student Response: The sequence is orange triangle, blue square, orange triangle, blue square.

Teacher Comment: **What shape comes next?**

Student Response: The next shape should be an orange triangle.

Teacher Comment: **Draw a circle around the orange triangle.**

Teacher Comment: **In the next box you will draw the next shape in a sequence. What is this sequence?**

Student Response: The sequence is purple circle, purple triangle, purple triangle, yellow circle.

Teacher Comment: **What shape comes next?**

Student Response: A yellow triangle should come next.

Teacher Comment: **Draw a yellow triangle in the dotted box.**

• Check students' work. Continue this dialog to discuss students' answers.

Thinking About Thinking

Teacher Comment: **What did you pay attention to when you decided which shape came next?**

Student Response:

1. I looked carefully at the colors and the shapes.
2. I saw that the same sequence of color and shape was repeated.
3. I figured out, if the sequence continued, what the next one would be.

Personal Application

Teacher Comment: **When do you need to finish a sequence?**

Student Response: I need to finish a sequence when I draw brick walls, leaves, floor or ceiling tiles, etc.

Page 47: DRAWING A SEQUENCE OF POLYGONS

LESSON

Introduction

Teacher Comment: **We have described many kinds of polygons. The word for each kind of polygon tells the number of its sides.**

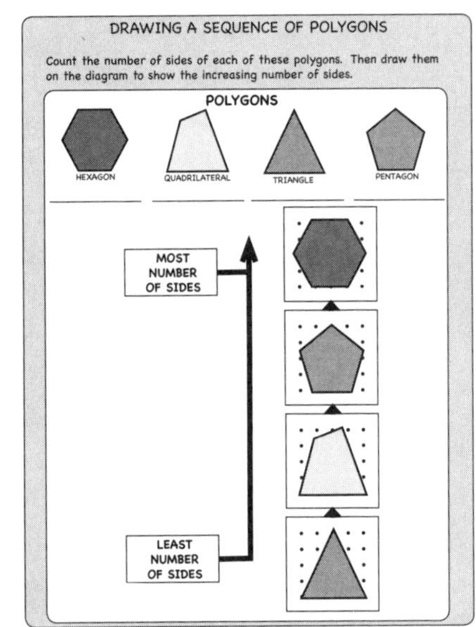

Explaining the Objective

Teacher Comment: **In this exercise you will identify four polygons in order of their number of sides.**

Conducting the Lesson

Teacher Comment: **Count the number of sides of each of these polygons. Draw and color them on the diagram to show the increasing number of sides. Which polygon has the least number of sides?**

Student Response: A triangle has three sides, the least number of sides.

Teacher Comment: **Draw a green triangle in the bottom box.**

• Check students' work. Continue this dialog to discuss students' answers.

Thinking About Thinking

Teacher Comment: **What did you pay attention to when you arranged polygons in order?**

Student Response:

1. I counted the number of sides.
2. I named the polygons in the order of the number of their sides.
3. I drew the polygons in order.

 © 2016 The Critical Thinking Co.™ • www.CriticalThinking.com • 800-458-4849

Personal Application

Teacher Comment: **When do you need to know the number of the sides of a polygon?**

Student Response: I need to know the number of sides of a polygon to name it correctly.

Page 48: DESCRIBING A SEQUENCE OF SHAPES

LESSON

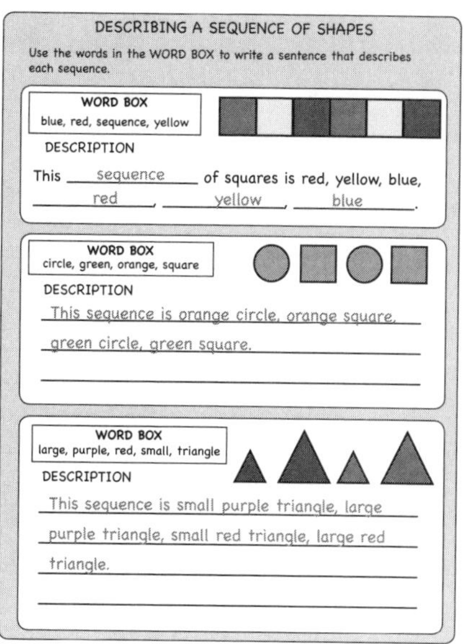

Introduction

Teacher Comment: **We have drawn the shapes that continue a sequence.**

Explaining the Objective

Teacher Comment: **In this exercise you will write sentences that describe sequences.**

Conducting the Lesson

Teacher Comment: **In the first box notice how the sequence is described. Use this as a model to describe a sequence. Describe the sequence you see in the first box.**

Student Response: I see a sequence of squares that are red, yellow, blue, red, yellow, blue.

Teacher Comment: **Complete the sentence in the first box.**

- Check students' work. Continue this dialog to discuss students' answers.

Thinking About Thinking

Teacher Comment: **What did you pay attention to when you wrote a description?**

Student Response:

1. I looked for a pattern of colors and shapes.
2. I found the words for size, color, and shape.
3. I wrote a description of the sequence.

Personal Application

Teacher Comment: **When do you need to write a sequence?**

Student Response: I need to write a sequence to write directions.

Page 49: SHOWING A SEQUENCE OF FRACTIONS

SHOWING A SEQUENCE OF FRACTIONS

Color one-third of the rectangle green. Mark the green part as 1/3 of the rectangle. | 1/3 |

Color two-thirds of the rectangle green. Mark each green square as 1/3 of the rectangle. The green part is 2/3 of the rectangle. | 1/3 | 1/3 |

Color the boxes green to show the next fraction in the sequence. Mark each green square as the fraction 1/3. The rectangle is 3/3 green. | 1/3 | 1/3 | 1/3 |

Color one-fourth of the rectangle yellow. Mark the yellow part as 1/4 of the rectangle. | 1/4 |

Color two-fourths of the rectangle yellow. Mark each yellow part as 1/4 of the rectangle. The yellow part is 2/4 of the rectangle. | 1/4 | 1/4 |

Color three-fourths of the rectangle yellow. Mark each yellow part as 1/4 of the rectangle. The yellow part is 3/4 of the rectangle. | 1/4 | 1/4 | 1/4 |

Color the boxes yellow to show the next fraction in the sequence. Mark each yellow square as the fraction 1/4. The rectangle is 4/4 yellow. | 1/4 | 1/4 | 1/4 | 1/4 |

LESSON

Introduction

Teacher Comment: **We have described a sequence of shapes.**

Explaining the Objective

Teacher Comment: **In this exercise you will color sequences of fractions.**

Conducting the Lesson

Teacher Comment: **In the top box color one-third of the first rectangle green. Mark the green part as 1/3 of the rectangle.**

• Check students' work.

Teacher Comment: **In the top box color two-thirds of the second rectangle green. Mark each green part as 1/3 of the rectangle.**

• Check students' work.

Teacher Comment: **To show the next fraction in the sequence, color the boxes of the third rectangle green. Mark each green part as 1/3 of the rectangle. The rectangle is 3/3 green.**

• Note: Repeat the directions for "fourths." After 2/4s, explain that we have also colored 1/2 of the rectangle.

Thinking About Thinking

Teacher Comment: **What did you pay attention to when you showed a sequence of fractions?**

Student Response:

1. I checked the directions and colored each part.
2. I saw how the colored part grew when I followed the sequence.

Personal Application

Teacher Comment: **When do you need to show fractions?**

Student Response: I need to show fractions to make designs or divide food or other objects.

© 2016 The Critical Thinking Co.™ • www.CriticalThinking.com • 800-458-4849

Page 50: SHOWING A SEQUENCE OF FRACTIONS

LESSON

Introduction

Teacher Comment: **In the last exercise we divided rectangles to describe a sequence of fractions.**

Explaining the Objective

Teacher Comment: **In this exercise you will color trapezoids, hexagons, and parallelograms to show sequences of fractions.**

Conducting the Lesson

Teacher Comment: **In the top box, what part of the trapezoid is orange?**

Student Response: One-third of the trapezoid is orange.

Teacher Comment: **Write "1/3" on the blank.**

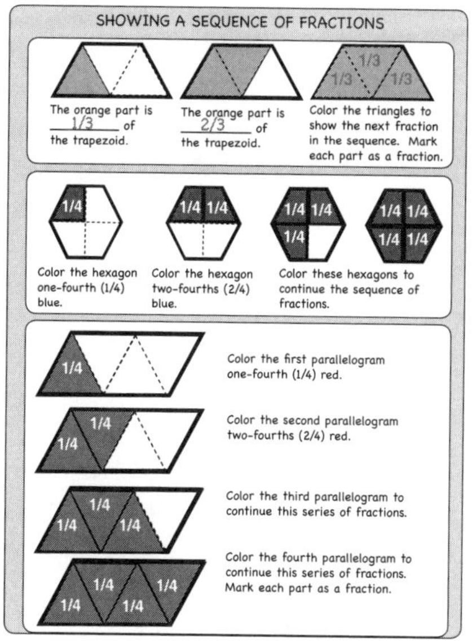

- Check students' work. Read the directions for the next two trapezoids.

Teacher Comment: **In the second box, color the first hexagon one-fourth blue. Mark each blue part as 1/4 of the hexagon.**

- Check students' work. Repeat the directions for the rest of the hexagons. After 2/4s, explain that we have also colored 1/2 of the hexagon.

Teacher Comment: **In the third box, color one-fourth of the parallelogram red. Mark each red part as 1/4 of the parallelogram.**

- Repeat the directions for the remaining parts of the parallelograms. After 2/4s, explain that we have also colored 1/2 of the parallelogram.

Thinking About Thinking

Teacher Comment: **What did you pay attention to when you showed a sequence of fractions?**

Student Response:

1. I checked the directions and colored each part.
2. I saw how the colored part grew when I followed the sequence.

Personal Application

Teacher Comment: **When do you need to show fractions?**

Student Response: I need to show fractions to make designs or divide food or other objects.

© 2016 The Critical Thinking Co.™ • www.CriticalThinking.com • 800-458-4849

Page 51: TUMBLING

LESSON

Introduction

Teacher Comment: **In the last exercises we showed sequences of fractions.**

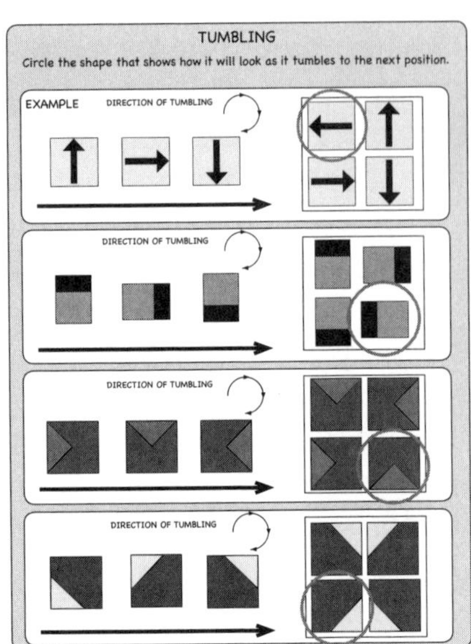

Explaining the Objective

Teacher Comment: **In this exercise the sequence shows how something looks when it is being turned. You will select the drawing that shows what the shape looks like when it rolls or tumbles to the next position.**

Conducting the Lesson

Teacher Comment: **In the example you see that the direction of the arrow changes as the square tumbles to the next position. First the arrow points up. Next it points to the right. Then it points down. Next the arrow should point to the left, the drawing that is circled.**

Teacher Comment: **Circle the drawing that shows what the rectangle will look like in the next position.**

- Check students' work. Continue this dialog to discuss students' answers.

Thinking About Thinking

Teacher Comment: **What did you pay attention to when you chose how the drawing would look in the next position?**

Student Response:

1. I noticed the direction the drawing turns.
2. I decided what the next turn would look like.

Personal Application

Teacher Comment: **When do you need to know what something will look like when it is turned?**

Student Response: I need to know what something will look like when it is turned to use a map or draw a design.

© 2016 The Critical Thinking Co.™ • www.CriticalThinking.com • 800-458-4849

Pages 52-53: TUMBLING

LESSON

Introduction

Teacher Comment: **In the last exercises we selected the drawing that shows what a shape looks like when it rolls or tumbles to the next position.**

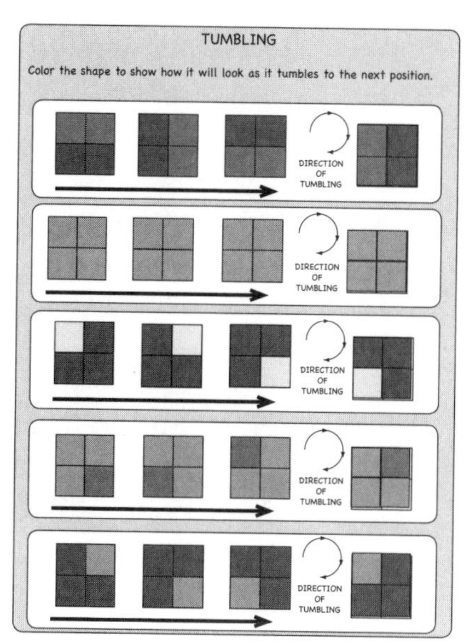

Explaining the Objective

Teacher Comment: **In this exercise the sequence shows how a colored square looks when it is being turned. You will draw what the square looks like when it rolls or tumbles to the next position.**

Conducting the Lesson

Teacher Comment: **How is the red part of the square changing?**

Student Response: First the red part is on top. Next it is on the right side. Then it is on the bottom.

Teacher Comment: **Where should the red part be in your drawing?**

Student Response: The red part should be on the left.

Teacher Comment: **Color the square with the left half red and the right half blue.**

- Check students' work. Continue this dialog to discuss students' answers.

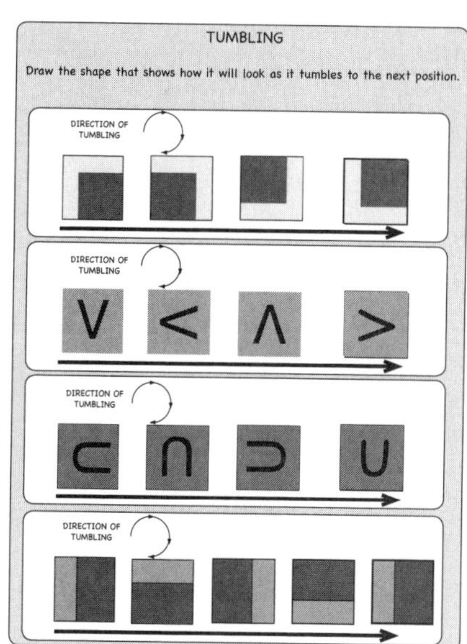

Thinking About Thinking

Teacher Comment: **What did you pay attention to when you drew how a square would look in the next position?**

Student Response:

1. I saw how the drawing changed with each turn.
2. I decided what the next turn would look like.
3. I drew what I decided.

Personal Application

Teacher Comment: **When do you need to know what something will look like when it is turned?**

Student Response: I need to know what something will look like when it is turned to use a map or draw a design.

Page 54: PAPER FOLDING

LESSON

- Use construction paper to make a model of each item in this lesson. Use the same color and rub chalk to make a mark along the fold line.

Introduction

Teacher Comment: **In the last exercises we drew what a shape looks like when it has been turned.**

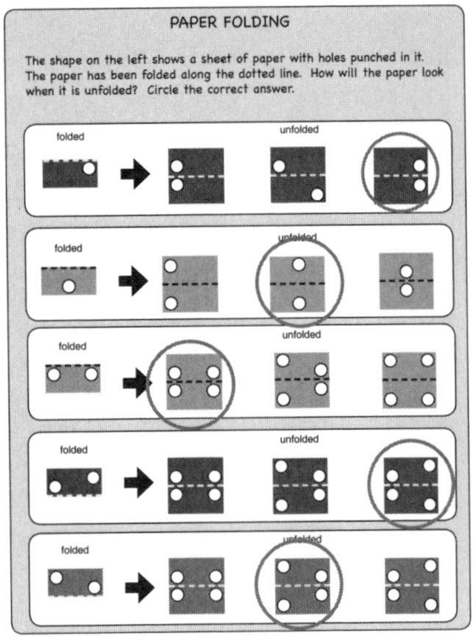

Explaining the Objective

Teacher Comment: **In this exercise you will decide what the paper looks like when it is unfolded.**

Conducting the Lesson

- Hold up the blue model.
  Teacher Comment: **This piece of paper has been folded and a hole punched in it. The fold line is on top.**
- Run your finger along the fold line.
  Teacher Comment: **Where is the hole located on the folded paper?**
  Student Response: The hole is near the top, right corner of the folded paper.
  Teacher Comment: **Remember where the hole is located as I unfold the paper. Tell your partner how the paper should look when it is unfolded.**
  Student Response: When the paper is unfolded, there will be two holes on the right side along the fold line.
- Unfold the paper.
  Teacher Comment: **Notice that the holes are on the right side near the fold line.**
- Point to the two holes along the fold line.
  Teacher Comment: **Explain why the other drawings are not correct.**
  Student Response: In the first drawing the holes are on the left side. In the second drawing the holes are on opposite sides of the paper.
  Teacher Comment: **Decide how each paper will look when it is unfolded. Circle the correct answer.**

- Check students' work. Continue this dialog to discuss students' answers.

Thinking About Thinking

Teacher Comment: **What did you pay attention to when you found the correct unfolded paper?**

Student Response:

1. I saw where the hole was located: left, right, or middle.
2. I saw where the hole was located: top or bottom.
3. I remembered where the hole would be when the paper was unfolded.
4. I checked that the other drawings could not be correct.

© 2016 The Critical Thinking Co.™ • www.CriticalThinking.com • 800-458-4849

Personal Application

Teacher Comment: **When do you need to know what a folded paper will look like when it is unfolded?**

Student Response: I need to know what a paper will look like when it is unfolded when I make decorations.

Page 55: PAPER FOLDING

LESSON

- Use construction paper to make a model of each item in this lesson. Use the same color and rub chalk to make a mark along the fold line.

Introduction

Teacher Comment: **In the last exercises we decided what a folded piece of paper in it looks like when it is unfolded.**

Explaining the Objective

Teacher Comment: **In this exercise you will decide what a paper will look like when it is folded.**

Conducting the Lesson

- Hold up the orange model.

Teacher Comment: **To make this design, a piece of paper has been folded and a hole punched in it. The fold line runs across the middle. Remember where the holes are located as I fold the paper. Tell your partner how the paper should look when it is folded.**

Student Response: When the paper is folded, there will be one hole in the middle of the bottom.

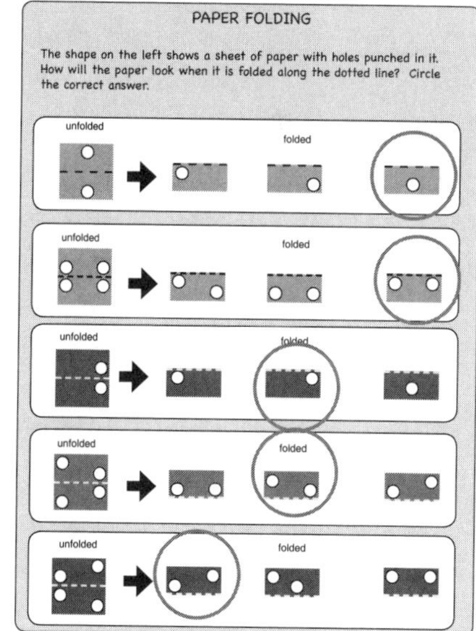

- Unfold the paper.

Teacher Comment: **Notice that the hole is in the middle of the bottom. Explain why the other drawings are not correct.**

Student Response: In the first drawing the hole is on the top of the left side. In the second drawing the hole is on the bottom right side.

Teacher Comment: **Decide how each paper will look when it is folded. Circle the correct answer.**

- Check students' work. Continue this dialog to discuss students' answers.

© 2016 The Critical Thinking Co.™ • www.CriticalThinking.com • 800-458-4849

Thinking About Thinking

Teacher Comment: **What did you pay attention to when you found the correct folded paper?**

Student Response:

1. I saw where the hole was located: left, right, or middle.
2. I saw where the hole was located: top or bottom.
3. I remembered where the hole would be when the paper was folded.
4. I checked that the other drawings could not be correct.

Personal Application

Teacher Comment: **When do you need to know what a paper will look like when it is folded?**

Student Response: I need to know what a paper will look like when it is folded when I make decorations.

Page 56: ANALOGIES WITH SHAPES

LESSON

Introduction

Teacher Comment: **We have learned how to compare shapes.**

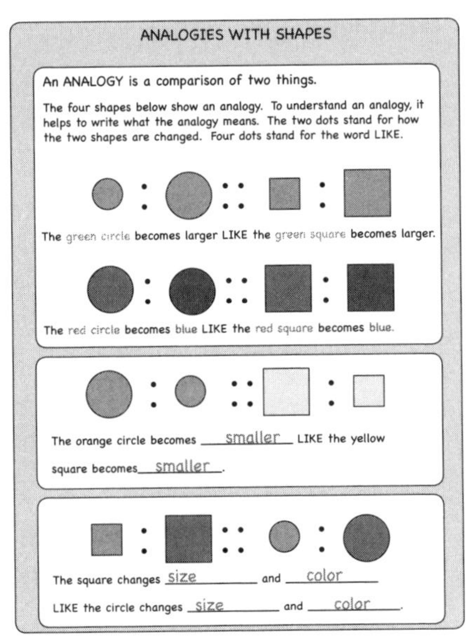
ANALOGIES WITH SHAPES

An ANALOGY is a comparison of two things.

The four shapes below show an analogy. To understand an analogy, it helps to write what the analogy means. The two dots stand for how the two shapes are changed. Four dots stand for the word LIKE.

The green circle becomes larger LIKE the green square becomes larger.

The red circle becomes blue LIKE the red square becomes blue.

The orange circle becomes smaller LIKE the yellow square becomes smaller.

The square changes size and color LIKE the circle changes size and color.

Explaining the Objective

Teacher Comment: **In this lesson you will compare two pairs of shapes, called an analogy.**

Conducting the Lesson

Teacher Comment: **An analogy is a comparison of two pairs of things. The two dots in an analogy show how the two objects are related. Four dots represent the word "LIKE." In this exercise you see four shapes. The second pair of shapes is related in the same way as the first pair. In the first box, you see that the green circle becomes larger like the green square becomes larger.**

Teacher Comment: **Next you see that the red circle becomes blue like the the red square becomes blue.**

Teacher Comment: **In the second box write the words to explain this analogy.**

Student Response: The orange circle becomes smaller LIKE the yellow square becomes smaller.

- Check students' work. Continue this dialog to discuss students' answers.

© 2016 The Critical Thinking Co.™ • www.CriticalThinking.com • 800-458-4849

Thinking About Thinking

Teacher Comment: **What did you pay attention to when you explained the analogy?**

Student Response:

1. I decided how the first pair of shapes changed.
2. I checked that the second pair were changed the same way.
3. I wrote how the shapes changed.

Personal Application

Teacher Comment: **When do you need to show how pairs of shapes are changed?**

Student Response: I need to know how shapes are changed to make a picture or drawing larger or smaller.

Page 57: ANALOGIES WITH SHAPES

LESSON

Introduction

Teacher Comment: **We learned that analogies can show change in size or color.**

Explaining the Objective

Teacher Comment: **In this lesson you will find the shape that completes each analogy.**

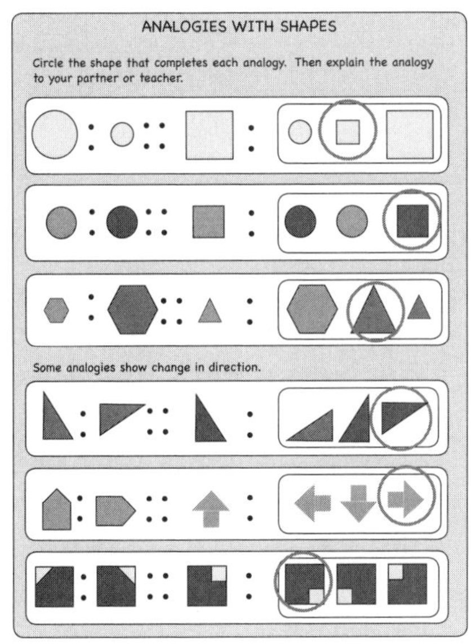

Conducting the Lesson

Teacher Comment: **In the first box, the yellow circle becomes smaller. The second pair of shapes will also change in the same way. Which shape shows the same change and completes the analogy?**

Student Response: The small yellow square completes the analogy.

Teacher Comment: **Explain the analogy.**

Student Response: The large yellow circle becomes smaller like the large yellow square becomes smaller.

Teacher Comment: **In the next two rows circle the shape that completes the analogy. Explain each analogy to your partner.**

- Check students' work. Continue this dialog for the next two exercises.

Teacher Comment: **In the next analogies the shapes change direction. Decide how the first shapes have been turned. Circle the shape that shows what the third shape will look like when it has been turned in the same way.**

- Check students' work. Continue this dialog to discuss students' answers.

Thinking About Thinking

Teacher Comment: **What did you pay attention to when you found the shape that completed the analogy?**

Student Response:

1. I decided how the first pair of shapes changed.
2. I looked at the third shape and decided which shape would show the same change.
3. I found the shape that completed the analogy.

Personal Application

Teacher Comment: **When do you need to know how pairs of shapes are changed?**

Student Response: I need to know how shapes are changed to make a picture or drawing larger or smaller.

Page 58: ANALOGIES WITH SHAPES

LESSON

• Students should know that the term "double" means making a size or amount twice as large.

Introduction

Teacher Comment: **In the last lesson we learned about analogies that show change in size, color, or direction.**

Explaining the Objective

Teacher Comment: **In this exercise you will complete analogies that show a change in number.**

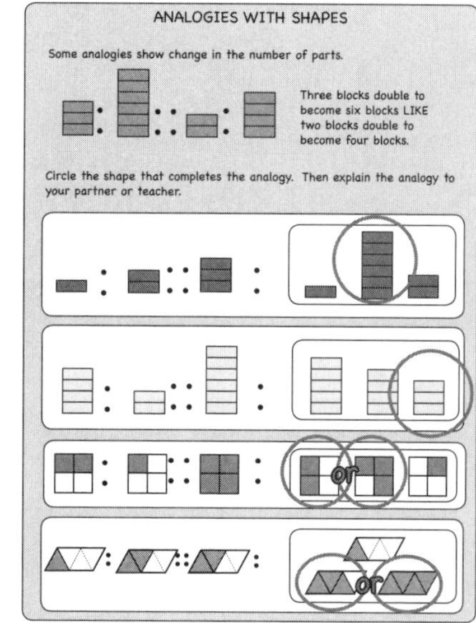

Conducting the Lesson

Teacher Comment: **In the analogy of the orange blocks, the first stack doubles from three blocks to six blocks. To change the same way, the stack of two blocks will double to become four blocks. We read the analogy, "Three blocks double to become six blocks like two blocks double to become four blocks." Look at the red blocks. How does the first pair change?**

Student Response: One block doubles to become two blocks.

Teacher Comment: **The three blocks should double to complete the analogy. Circle the stack that shows the analogy. Explain the analogy to your partner.**

Student Response: One block doubles to two blocks like three blocks doubles to six blocks.

• Check students' work. Continue this dialog to discuss students' answers.

© 2016 The Critical Thinking Co.™ • www.CriticalThinking.com • 800-458-4849

Thinking About Thinking

Teacher Comment: **What did you pay attention to when you completed the analogy?**

Student Response:

1. I decided how the first number changed.
2. I looked at the third number and decided how it would change the same way.
3. I found the number of shapes that completed the analogy.

Personal Application

Teacher Comment: **When do you need to show analogies with numbers?**

Student Response: I need to know how to show analogies with numbers to show fractions are equal.

© 2016 The Critical Thinking Co.™ • www.CriticalThinking.com • 800-458-4849

CHAPTER FIVE – FIGURAL CLASSIFICATIONS (Pages 59-72)
GENERAL INTRODUCTION

CURRICULUM APPLICATIONS
Mathematics: Recognize properties of polygons and pattern recognition.
Science: Classify natural objects by shape (leaves, fish, shells, etc.). Read charts with rows and columns.
Social Studies: Identify road signs from their shape. Recognize map symbols.

TEACHING SUGGESTIONS
- Notice that the terms "shape" and "polygon" are used interchangeably where appropriate. If students use the term "polygon" easily, use that term throughout the lessons.
- Notice that the terms "group" and "class" are used interchangeably where appropriate. If students use the term "class" easily, use that term throughout the lessons.
- Identify plants or animals in the same classification that have the same shape (butterflies, leaves, flowers, insects, etc.).

Page 60: CLASSIFYING SHAPES – MATCHING

LESSON

Introduction
Teacher Comment: **We call ourselves a "class" of students. In this class students are about the same age, meet in the same place, study the same things, and have the same teacher. Class also means a group that has an important common characteristic. When we describe a group by its common characteristic, we are classifying it. When we classify things, we describe how all the things in the group are alike.**

Explaining the Objective
Teacher Comment: **In this lesson you will match a shape to a group with the same shape.**

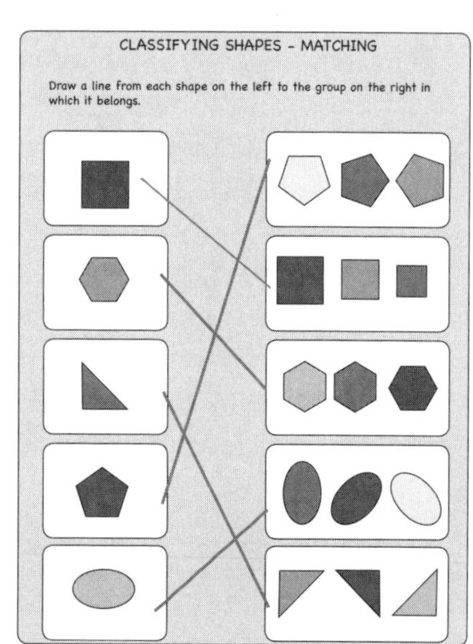

Conducting the Lesson
Teacher Comment: **Look at the purple square in the top left corner. It belongs to the group of squares. Notice a line has been drawn to the group of squares. Name the next shape.**

Student Response: The next shape below is a green hexagon.

Teacher Comment: **To which group does the green hexagon belong?**

Student Response: The green hexagon belongs to the group of hexagons.

Teacher Comment: **Draw a line from the green hexagon to the third group of shapes on the right, which are all hexagons.**

- Check students' work. Continue this dialog to discuss students' answers.

© 2016 The Critical Thinking Co.™ • www.CriticalThinking.com • 800-458-4849

Thinking About Thinking

Teacher Comment: **What did you pay attention to when you decided which group a shape fit?**

Student Response:

1. I looked at the shape and named it.
2. I looked for the group with the same shape.

Personal Application

Teacher Comment: **When do you need to fit something into a group?**

Student Response: I fit things into a group when I match socks, do puzzles, or draw flowers, animals, or objects.

Pages 61: CLASSIFYING SHAPES – FIND THE EXCEPTION

LESSON

Introduction

Teacher Comment: **We have matched shapes to their groups.**

Explaining the Objective

Teacher Comment: **In this lesson you will decide how most of the shapes are alike, and cross out the shape that does not belong to the group.**

Conducting the Lesson

Teacher Comment: **To what class do five of these shapes belong?**

Student Response: Five of these shapes are triangles with a square corner (right triangles).

Teacher Comment: **Notice that the yellow triangle is crossed out. It is not in the class of right triangles.**

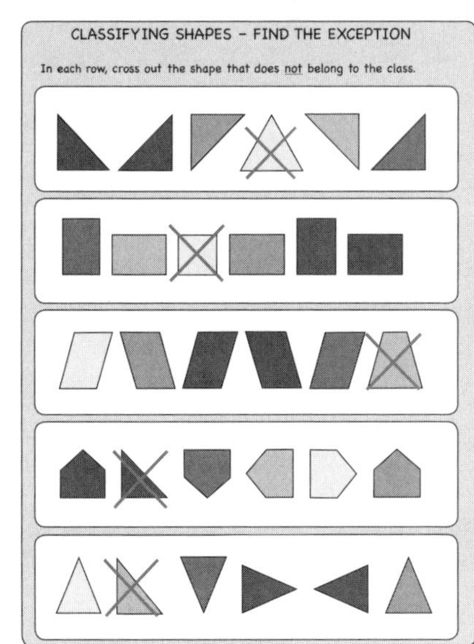

- Check students' work. Continue this dialog to discuss students' answers.

Thinking About Thinking

Teacher Comment: **What did you pay attention to in order to find the shape that was not in the same class as the others?**

Student Response:

1. I looked to see how five of the shapes were alike.
2. I named their class.
3. I looked to see which shape was different from the five.
4. I crossed out the shape that didn't belong to that class.

Personal Application

Teacher Comment: **When do you need to find an object that is not like the others?**

Student Response: I need to find an object that is not like the others when I sort eating or cooking utensils, construction toys or tools, edge pieces from interior pieces in a picture puzzle, and when I organize objects or materials at home or in school.

Page 62: CLASSIFYING SHAPES

LESSON

Introduction

Teacher Comment: **We described a group of shapes by their class.**

Explaining the Objective

Teacher Comment: **In this lesson you will sort polygons into three groups.**

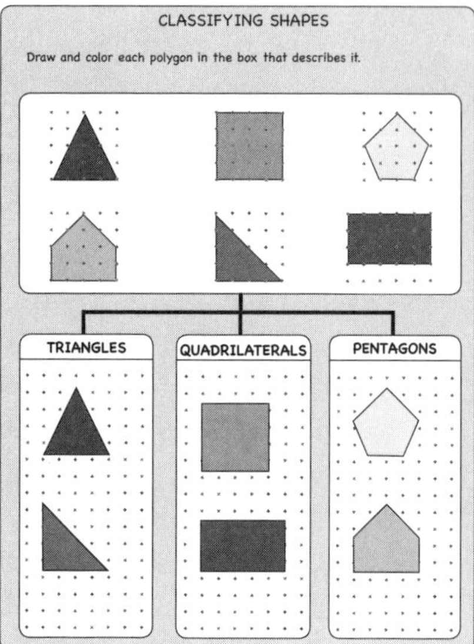

Conducting the Lesson

Teacher Comment: **Name the polygon in the top left corner.**

Student Response: The shape is a purple triangle.

Teacher Comment: **To what group does the purple triangle belong?**

Student Response: The purple triangle belongs with the group of triangles.

Teacher Comment: **Draw a purple triangle in the box marked "triangles."**

Teacher Comment: **Draw and color each polygon in the box that describes it.**

• Check students' work. Continue this dialog to discuss students' answers.

Thinking About Thinking

Teacher Comment: **What did you pay attention to when you drew polygons that belong to the same class.**

Student Response:

1. I named the shape.
2. I named the class of that polygon.
3. I found the box for that class.
4. I drew the shape with others of that class.

Personal Application

Teacher Comment: **When do you need to sort things by shape?**

Student Response: I sort things by shape when I match socks, do puzzles, or build with blocks.

© 2016 The Critical Thinking Co.™ • www.CriticalThinking.com • 800-458-4849

Page 63: CLASSIFYING QUADRILATERALS

LESSON

Introduction

Teacher Comment: **In the last lesson we sorted shapes into groups of triangles, quadrilaterals, and pentagons.**

Explaining the Objective

Teacher Comment: **In this lesson you will sort quadrilaterals into three groups.**

Conducting the Lesson

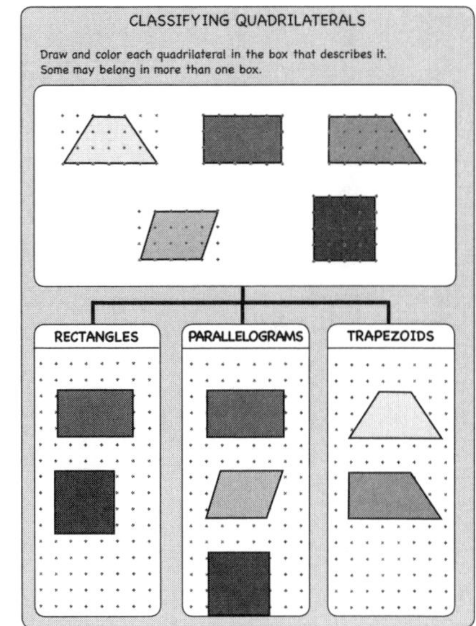

Teacher Comment: **Name the three groups in which the shapes will be sorted.**

Student Response: The shape groups are rectangles, parallelograms, and trapezoids.

Teacher Comment: **Name the first shape on the left.**

Student Response: The first shape is a yellow trapezoid.

Teacher Comment: **Draw a yellow trapezoid in the trapezoid box.**

• Check students' work.

Teacher Comment: **Name the red shape.**

Student Response: The red shape is a rectangle.

Teacher Comment: **Draw a red rectangle in the rectangle box.**

• Check students' work.

Teacher Comment: **The red rectangle also belongs in another box. Which one?**

Student Response: The red rectangle is also a parallelogram because its opposite sides are parallel.

Teacher Comment: **Draw a red rectangle in the parallelogram box.**

• Check students' work. Continue this dialog to discuss students' answers.

Teacher Comment: **Name the green shape.**

Student Response: The green shape is a trapezoid because it has one pair of parallel sides, the top and the bottom.

Teacher Comment: **Draw a green trapezoid in the trapezoid box.**

• Check students' work.

Teacher Comment: **Name the orange shape.**

Student Response: The orange shape is a parallelogram.

Teacher Comment: **Draw an orange parallelogram in the parallelogram box.**

• Check students' work.

© 2016 The Critical Thinking Co.™ • www.CriticalThinking.com • 800-458-4849

Teacher Comment: **Name the purple shape.**

Student Response: The purple shape is a square.

Teacher Comment: **Where does the square belong?**

Student Response: A square is a rectangle with equal sides. Rectangles are also parallelograms.

Teacher Comment: **Draw a purple square in both the rectangle box and the parallelogram box.**

Thinking About Thinking

Teacher Comment: **What did you pay attention to when you matched shapes to groups?**

Student Response:

1. I named the shape.
2. I named the group that had the same shape.
3. I checked that it belonged in that group.

Personal Application

Teacher Comment: **When do you need to sort things by shape?**

Student Response: I sort things by shape when I match socks, do puzzles, or build with blocks.

Page 64 - CLASSIFYING SHAPES

LESSON

Introduction

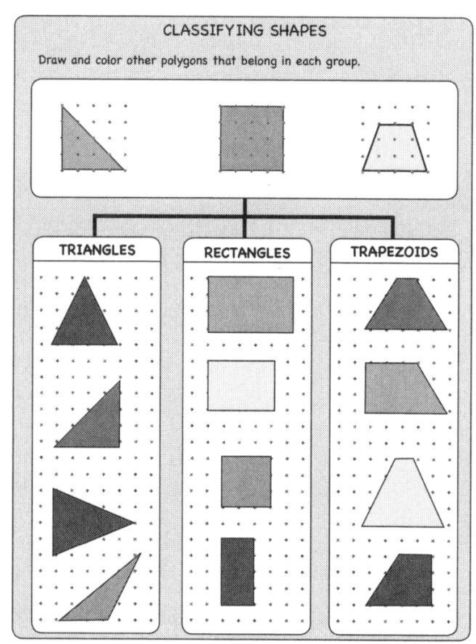

Teacher Comment: **In the last lesson we sorted a group of quadrilaterals into rectangles, parallelograms, and trapezoids. What did you learn about quadrilaterals?**

Student Response: I learned that a rectangle is a parallelogram and a square is a rectangle and a parallelogram.

Explaining the Objective

Teacher Comment: **In this lesson you will draw polygons that are triangles, rectangles, or trapezoids.**

Conducting the Lesson

Teacher Comment: **In the first box draw and color at least three other triangles.**

• Check students' work. Students may draw and color any type of triangle.

Teacher Comment: **In the second box draw at least three other rectangles.**

Teacher Comment: **In the third box draw at least three other trapezoids.**

• Check students' work.

© 2016 The Critical Thinking Co.™ • www.CriticalThinking.com • 800-458-4849

Thinking About Thinking

Teacher Comment: **What did you pay attention to when you drew polygons that belonged to the same class.**

Student Response:

1. I named the shape.
2. I named the class of that polygon.
3. I found the box for that class.
4. I drew the shape with others of that class.

Personal Application

Teacher Comment: **When do you need to sort things by shape?**

Student Response: I sort things by shape when I match socks, do puzzles, or build with blocks.

Page 65: CLASSIFYING SHAPES – FORMING GROUPS

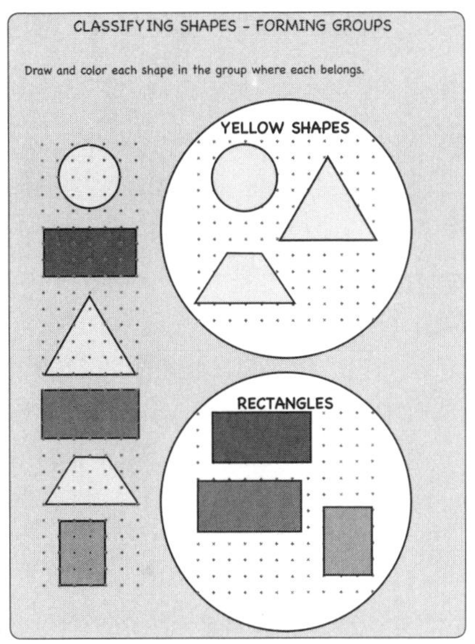

LESSON

Introduction

Teacher Comment: **In the last lesson we drew groups of polygons.**

Explaining the Objective

Teacher Comment: **In this lesson you will sort shapes that are either yellow or rectangles.**

Conducting the Lesson

Teacher Comment: **Name the first shape.**

Student Response: The first shape is a yellow circle.

Teacher Comment: **Draw a yellow circle in the group "YELLOW SHAPES."**

Teacher Comment: **Name the second shape.**

Student Response: The second shape is a blue rectangle.

Teacher Comment: **Draw a blue rectangle in the group "RECTANGLES."**

• Check students' work.

Teacher Comment: **Draw and color each shape in the group where each belongs.**

Thinking About Thinking

Teacher Comment: **What did you pay attention to when you sorted shapes?**

Student Response:

1. I named the shape and color.
2. I decided in which group it belonged.
3. I copied the shape and color in the correct group.

Personal Application

Teacher Comment: **When do you need to sort shapes?**

Student Response: I sort things by shape when I match socks, do puzzles, or build with blocks.

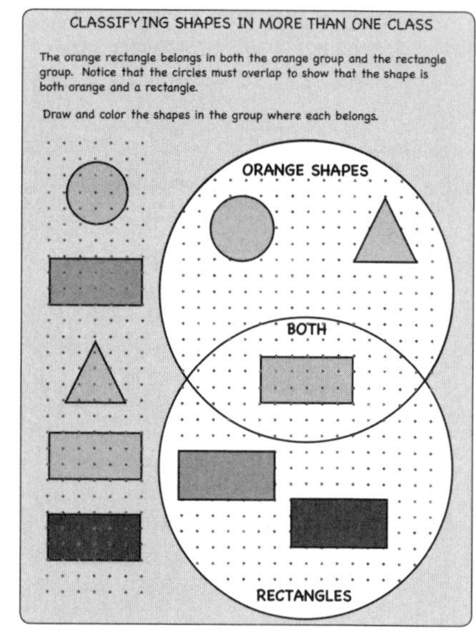

Pages 66-68: CLASSIFYING SHAPES IN MORE THAN ONE CLASS

LESSON

- These lessons may take more than one class session. Repeat the directions and check students' work.

Introduction

Teacher Comment: **In the last lessons we sorted shapes into two groups.**

Explaining the Objective

Teacher Comment: **In this lesson you will learn that some shapes can belong in two groups.**

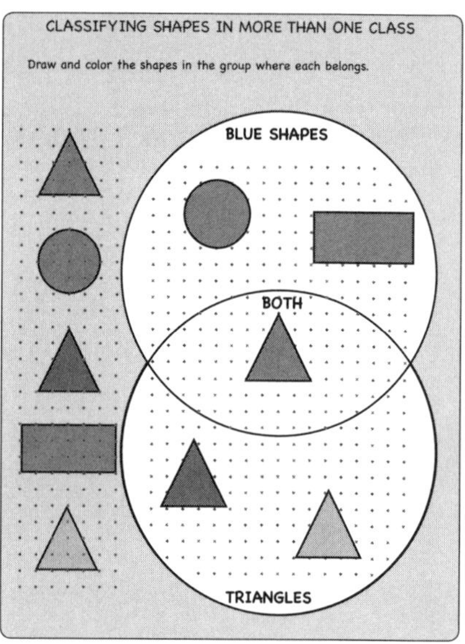

Conducting the Lesson

Teacher Comment: **The orange rectangle belongs in both the orange group and the rectangle group. Notice that the circles must overlap to show that the shape is both orange and a rectangle. Draw and color the rest of the shapes in the group where each belongs.**

- Check students' work.

Teacher Comment: **On pages 67 and 68, draw and color the shapes in the group where each belongs.**

- Check students' work.

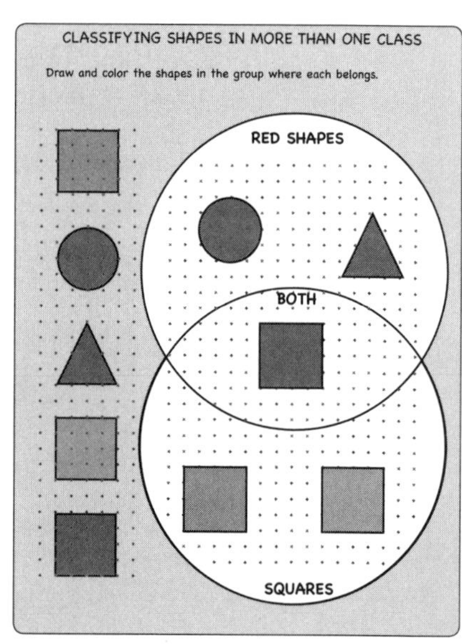

Thinking About Thinking

Teacher Comment: **What did you pay attention when you sorted shapes?**

Student Response:

1. I named the shape and color.
2. I decided in which group it belonged.
3. I copied the shape and color in the correct group.

Personal Application

Teacher Comment: **When do you need to sort shapes?**

Student Response: I sort things by shape when I match socks, do puzzles, or build with blocks.

© 2016 The Critical Thinking Co.™ • www.CriticalThinking.com • 800-458-4849

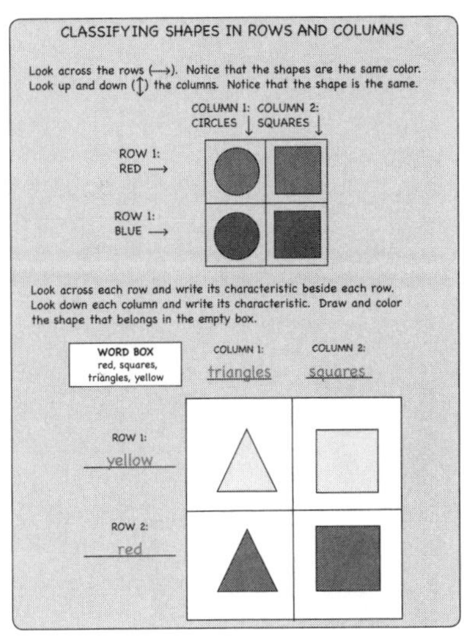
CLASSIFYING SHAPES IN ROWS AND COLUMNS

Look across the rows (⟶). Notice that the shapes are the same color. Look up and down (↕) the columns. Notice that the shape is the same.

COLUMN 1: CIRCLES ↓ COLUMN 2: SQUARES ↓

ROW 1: RED ⟶

ROW 1: BLUE ⟶

Look across each row and write its characteristic beside each row. Look down each column and write its characteristic. Draw and color the shape that belongs in the empty box.

WORD BOX: red, squares, triangles, yellow

COLUMN 1: triangles COLUMN 2: squares

ROW 1: yellow

ROW 2: red

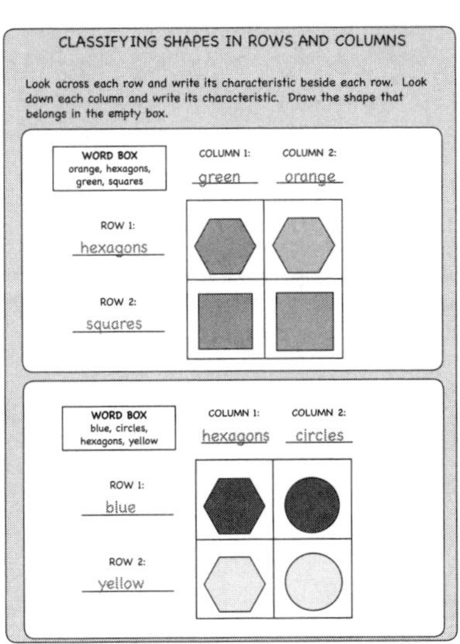
CLASSIFYING SHAPES IN ROWS AND COLUMNS

Look across each row and write its characteristic beside each row. Look down each column and write its characteristic. Draw the shape that belongs in the empty box.

WORD BOX: orange, hexagons, green, squares

COLUMN 1: green COLUMN 2: orange

ROW 1: hexagons

ROW 2: squares

WORD BOX: blue, circles, hexagons, yellow

COLUMN 1: hexagons COLUMN 2: circles

ROW 1: blue

ROW 2: yellow

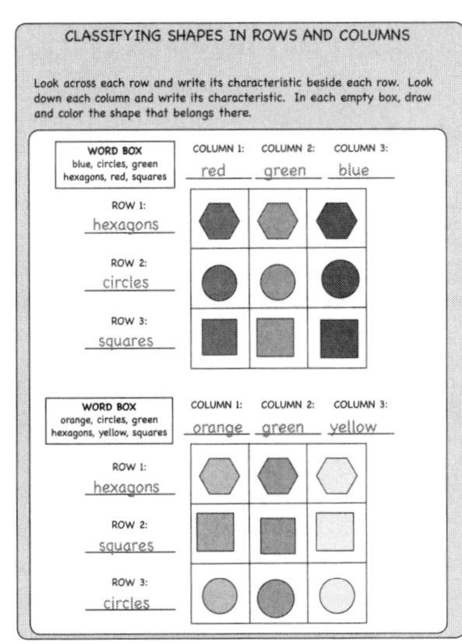
CLASSIFYING SHAPES IN ROWS AND COLUMNS

Look across each row and write its characteristic beside each row. Look down each column and write its characteristic. In each empty box, draw and color the shape that belongs there.

WORD BOX: blue, circles, green hexagons, red, squares

COLUMN 1: red COLUMN 2: green COLUMN 3: blue

ROW 1: hexagons

ROW 2: circles

ROW 3: squares

WORD BOX: orange, circles, green hexagons, yellow, squares

COLUMN 1: orange COLUMN 2: green COLUMN 3: yellow

ROW 1: hexagons

ROW 2: squares

ROW 3: circles

Pages 69-71: CLASSIFYING SHAPES IN ROWS AND COLUMNS

LESSON

- These lessons may take more than one class session. Repeat the directions and check students' work.

Introduction

Teacher Comment: **In the last lessons we sorted shapes into groups.**

Explaining the Objective

Teacher Comment: **In this lesson you will identify rows and columns to show two characteristics of a shape.**

Conducting the Lesson

Teacher Comment: **In the lower box what are the characteristics of columns one and two?**

Student Response: Column one is for triangles and column two is for squares.

Teacher Comment: **What are the characteristics of rows one and two?**

Student Response: Row one is for yellow shapes and row two is for red shapes.

Teacher Comment: **Draw and color the shape that belongs in the empty box.**

- Check students' work. Continue this dialog to discuss students' answers on pages 70 and 71.

Thinking About Thinking

Teacher Comment: **What did you pay attention to when you classified shapes two ways?**

Student Response:

1. I decided the characteristics of the rows.
2. I decided the characteristics of the columns.
3. I drew shapes in the blanks that fit the characteristics of the rows and columns.

Personal Application

Teacher Comment: **When do you need to understand the characteristics of shapes in rows and columns?**

Student Response: I need to understand rows and columns to read charts or schedules.

Page 72: WRITING DESCRIPTIONS OF CLASSES

LESSON

Introduction
Teacher Comment: **We have classified shapes.**

Explaining the Objective
Teacher Comment: **In this lesson you will describe classes of shapes.**

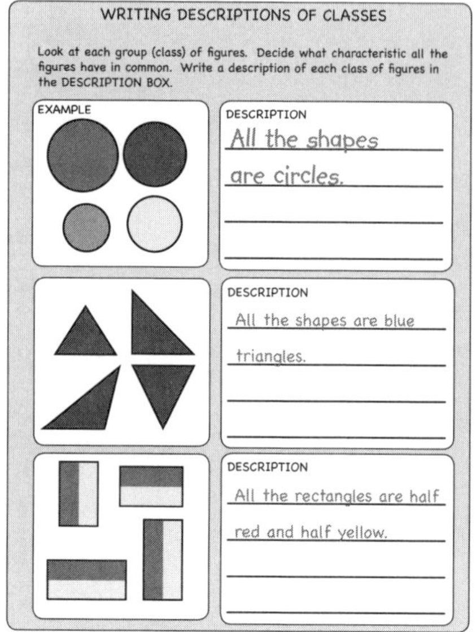

Conducting the Lesson
Teacher Comment: **In the example box what shapes do you see?**
Student Response: I see four circles of different sizes and colors.
Teacher Comment: **What characteristic do they all have in common?**
Student Response: They are all circles.
Teacher Comment: **In the description box you see "All the shapes are circles." What do all the shapes in the second box have in common?**
Student Response: All the shapes are blue triangles.
Teacher Comment: **Write the description that describes this class of shapes.**

• Check students' work. Continue this dialog to discuss students' answers.

Thinking About Thinking
Teacher Comment: **What did you pay attention to when you described a group of shapes?**
Student Response:
1. I decided how all the shapes were alike.
2. I wrote a sentence that described that group.

Personal Application
Teacher Comment: **When do you need to describe groups of shapes?**
Student Response: I describe groups of shapes to tell someone else their characteristics.

© 2016 The Critical Thinking Co.™ • www.CriticalThinking.com • 800-458-4849

CHAPTER SIX – THINKING ABOUT MATTER, WATER, AND WEATHER (Pages 73-80)
GENERAL INTRODUCTION

CURRICULUM APPLICATIONS
Language Arts: Identify the significance of matter, water, and weather in myths and stories. Discuss grade two topics and texts with peers and adults in large and small groups. Compare and contrast the most important points in describing two concepts. Produce complete sentences in order to provide adequate detail and clarification. Use appropriate adjectives, adverbs, and verbs to describe key concepts. Describe the connections between a series of events, concepts, or steps.
Mathematics: Identify how measurement is important in describing weather.
Science: Identify solids, liquids, and gases. Understand the structure and properties of matter before and after they undergo change. Explain the water cycle. Identify weather conditions and instruments that measure them. Understand patterns of weather and factors that affect weather.
Social Studies: Identify how water conditions and climate effect food, clothing, shelter, and cultures.
Art: Identify how weather is depicted in works of art.

TEACHING SUGGESTIONS
- Introduce lessons by reading non-fiction picture books that feature states of matter, water, and weather.

Page 74: DESCRIBING MATTER

LESSON

DESCRIBING MATTER

Matter is anything that takes up space and has weight. It can be a solid, a liquid, or a gas. If a liquid is heated, it becomes so light that you do not see it. It has become a gas. Circle the picture of matter that your teacher describes.*

blocks · orange juice · steam

smoke · bricks · paint

waterfall · fog · rocks

*Descriptions are available on page 19 of the free answer guide.

Introduction
Teacher Comment: **Matter is anything that takes up space and has weight. Some matter is solid, something that is hard and has shape such as this book. Some matter is liquid. A liquid is anything wet that you can pour, such as water. Milk and oil are liquids. If a liquid is heated, it becomes so light that you do not see it. It has become a gas. A gas is something such as air that does not have a shape and cannot be poured. Air is made of different gases mixed together.**

Explaining the Objective
Teacher Comment: **In this lesson you will circle the picture of matter that your teacher describes.**

Conducting the Lesson
Teacher Comment: **Which picture in the first row shows a healthy breakfast drink?**
Student Response: The breakfast drink is orange juice.
Teacher Comment: **What form of matter is orange juice?**

Student Response: Orange juice is a liquid.
Teacher Comment: **Circle the picture of orange juice.**

Teacher Comment: **What form of matter are the blocks?**
Student Response: The blocks are solid.
Teacher Comment: **What form of matter is the steam?**
Student Response: The steam is a gas.

Teacher Comment: **Which picture in the second row shows a solid that is used to build houses?**
Student Response: Bricks are used to build houses.
Teacher Comment: **What form of matter are bricks?**
Student Response: Bricks are solid.
Teacher Comment: **Circle the picture of the bricks.**

Teacher Comment: **What form of matter is the smoke?**
Student Response: The smoke is a gas.
Teacher Comment: **What form of matter is the paint?**
Student Response: The paint is a liquid.

Teacher Comment: **Which picture in the third row shows weather that makes it hard to see?**
Student Response: Fog makes it hard to see.
Teacher Comment: **What form of matter is the fog?**
Student Response: The fog is a gas.
Teacher Comment: **Circle the picture of fog.**

Teacher Comment: **What form of matter is the waterfall?**
Student Response: The waterfall is a liquid.
Teacher Comment: **What form of matter are the rocks?**
Student Response: The rocks are solid.

Thinking About Thinking

Teacher Comment: **What did you pay attention to when you decided whether something was a solid, a liquid, or a gas?**
Student Response:
1. I remembered whether I could hold it, pour it, or barely see it.
2. I remembered whether I should call it a solid, a liquid, or a gas.

Personal Application

Teacher Comment: **When do you need to decide whether something is a solid, a liquid, or a gas?**
Student Response: I need to decide whether something is a solid, a liquid, or a gas to know how to use it and whether it may change.

© 2016 The Critical Thinking Co.™ • www.CriticalThinking.com • 800-458-4849

Page 75: CHANGING FORMS OF MATTER

LESSON

Introduction

Teacher Comment: **We have identified the three forms of matter. Some kinds of matter can change from a solid to a liquid by heating. A liquid can change to a solid by cooling.**

Explaining the Objective

Teacher Comment: **In this lesson you will tell whether the object shown in a picture is a solid or a liquid. You will also tell if a change is caused by heating or cooling.**

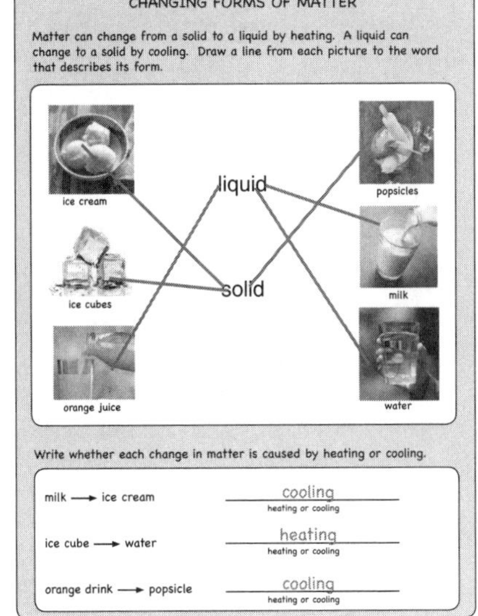

CHANGING FORMS OF MATTER

Matter can change from a solid to a liquid by heating. A liquid can change to a solid by cooling. Draw a line from each picture to the word that describes its form.

Write whether each change in matter is caused by heating or cooling.

milk → ice cream	cooling (heating or cooling)
ice cube → water	heating (heating or cooling)
orange drink → popsicle	cooling (heating or cooling)

Conducting the Lesson

Teacher Comment: **Is the ice cream a solid or liquid?**

Student Response: Ice cream is a solid.

Teacher Comment: **Draw a line from the ice cream to "solid."**

- Continue this dialog to discuss students' answers. When the first part of lesson is complete continue with the second part.

Teacher Comment: **Write whether each change in matter caused by heating or cooling. When milk is changed into ice cream, is this caused by heating or cooling?**

Student Response: Milk is changed to ice cream by cooling.

Teacher Comment: **Write "cooling" on the first blank.**

- Check students' work. Continue this dialog to discuss students' answers.

Thinking About Thinking

Teacher Comment: **What did you pay attention to when you decided whether something was a solid, a liquid, or a gas?**

Student Response:

1. I remembered whether I could hold something, pour it, or barely see it.
2. I remembered whether I should call it a solid, a liquid, or a gas.

Personal Application

Teacher Comment: **When do you need to decide whether something is a solid, a liquid, or a gas?**

Student Response: I need to decide whether it is a solid, a liquid, or a gas to know how heating or cooling it will keep or change its shape.

Page 76: SOLIDS, LIQUIDS, AND GASES

LESSON

- Remind students of words that describe heating (boil, thaw, defrost) or cooling (freeze).
- Explain to students that gasoline is a liquid. We call it "gas" as a short word for gasoline.

Introduction

Teacher Comment: **We have identified liquids and solids and how they change.**

Explaining the Objective

Teacher Comment: **In this lesson you will learn about gases and how solids, liquids, and gases are different.**

- Read the information in the white box.

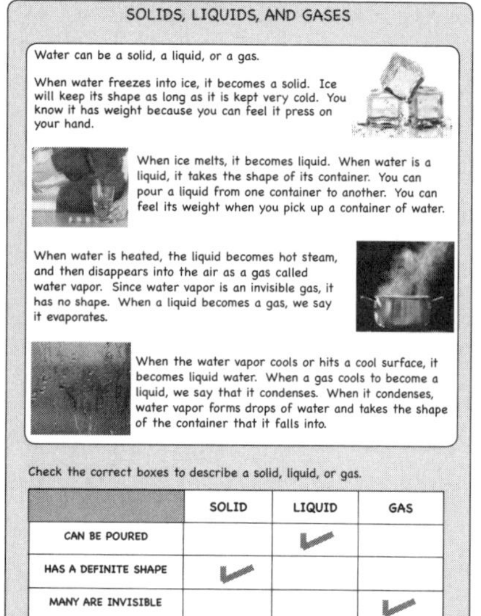

SOLIDS, LIQUIDS, AND GASES

Water can be a solid, a liquid, or a gas.

When water freezes into ice, it becomes a solid. Ice will keep its shape as long as it is kept very cold. You know it has weight because you can feel it press on your hand.

When ice melts, it becomes liquid. When water is a liquid, it takes the shape of its container. You can pour a liquid from one container to another. You can feel its weight when you pick up a container of water.

When water is heated, the liquid becomes hot steam, and then disappears into the air as a gas called water vapor. Since water vapor is an invisible gas, it has no shape. When a liquid becomes a gas, we say it evaporates.

When the water vapor cools or hits a cool surface, it becomes liquid water. When a gas cools to become a liquid, we say that it condenses. When it condenses, water vapor forms drops of water and takes the shape of the container that it falls into.

Check the correct boxes to describe a solid, liquid, or gas.

	SOLID	LIQUID	GAS
CAN BE POURED		✓	
HAS A DEFINITE SHAPE	✓		
MANY ARE INVISIBLE			✓

Conducting the Lesson

Teacher Comment: **Which form of matter can be poured?**

Student Response: A liquid can be poured.

Teacher Comment: **Put a check mark in the box to show that a liquid can be poured.**

- Check students' work. Continue this dialog to discuss students' answers.

Thinking About Thinking

Teacher Comment: **What did you pay attention to when you decided that something is a solid, liquid, or gas?**

Student Response:

1. I decided whether the object kept its shape, was poured, or became hard to see.
2. I remembered whether it changed when heated or cooled.

Personal Application

Teacher Comment: **When do you need to pay attention to know whether something is a solid, liquid, or gas?**

Student Response: I need to know whether something is a solid, liquid, or gas to keep or change its shape.

© 2016 The Critical Thinking Co.™ • www.CriticalThinking.com • 800-458-4849

Page 77: HEATING AND COOLING WATER

LESSON

Introduction

Teacher Comment: **We have learned how solids, liquids, and gases are different.**

Explaining the Objective

Teacher Comment: **In this lesson you will tell how water changes when it is heated or cooled.**

• Read the paragraph at the top of the page.

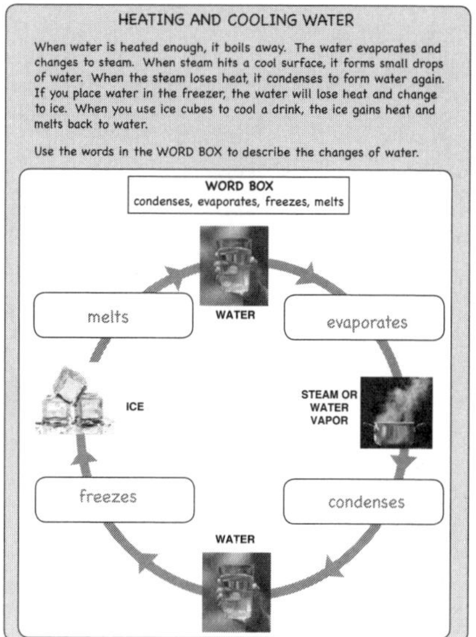

HEATING AND COOLING WATER

When water is heated enough, it boils away. The water evaporates and changes to steam. When steam hits a cool surface, it forms small drops of water. When the steam loses heat, it condenses to form water again. If you place water in the freezer, the water will lose heat and change to ice. When you use ice cubes to cool a drink, the ice gains heat and melts back to water.

Use the words in the WORD BOX to describe the changes of water.

WORD BOX
condenses, evaporates, freezes, melts

Conducting the Lesson

Teacher Comment: **We use the words "condenses," "evaporates," "freezes," and "melts" to describe how water changes form. When water is heated enough, it boils away. What do we call the change of water into steam?**

Student Response: When water changes to steam, it evaporates.

Teacher Comment: **Write "evaporates" in the box between "water" and "steam."**

Teacher Comment: **When steam cools, it forms small drops of water. What do we call the change of steam to water?**

Student Response: When steam changes to water it condenses.

Teacher Comment: **Write "condenses" in the box between "steam" and "water."**

Teacher Comment: **If you place water in the freezer, the water will lose heat and change to ice. What do we call the change from water to ice?**

Student Response: When water changes to ice it freezes.

Teacher Comment: **Write "freezes" in the box between "water" and "ice."**

Teacher Comment: **When you use ice cubes to cool a drink, the ice gains heat and changes back to water. What do we call the change from ice to water?**

Student Response: When ice changes to water the ice melts.

Teacher Comment: **Write "melts" in the box between ice and water.**

Thinking About Thinking

Teacher Comment: **What did you pay attention to when you told how water changed?**

Student Response:

1. I thought about what happens when water is heated or cooled.
2. I found the right word to describe the change.

Personal Application

Teacher Comment: **When do you need to tell how water changes form?**

Student Response: I need to tell how water changes to know how to use it.

Page 78: THE WATER CYCLE

LESSON

- Students may need to be reminded that when water becomes a gas, it is called "steam" or "water vapor."

Introduction

Teacher Comment: **We have learned how heating and cooling changes the form of water.**

Explaining the Objective

Teacher Comment: **In this lesson you will show how heating and cooling water works in nature.**

Conducting the Lesson

Teacher Comment: **Look at the diagram while I explain how heating and cooling water works in nature. Heat from the sun causes water to evaporate from lakes and oceans. The warm, invisible water vapor rises higher and higher. As it rises, it cools. When moist air is cooled, tiny water droplets condense into clouds. When the water droplets grow large enough, they fall as rain. The rain runs off the land into rivers. The rivers flow into the ocean. What happens when the sun heats water in the ocean?**

Student Response: When the sun heats the ocean, the water evaporates to become water vapor.

Teacher Comment: **Write "evaporates" in the box to show that the sun heats the ocean water to change it to a vapor.**

Teacher Comment: **When warm, invisible water vapor rises higher and higher, it cools. When moist air is cooled, tiny water droplets condense into clouds. What word tells what happens when water vapor changes into water droplets?**

Student Response: The water vapor condenses.

Teacher Comment: **Write "condenses" in the next box.**

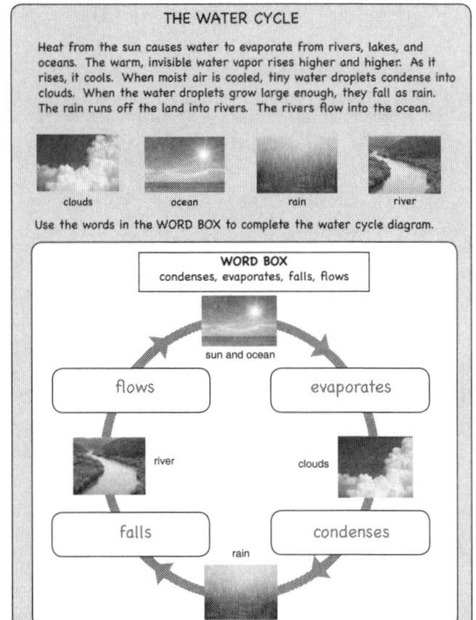

THE WATER CYCLE

Heat from the sun causes water to evaporate from rivers, lakes, and oceans. The warm, invisible water vapor rises higher and higher. As it rises, it cools. When moist air is cooled, tiny water droplets condense into clouds. When the water droplets grow large enough, they fall as rain. The rain runs off the land into rivers. The rivers flow into the ocean.

clouds ocean rain river

Use the words in the WORD BOX to complete the water cycle diagram.

WORD BOX
condenses, evaporates, falls, flows

Teacher Comment: **When the water droplets grow large enough, they fall as rain. What word tells what happens when water droplets become large?**

Student Response: The water in the cloud falls as rain.

Teacher Comment: **Write "falls" in the next box.**

Teacher Comment: **The rain runs off the land into rivers. What word tells what happens when the rain runs into rivers?**

Student Response: The rivers flow into the ocean.

Teacher Comment: **Write "flows" in the last box.**

- Help students understand that this cycle repeats.

© 2016 The Critical Thinking Co.™ • www.CriticalThinking.com • 800-458-4849

Thinking About Thinking

Teacher Comment: **What did you pay attention to when you showed water evaporating and condensing in nature?**

Student Response:

1. I listened carefully to the explanation.
2. I matched the explanation to each step in the diagram.
3. I showed that water evaporating and condensing was a cycle that keeps repeating.

Personal Application

Teacher Comment: **When do you need to know about the water cycle?**

Student Response: I need to know about the water cycle to understand that heating and cooling affects the weather and the amount of water that people, plants, and animals need.

Page 79: PRECIPITATION

LESSON

Introduction

Teacher Comment: **We have learned how water changes in a cycle. When water vapor in clouds condenses back into water, it falls to the ground in different forms called precipitation. It can fall as solid snow flakes, solid hail, liquid rain, or as fog–a cloud on the ground.**

Explaining the Objective

Teacher Comment: **In this lesson you will identify different kinds of precipitation.**

Conducting the Lesson

Teacher Comment: **What is precipitation?**

Student Response: Precipitation is water in one of its forms that falls from the sky.

Teacher Comment: **What do we call the large water drops that fall from clouds above Earth?**

Student Response: Rain falls from the clouds.

Teacher Comment: **Write "Rain" in the first blank.**

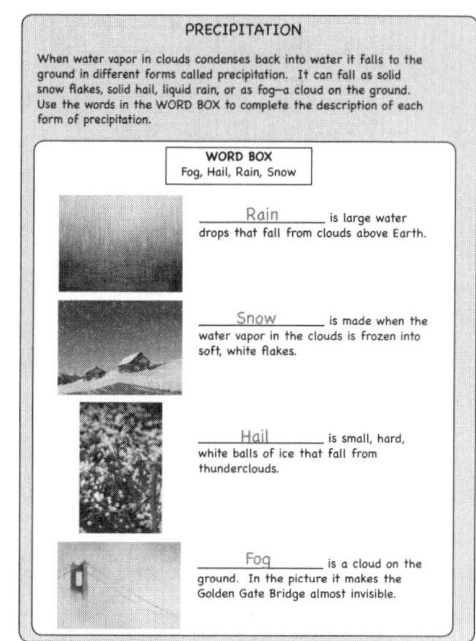

PRECIPITATION

When water vapor in clouds condenses back into water it falls to the ground in different forms called precipitation. It can fall as solid snow flakes, solid hail, liquid rain, or as fog—a cloud on the ground. Use the words in the WORD BOX to complete the description of each form of precipitation.

WORD BOX
Fog, Hail, Rain, Snow

Rain is large water drops that fall from clouds above Earth.

Snow is made when the water vapor in the clouds is frozen into soft, white flakes.

Hail is small, hard, white balls of ice that fall from thunderclouds.

Fog is a cloud on the ground. In the picture it makes the Golden Gate Bridge almost invisible.

Teacher Comment: **What do we call the precipitation that is made when the water vapor in the clouds is frozen into soft, white flakes.**

Student Response: Snow is formed when the water vapor in the clouds is frozen into soft, white flakes.

Teacher Comment: **Write "Snow" in the second blank.**

Teacher Comment: **What do we call the precipitation that is made when the water in thunderclouds is frozen into small, hard, white balls of ice that fall to the ground?**

Student Response: Hail is formed when the water in the clouds is frozen into hard, white balls of ice.

© 2016 The Critical Thinking Co.™ • www.CriticalThinking.com • 800-458-4849

Teacher Comment: **Write "Hail" in the third blank.**

- If needed, clarify the difference between snow and hail. Snow flakes are small individual crystals of ice. Hailstones are large balls of ice.

Teacher Comment: **What do we call a cloud that is formed on the ground?**
Student Response: Fog is a cloud formed on the ground.
Teacher Comment: **Write "Fog" in the fourth blank.**

- Optional extension: Discuss the difference between naturally occurring precipitation and storms.

Thinking About Thinking

Teacher Comment: **What did you look for when you identified forms of precipitation?**
Student Response:
1. I listened carefully to the description.
2. I found the picture that matched the description.

Personal Application

Teacher Comment: **When do you need to understand different kinds of precipitation?**
Student Response: I need to understand different kinds of precipitation to stay safe and dry.

Page 80: WEATHER INSTRUMENTS

LESSON

Introduction

Teacher Comment: **We have identified four kinds of precipitation.**

Explaining the Objective

Teacher Comment: **In this lesson you will learn what each weather instrument does and what it measures.**

Conducting the Lesson

Teacher Comment: **The first picture shows an anemometer that spins to measure how fast the wind is blowing. What does an anemometer measure?**
Student Response: The anemometer measures wind speed.
Teacher Comment: **Draw a line from the explanation to "WIND SPEED."**

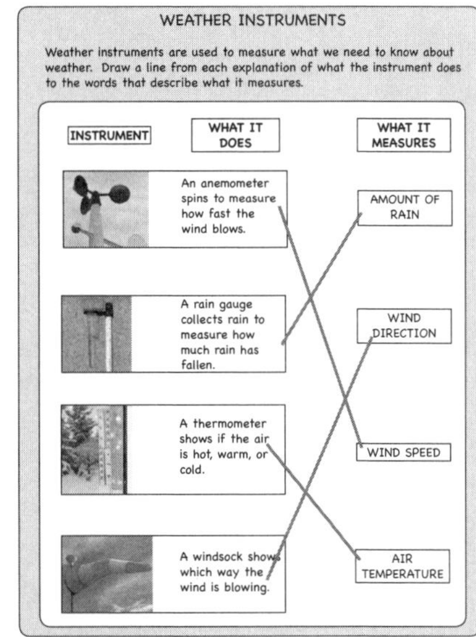
WEATHER INSTRUMENTS

Weather instruments are used to measure what we need to know about weather. Draw a line from each explanation of what the instrument does to the words that describe what it measures.

INSTRUMENT	WHAT IT DOES	WHAT IT MEASURES
	An anemometer spins to measure how fast the wind blows.	AMOUNT OF RAIN
	A rain gauge collects rain to measure how much rain has fallen.	WIND DIRECTION
	A thermometer shows if the air is hot, warm, or cold.	WIND SPEED
	A windsock shows which way the wind is blowing.	AIR TEMPERATURE

Teacher Comment: **The second picture shows a gauge that collects rain to measure how much has fallen. Which of the explanations tells what a rain gauge measures?**
Student Response: The rain gauge measures the amount of rain.
Teacher Comment: **Draw a line from the explanation to "AMOUNT OF RAIN."**

© 2016 The Critical Thinking Co.™ • www.CriticalThinking.com • 800-458-4849

Teacher Comment: **The third picture shows a thermometer that shows if air is hot, warm, or cold. Which of the explanations tells what a thermometer measures?**

Student Response: The thermometer shows if the air is hot, warm, or cold.

Teacher Comment: **Draw a line from the explanation to "AIR TEMPERATURE."**

Teacher Comment: **The last picture shows a windsock that shows which way the wind is blowing. Which of the explanations in the last column tells what a windsock measures?**

Student Response: The windsock measures wind direction.

Teacher Comment: **Draw a line from the explanation to "WIND DIRECTION."**

Thinking About Thinking

Teacher Comment: **What did you look for when you identified what each weather instrument measured?**

Student Response:

1. I listened to the explanation and looked at the picture for clues.
2. I matched the explanation to what it measured.

Personal Application

Teacher Comment: **When do you need to know how weather is measured?**

Student Response: I need to know how weather is measured to understand a weather report.

© 2016 The Critical Thinking Co.™ • www.CriticalThinking.com • 800-458-4849

CHAPTER SEVEN – THINKING ABOUT LAND FORMS AND BODIES OF WATER (Pages 81-94)
GENERAL INTRODUCTION

CURRICULUM APPLICATIONS

Language Arts: Identify the natural settings in myths and stories. Discuss grade two topics and texts with peers and adults in large and small groups. Compare and contrast the most important points in describing two concepts. Produce complete sentences in order to provide adequate detail and clarification. Use appropriate adjectives, adverbs, and verbs to describe key concepts.
Science: Identify terms for natural forms and their properties. Identify plants and animals that live in various ecosystems. Identify conditions that various plants and animals need to survive.
Social Studies: Identify land forms and bodies of water in local communities and on common maps. Give examples of ways in which people depend on the physical environment and natural resources to meet basic needs.
Enrichment: Create student art to depict local land forms and bodies of water.

TEACHING SUGGESTIONS

- In this chapter students learn the terms for various land forms and bodies of water. Identify local examples in order to relate the terms and the characteristics to the students' own communities.
- Second grade students can recognize continent and ocean, their country's map, and perhaps features of maps in their vicinity. Display and discuss these maps as the land forms and bodies of water are discussed in the lesson.
- Second grade students should understand that rivers and streams flow from their source to a larger body of water. Help students identify the source and flow of streams and rivers in their area.
- Students may have difficulty distinguishing the relative size of various bodies of water (streams and rivers, ponds and lakes). Identify local examples to clarify these terms.
- Students may not know which bodies of water contain fresh or salt water. Use picture books and familiar bodies of water to explain the difference. Discuss the plant and animal life in them.

MENTAL MODEL

A mental model outlines the characteristics that one must state to describe or define a concept. After completing this chapter, each student will have applied these mental models to land forms or bodies of water in the lessons. A mental model helps a student:

- anticipate what he or she needs to know to understand a new land form or body of water.
- remember the characteristics of a land form or body of water.
- state a clear definition or write an adequate description of a land form or body of water.
- explain a land form or body of water to someone else.

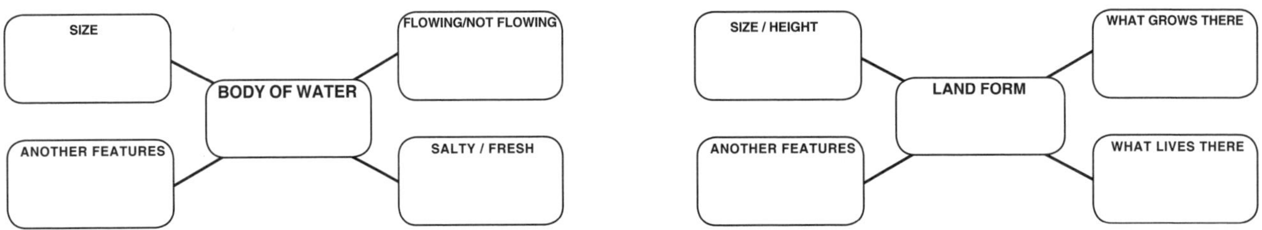

 © 2016 The Critical Thinking Co.™ • www.CriticalThinking.com • 800-458-4849

Page 82: DESCRIBING LAND FORMS AND BODIES OF WATER

LESSON

Introduction

Teacher Comment: **To understand nature, we need to recognize types of land and bodies of water. We need to know how high the land form is, how much water is available there for plants and animals, what plants and animals live there, and what people do there. To understand bodies of water, we need to know their size, whether or not the water is salty, what animals live there, and what people do around these bodies of water.**

Explaining the Objective

Teacher Comment: **In this lesson I will describe a land form or a body of water and you will select the picture that fits this description.**

Conducting the Lesson

Teacher Comment: **Look at the top row. We see a mountain, a plateau, and a valley. Listen to the clues and circle the land form that I describe. This high, flat land looks like a mountain that has had its top cut off. The flat land on top may be grassy. Its steep sides called "cliffs" may be rocky.**

- Ask students to decide with their partners which land form has been described.

DESCRIBING LAND FORMS AND BODIES OF WATER

Circle the picture of the land or water your teacher describes.*

mountain plateau valley

pond canal stream

wetlands river plain

lake ocean reservoir

*Descriptions are available on page 19 of the free answer guide.

Teacher Comment: **Which is the high, flat land form that looks like a mountain with a flat top?**

Student Response: The plateau is the high, flat land that looks like a mountain with a flat top.

Teacher Comment: **What clues let you know that the land form in this picture is a plateau?**

Student Response: The flat land has grass. The edge of the flat land is a rocky cliff that shows that the plateau is high ground.

Teacher Comment: **Why don't the other land forms fit the description?**

Student Response: The mountain has high, sharp tops. The valley is low and may not be flat.

Teacher Comment: **Circle the picture of the plateau.**

Teacher Comment: **Look at the second row. We see a pond, a canal, and a stream. Listen to the clues and circle the body of water that I describe. This long, thin body of water was built to move water where it is needed or to move ships from one large body of water to another.**

- Ask students to decide with their partners which body of water has been described.

Teacher Comment: **Which is the long, thin body of water that people built?**

Student Response: The canal is a long, thin body of water that people built.

Teacher Comment: **What clues let you know that the body of water in this picture is a canal?**

Student Response: I see how thin the canal is and the large body of water where the canal begins. I see that it has been built by people.

Teacher Comment: **Why don't the other bodies of water fit the description?**

Student Response: The pond is a small body of water that is surrounded by land. The stream is a small river. Both the pond and the stream are natural, not built by people.

Teacher Comment: **Circle the picture of the canal.**

Teacher Comment: **Look at the next row. We see wetlands, a river, and a plain. Listen to the clues and circle the land form that I describe. This flat land form contains so many streams and rivers that most of the ground is wet. It contains large areas of grass and some trees. Farmers cannot grow crops here, but people often fish and hunt in these large areas.**

- Ask students to decide with their partners which land form has been described.

Teacher Comment: **Which is the wet, flat land form?**

Student Response: The wetlands are a wet, flat land form.

Teacher Comment: **What clues let you know that this picture shows wetlands?**

Student Response: This flat, wet land has many streams and rivers. It has large areas of grass and some trees.

Teacher Comment: **Why don't the other pictures fit the description?**

Student Response: A river is a body of water that flows through plains, around mountains, and through the wetlands. The plain is not wet.

Teacher Comment: **Circle the picture of the wetlands.**

Teacher Comment: **Look at the bottom row. We see a lake, an ocean, and a reservoir. Listen to the clues and circle the body of water that I describe. This body of water is made when people build a very large dam across a river. The river water that collects behind the dam grows into a large lake that people use for recreation and for their water supply.**

- Ask students to decide with their partners which body of water has been described.

Teacher Comment: **Which is the large lake that people made by building a dam across a river?**

Student Response: The reservoir is a large lake that people made by building a dam across a river.

Teacher Comment: **What clues let you know that the body of water in this picture is a reservoir?**

Student Response: I see the dam that people built. I see the narrow river in front and the wide lake behind the dam.

Teacher Comment: **Why don't the other bodies of water fit the description?**

Student Response: A lake and an ocean are natural, not built, bodies of water.

Teacher Comment: **Circle the picture of the reservoir.**

© 2016 The Critical Thinking Co.™ • www.CriticalThinking.com • 800-458-4849

Thinking About Thinking

Teacher Comment: **What did you look for when you picked out the land form or body of water that was described?**

Student Response: I looked for its size, its surroundings, if plants or animals lived there and whether it was man-made.

Personal Application

Teacher Comment: **When is it important to understand land forms and bodies of water?**

Student Response: I need to understand land forms and bodies of water in order to know what plants or animals can live there.

Page 83: DESCRIBING LAND FORMS AND BODIES OF WATER

LESSON

Introduction

Teacher Comment: **We identified land forms and bodies of water from a description.**

Explaining the Objective

Teacher Comment: **In this lesson you will draw a line from each photograph to the word that describes it.**

Conducting the Lesson

Teacher Comment: **The first photograph shows a large, flat, grassy land. People often farm there. What is it called?**

Student Response: The large, flat, grassy land is a plain

Teacher Comment: **Draw a line from the picture to "plain."**

- Check students' work. Continue this dialog to discuss students' answers.

Thinking About Thinking

Teacher Comment: **What did you look for when you picked out the land form or body of water that was described?**

Student Response: I looked for its size, its surroundings, whether plants or animals lived there, and what people did there.

Personal Application

Teacher Comment: **When is it important to understand land forms and bodies of water?**

Student Response: I need to understand land forms and bodies of water in order to know what plants or animals can live there.

Page 84: DESCRIBING LAND FORMS

LESSON

Introduction

Teacher Comment: **We have identified land forms and bodies of water.**

Explaining the Objective

Teacher Comment: **In this lesson you will draw a line from each description to the picture of that land form. Look at the pictures of land forms. As I read the definition, decide which picture shows that landform.**

Conducting the Lesson

Teacher Comment: **What do we call a body of land completely surrounded by water?**
Student Response: Land that is surrounded by water is an island.
Teacher Comment: **Draw a line from the first definition to the picture of an island.**

Teacher Comment: **What do we call dry, sandy land where few plants and animals live?**
Student Response: Dry, sandy land where few plants or animals live is called a desert.
Teacher Comment: **Draw a line from the definition to the picture of a desert.**

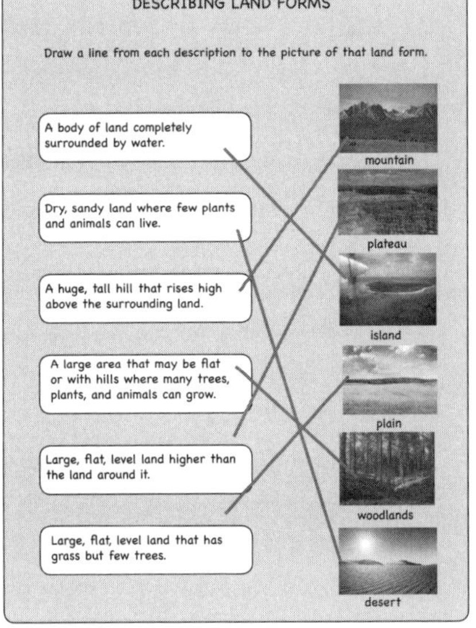

Teacher Comment: **What do we call a huge, tall hill that rises high above the surrounding land?**
Student Response: A huge, tall hill that rises high above the surrounding land is called a mountain.
Teacher Comment: **Draw a line from the definition to the picture of a mountain.**

Teacher Comment: **What do we call a large area that can be flat or hilly, and where many trees, plants, and animals can grow?**
Student Response: A large, flat or hilly area where many trees, plants, and animals live are woodlands.
Teacher Comment: **Draw a line from the definition to the picture of woodlands.**

Teacher Comment: **What do we call large, flat land that is higher than the land around it?**
Student Response: Large, flat land higher than the land around it is called a plateau.
Teacher Comment: **Draw a line from the definition to the picture of a plateau.**

Teacher Comment: **What do we call large, flat land that has grass, but few trees?**
Student Response: Large, flat land that has grass, but few trees, is called a plain.
Teacher Comment: **Draw a line from the last definition to the picture of a plain.**

© 2016 The Critical Thinking Co.™ • www.CriticalThinking.com • 800-458-4849

Thinking About Thinking

Teacher Comment: **What did you pay attention to when you described which land form was shown in the picture?**

Student Response:

1. I looked at the land form and compared it to the land around it to see how large or high it was.
2. I saw whether it was wet enough for plants and animals to live there.
3. I matched the photograph to the description for the land form.

Personal Application

Teacher Comment: **When do you need to know different land forms?**

Student Response: I need to know different land forms to understand what plants or animals can live there. I need to know the right word to describe a particular place to someone else. I need to know what the land form is like so that I understand stories that take place there.

Page 85: DESCRIBING BODIES OF WATER

LESSON

Introduction

Teacher Comment: **We have identified land forms and bodies of water.**

Explaining the Objective

Teacher Comment: **In this lesson you will match each description to the picture of that body of water.**

Conducting the Lesson

Teacher Comment: **What do we call a lake that people build by blocking a river to collect water for their use?**

Student Response: A lake that people build by blocking a river is called a reservoir.

Teacher Comment: **Draw a line from the first definition to the picture of a reservoir.**

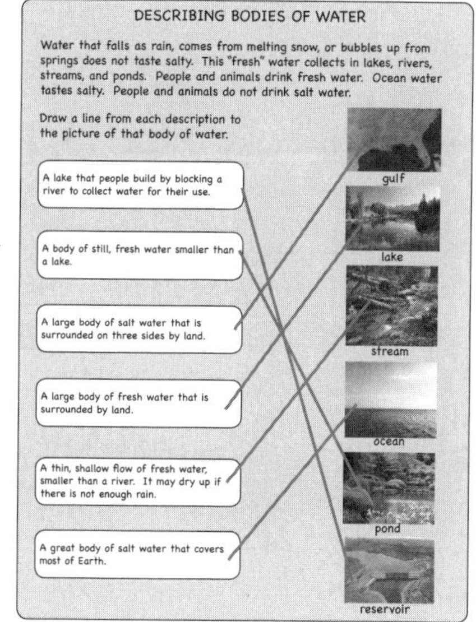

DESCRIBING BODIES OF WATER

Water that falls as rain, comes from melting snow, or bubbles up from springs does not taste salty. This "fresh" water collects in lakes, rivers, streams, and ponds. People and animals drink fresh water. Ocean water tastes salty. People and animals do not drink salt water.

Draw a line from each description to the picture of that body of water.

A lake that people build by blocking a river to collect water for their use.

A body of still, fresh water smaller than a lake.

A large body of salt water that is surrounded on three sides by land.

A large body of fresh water that is surrounded by land.

A thin, shallow flow of fresh water, smaller than a river. It may dry up if there is not enough rain.

A great body of salt water that covers most of Earth.

gulf

lake

stream

ocean

pond

reservoir

Teacher Comment: **What do we call a body of still, fresh water that is smaller than a lake?**

Student Response: A body of still, fresh water that is smaller than a lake is called a pond.

Teacher Comment: **Draw a line from the second definition to the picture of a pond.**

Teacher Comment: **What do we call a large body of salt water that is surrounded on three sides by land?**

Student Response: A large body of salt water that is surrounded on three sides by land is called a gulf.

Teacher Comment: **Draw a line from the definition to the picture of a gulf.**

Teacher Comment: **What do we call a large body of fresh water that is surrounded by land?**

Student Response: A large body of fresh water that is surrounded by land is called a lake.

Teacher Comment: **Draw a line from the definition to the picture of a lake.**

Teacher Comment: **What do we call a thin, shallow flow of fresh water smaller than a river? It may dry up if there is not enough rain.**

Student Response: A thin, shallow flow of fresh water smaller than a river is a stream.

Teacher Comment: **Draw a line from the definition to the picture of a stream.**

Teacher Comment: **What do you call a great body of salt water that covers most of Earth?**

Student Response: A body of salt water that covers most of Earth is called an ocean.

Teacher Comment: **Draw a line from the last definition to the picture of an ocean.**

Thinking About Thinking

Teacher Comment: **What did you pay attention to when you described which body of water was shown in the picture?**

Student Response:

1. I looked at the body of water and compared it to the land around it to see how large it was.
2. I thought about whether it was fresh or salt water.
3. I matched the photograph to the word for the body of water.
4. I matched the photograph to the word for its height.

Personal Application

Teacher Comment: **When do you need to know different bodies of water?**

Student Response: I need to know different bodies of water to understand which plants or animals can live there. I need to know the right word to describe a particular place to someone else. I need to know what the body of water is like so that I understand stories that take place there.

Page 86: HOW PEOPLE CHANGE THE LAND AND WATER

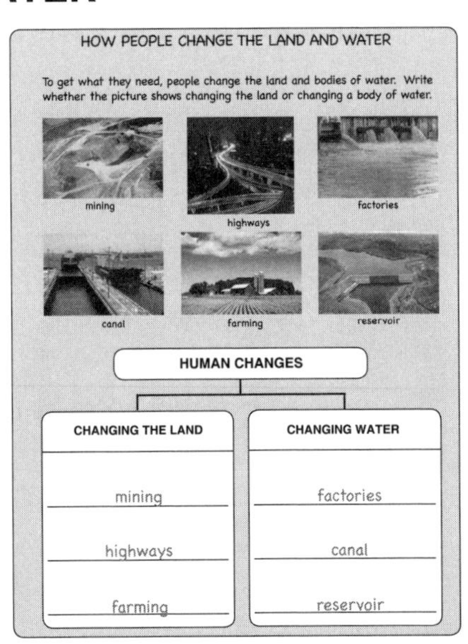
HOW PEOPLE CHANGE THE LAND AND WATER

To get what they need, people change the land and bodies of water. Write whether the picture shows changing the land or changing a body of water.

mining — highways — factories

canal — farming — reservoir

HUMAN CHANGES

CHANGING THE LAND	CHANGING WATER
mining	factories
highways	canal
farming	reservoir

LESSON

- Students may be unfamiliar with mining. Read a picture book about mining prior to the lesson.

Introduction

Teacher Comment: **We have matched descriptions to the pictures of land forms and bodies of water.**

Explaining the Objective

Teacher Comment: **In this lesson you will write how each picture shows how people have changed the land or a body of water.**

© 2016 The Critical Thinking Co.™ • www.CriticalThinking.com • 800-458-4849

Conducting the Lesson

Teacher Comment: **To have what they need, people change land and bodies of water. The first picture shows mining. Companies dig tunnels or huge holes to remove valuable minerals such as coal or gold. What does mining change?**

Student Response: Mining changes the land.

Teacher Comment: **Write "mining" on the first line of the "CHANGING THE LAND" box.**

• Check students' work. Continue this dialog to discuss students' answers.

Thinking About Thinking

Teacher Comment: **What did you pay attention to when you described how people changed the land and water?**

Student Response:

1. I looked at the picture to see what people made.
2. I decided whether it was a land form or a body of water that people changed.
3. I wrote the word to show whether people changed the land or the water

Personal Application

Teacher Comment: **When do you need to understand how people have changed land or bodies of water?**

Student Response: I need to understand how people have changed land or bodies of water to fit their needs.

Page 87: DESCRIBING LAND FORMS

LESSON

Introduction

Teacher Comment: **We have described land forms and bodies of water.**

Explaining the Objective

Teacher Comment: **In this lesson you will complete sentences to describe land forms.**

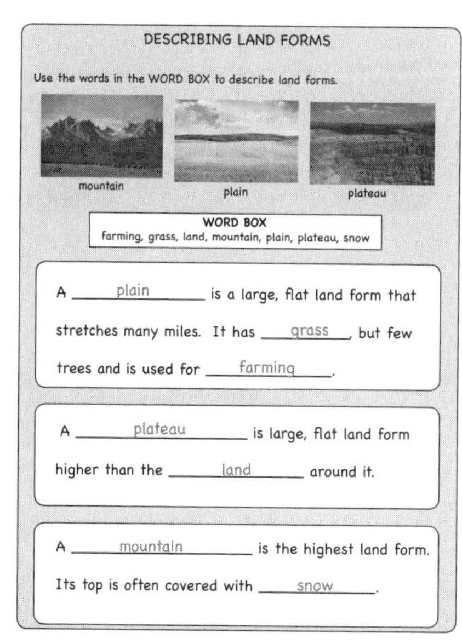

Conducting the Lesson

Teacher Comment: **The first sentence describes a large, flat land form that stretches many miles. Which picture fits this sentence?**

Student Response: A plain is a large, flat land form that stretches many miles.

Teacher Comment: **Write "plain" in the first blank.**

Teacher Comment: **Write words from the WORD BOX to describe a plain.**

• Continue this dialog to discuss students' answers.

Thinking About Thinking

Teacher Comment: **What did you pay attention to when you described which land form was shown in the picture?**

Student Response:

1. I looked at the land form to compare it to the land around it to see how large or high it is.
2. I matched the photograph to the word for the land form.
3. I wrote the words to describe it.

Personal Application

Teacher Comment: **When do you need to know different land forms?**

Student Response: I need to know different land forms to understand which plants or animals can live there. I need to know the right word to describe a particular place to someone else. I need to know what the land form is like so that I understand stories that take place there.

Page 88: DESCRIBING BODIES OF WATER

LESSON

- Students should know that "flowing" means that the water moves from place to place.

Introduction

Teacher Comment: **We have described land forms.**

Explaining the Objective

Teacher Comment: **In this lesson you will describe bodies of water.**

Conducting the Lesson

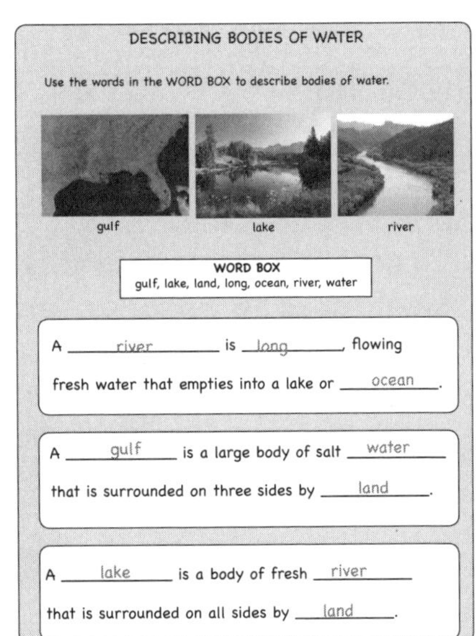
DESCRIBING BODIES OF WATER

Use the words in the WORD BOX to describe bodies of water.

gulf lake river

WORD BOX
gulf, lake, land, long, ocean, river, water

A __river__ is __long__, flowing fresh water that empties into a lake or __ocean__.

A __gulf__ is a large body of salt __water__ that is surrounded on three sides by __land__.

A __lake__ is a body of fresh __river__ that is surrounded on all sides by __land__.

Teacher Comment: **In the first sentence, what are the key words that describe this body of water?**

Student Response: "Long" tells its shape. "Flowing" tells that the water moves. "Fresh" tells that the water is not from an ocean, but flows to a lake or to the ocean.

Teacher Comment: **What long, flowing body of fresh water empties into a lake or ocean?**

Student Response: A river is a long, flowing body of water that empties into a lake or ocean.

Teacher Comment: **Write words from the WORD BOX to complete the first sentence. Write "river" on the first blank.**

Teacher Comment: **What are the key words in the second sentence to describe a body of water?**

Student Response: "Salt" tells that this is part of an ocean. "Three sides" tells that land separates this body of water from the rest of the ocean.

Teacher Comment: **What body of water is surrounded on three sides by land?**

Student Response: A gulf is a body of salt water surrounded on three sides by land.

Teacher Comment: **Write "gulf" on the first blank.**

 © 2016 The Critical Thinking Co.™ • www.CriticalThinking.com • 800-458-4849

Teacher Comment: **What are the key words in the third sentence to describe a body of water?**

Student Response: "Fresh" tells that it is not part of an ocean. "Surrounded on all sides" tells that the water does not flow from one place to another.

Teacher Comment: **Which body of fresh water is surrounded on all sides?**

Student Response: The lake is a body of fresh water surrounded on all sides by land.

Teacher Comment: **Write lake on the first blank.**

Thinking About Thinking

Teacher Comment: **What did you pay attention to when you described which body of water was shown in the picture?**

Student Response:

1. I looked at the body of water and compared it to the land around it in order to see how large or long it was.
2. I looked for land around it to understand whether or not it had fresh or salty water.
3. I matched the photograph to the words for that body of water.

Personal Application

Teacher Comment: **When do you need to know how to describe bodies of water?**

Student Response: I need to know about different bodies of water in order to understand which plants or animals can live there. I need to know the right word to describe a particular place to someone else. I need to know what a body of water is like in order to understand stories that take place there.

Page 89: KINDS OF LAND AND WATER

LESSON

Introduction

Teacher Comment: We have described land forms and bodies of water.

Explaining the Objective

Teacher Comment: **In this lesson you will write examples of different kinds of land forms or bodies of water.**

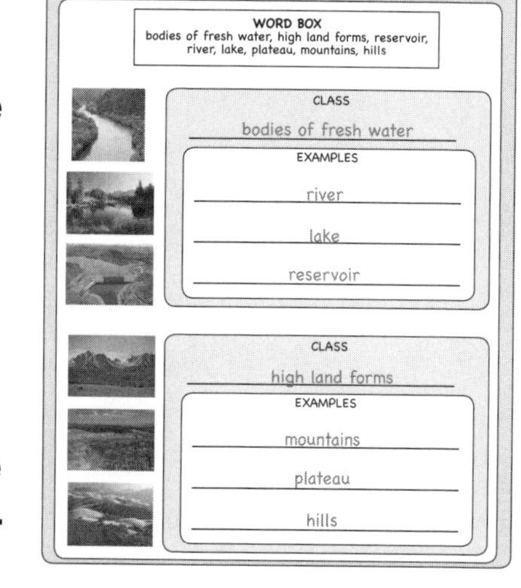

KINDS OF LAND AND WATER

Using the WORD BOX write the words that describe the kinds of land forms or bodies of water. Write the names of the examples on the lines below it.

WORD BOX
bodies of fresh water, high land forms, reservoir, river, lake, plateau, mountains, hills

CLASS
bodies of fresh water
EXAMPLES
river
lake
reservoir

CLASS
high land forms
EXAMPLES
mountains
plateau
hills

Conducting the Lesson

Teacher Comment: **The first group of pictures shows three bodies of water. Use words from the WORD BOX to write the group on the top line. List the examples of bodies of fresh water.**

- Check students work

Teacher Comment: **The second group of pictures shows three land forms. Use words from the WORD BOX to write the group on the top line. List the examples of land forms.**

- Check students' work.

Thinking About Thinking

Teacher Comment: **What did you pay attention to when you told the difference between words that described the kind and words for examples?**

Student Response:

1. I decided whether the pictures showed land forms or bodies of water.
2. I wrote the words for the kind of land or water.
3. I wrote the words for the examples.

Personal Application

Teacher Comment: **When do you need to know the difference between kinds of land and water and examples of them?**

Student Response: I need to know kinds of land and water to tell or write about them.

Page 90: SIMILAR LAND OR WATER

LESSON

Introduction

Teacher Comment: **We have described kinds of land and bodies of water.**

Explaining the Objective

Teacher Comment: **In this lesson you will describe how two land forms or bodies of water are alike.**

Conducting the Lesson

- Note to teachers: Remind students that word "both" signals that the sentence will describe how two things are alike.

SIMILAR LAND OR WATER

Use the words in the WORD BOX to write sentences telling how the two land forms or bodies are alike.

WORD BOX
flowing, fresh, river, stream, water

Both a river and a stream have flowing fresh water.

WORD BOX
flat, land, large, plain, plateau, forms

Both a plain and a plateau are large, flat land forms.

WORD BOX
fresh, hold, lake, pond, water

Both a lake and a pond hold fresh water.

WORD BOX
canal, man-made, reservoir

Both a canal and a reservoir are man-made.

Teacher Comment: **The first pictures show a river and a stream. Tell your partner how these two bodies of water are alike.**

Student Response: Both contain fresh water. Both have water that flows from one place to another.

Teacher Comment: **Use the words in the WORD BOX to write a sentence that tells how these bodies of water are alike.**

Teacher Comment: **The next pictures show a plain and a plateau. Tell your partner how these land forms are alike.**

Student Response: Both are large land forms. Both are flat.

Teacher Comment: **Use the words in the WORD BOX to write a sentence that tells how these land forms are alike.**

Teacher Comment: **The next pictures show a pond and a lake. Tell your partner how these two bodies of water are alike.**

Student Response: Both hold fresh water.

© 2016 The Critical Thinking Co.™ • www.CriticalThinking.com • 800-458-4849

Teacher Comment: **Use the words in the WORD BOX to write a sentence that tells how these bodies of water are alike.**

Teacher Comment: **The next pictures show a canal and a reservoir. Tell your partner how these two bodies of water are alike.**

Student Response: Both are man-made.

Teacher Comment: **Use the words in the WORD BOX to write a sentence that tells how these bodies of water are alike.**

Thinking About Thinking

Teacher Comment: **What did you think about when you described how the land forms or bodies of water were alike?**

Student Response:

1. For the land forms, I thought about their size, their height, how much water was there, what plants and animals lived there, and what people did there.
2. For bodies of water, I thought about their size, the land around them, whether they were deep or shallow, what plants and animals lived in or around them, and what people did there.

Personal Application

Teacher Comment: **When is it important to understand how land forms or bodies of water are alike?**

Student Response: I need to understand how land forms and bodies of water are alike in order to tell or write about them.

Page 91: COMPARING LAND FORMS OR BODIES OF WATER

LESSON

Introduction

Teacher Comment: **When we described how two things are alike, we were comparing them. Another way to compare things is to arrange them in order of their size.**

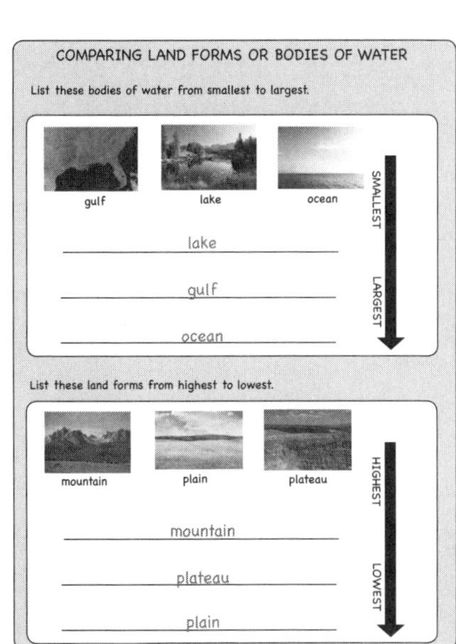

Explaining the Objective

Teacher Comment: **In this lesson we will arrange bodies of water or land forms in order of their size or height.**

Conducting the Lesson

Teacher Comment: **Name the bodies of water in the top box.**

Student Response: They are a gulf, a lake, and an ocean.

Teacher Comment: **List these bodies of water from smallest to largest. Which body of water is the smallest?**

Student Response: The lake is the smallest body of water.

Teacher Comment: **Write "lake"on the top line.**

Teacher Comment: **Which body of water is a little larger than a lake?**
Student Response: The gulf is larger than a lake.
Teacher Comment: **Write "gulf" on the second line.**

Teacher Comment: **Which body of water is the largest?**
Student Response: The ocean is the largest body of water.
Teacher Comment: **Write "ocean" on the third line.**

Teacher Comment: **Name the land forms in the bottom box.**
Student Response: They are a mountain, a plain, and a plateau.
Teacher Comment: **List these land forms from highest to lowest. Which land form is the highest?**
Student Response: The mountain is the highest land form.
Teacher Comment: **Write "mountain" on the top line.**

Teacher Comment: **Which land form is lower than a mountain?**
Student Response: The plateau is lower than a mountain.
Teacher Comment: **Write "plateau" on the second line.**

Teacher Comment: **Which land form is the lowest land form?**
Student Response: The plain is the lowest land form.
Teacher Comment: **Write "plain" on the third line.**

Thinking About Thinking

Teacher Comment: **What did you think about when you compared these bodies of water or land forms?**
Student Response:
1. I thought about the size or height of each example.
2. I remembered to start with the smallest size or the highest height.
3. I compared the other two examples to it.

Personal Application

Teacher Comment: **When is it important to compare bodies of water or land forms?**
Student Response: I need to compare bodies of water or land forms to tell or write about them.

© 2016 The Critical Thinking Co.™ • www.CriticalThinking.com • 800-458-4849

Page 92: CANAL & RESERVOIR – HOW ALIKE AND HOW DIFFERENT

LESSON

Introduction

Teacher Comment: **We have compared the sizes of bodies of water.**

Explaining the Objective

Teacher Comment: **In this lesson you will compare two bodies of water. You will write how they are alike. You will also contrast them. You will write how they are different.**

Conducting the Lesson

Teacher Comment: **The first picture shows a canal. A canal is built to move ships between two bodies of water. The second picture shows a reservoir. A reservoir is made by blocking a river to make a large lake to hold water until it is used. How are a canal and a reservoir alike?**

Student Response: They are both man-made. People changed bodies of water to do what they need.

Teacher Comment: **Write how they are alike in the top box.**

• Check students' work.

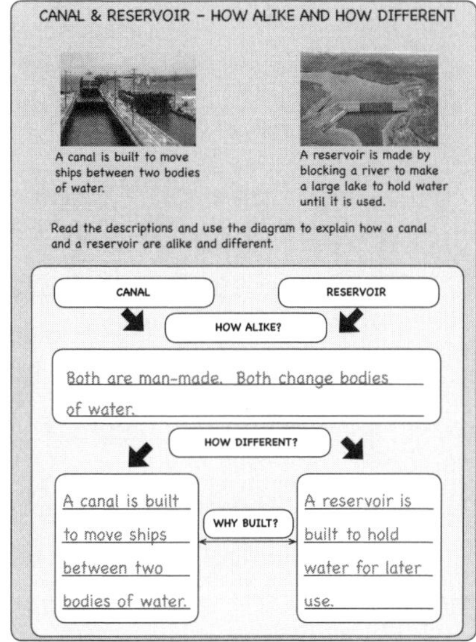

Teacher Comment: **How are a canal and a reservoir different?**

Student Response: A canal is built to move ships between two bodies of water, but a reservoir is built to hold water for people to use.

Teacher Comment: **Write how they are different in the bottom boxes.**

• Check students' work.

Thinking About Thinking

Teacher Comment: **What did you pay attention to when you compared and contrasted these bodies of water?**

Student Response:

1. I remembered and wrote how they are both man-made and changed bodies of water.
2. I remembered and wrote how they are built differently.

Personal Application

Teacher Comment: **When do you need to tell how bodies of water are alike or different?**

Student Response: I need to tell how bodies of water are alike or different to understand why people need or change them.

Page 93: PLAIN & DESERT – HOW ALIKE AND HOW DIFFERENT

LESSON

Introduction

Teacher Comment: **In the previous lesson we compared and contrasted two bodies of water.**

Explaining the Objective

Teacher Comment: **In this lesson you will compare and contrast two land forms.**

Conducting the Lesson

Teacher Comment: **We will compare and contrast a plain and a desert. A plain is very large, flat land that is often planted to provide food. There is enough water that large fields of grass and can grow there. Small animals can live there. A desert is very large, flat, dry, sandy land. Only a few plants or small animals can live there. How are a plain and a desert alike?**

Student Response: A plain and a desert are both very large, flat lands.

Teacher Comment: **Write how they are alike in the top box.**

Teacher Comment: **How are a plain and a desert different with regard to water?**

Student Response: A plain has enough water to grow grass and food, but a desert has little water.

Teacher Comment: **Write how the amount of water is different.**

Teacher Comment: **How are a plain and a desert different with regard to plants?**

Student Response: Grass and food can grow on a plain, but most of the desert is too dry for plants.

Teacher Comment: **Write whether plants grow there.**

Teacher Comment: **How are a plain and a desert different with regard to animals?**

Student Response: Many small animals can live on the plain, but very few animals can live in a desert.

Teacher Comment: **Write whether animals live there.**

Thinking About Thinking

Teacher Comment: **What did you pay attention to when you compared and contrasted these land forms?**

Student Response:

1. I thought about their size, the amount of water, and the plants or animals that lived there.
2. I remembered how they were alike.
3. I remembered how they were different.

 © 2016 The Critical Thinking Co.™ • www.CriticalThinking.com • 800-458-4849

Personal Application

Teacher Comment: **When do you need to tell how land forms are alike or different?**

Student Response: I need to tell how land forms are alike or different to understand whether plants or animals can live there.

Page 94: DESCRIBING A LAND FORM

LESSON

Introduction

Teacher Comment: **To describe a land form or a body of water, we need to explain all the important characteristics that make that example different from others.**

Explaining the Objective

Teacher Comment: **In this lesson you will recall the details of the important characteristics needed to describe any land form or body of water and put those details together to make a description.**

Conducting the Lesson

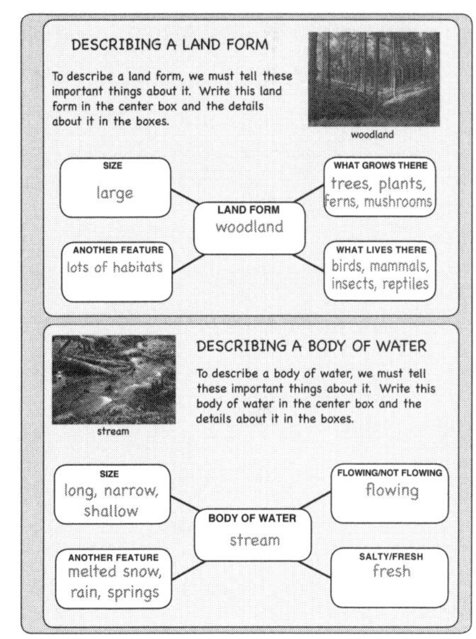

Teacher Comment: **The diagram shows the four characteristics that we need to describe any land form: Its size or height compared to the land around it, the amount of water, the plants or animals that can live there, and special features that make it different from other land forms. The picture shows woodlands. Write "woodlands" in the center box.**

Teacher Comment: **We begin by telling its size and height. How do we describe the size and height of woodlands?**

Student Response: Woodlands are very large and hilly.

Teacher Comment: **Write "large and hilly" in the "size" box.**

Teacher Comment: **What type of things grow here compared to other land forms?**

Student Response: Many types of trees and plants, ferns and fungus.

Teacher Comment: **Write "trees, moss, ferns, mushrooms" in the "what grows there" box.**

Teacher Comment: **What types of animals live in the woodlands?**

Student Response: Many types of birds, mammals, reptiles, and insects.

Teacher Comment: **Write "birds, mammals, insects, reptiles" in the "what lives there" box.**

Teacher Comment: **What is special about woodlands compared to other land forms?**

Student Response: Many different habitats for animals.
Teacher Comment: **Write "lots of habitats" in the "another feature" box.**

Teacher Comment: **Put these details together to describe a woodland to your partner.**

• Continue this dialog to describe a stream. Check students' work.

Thinking About Thinking

Teacher Comment: **What did you think about when you described a land form or a body of water?**

Student Response:

1. I identified the kind of land form or body of water.
2. I looked at the photograph to see how large it was.
3. I described the amount of water in the land form. When I described a body of water I described whether the water flowed and if it fresh or salt water.
4. I describe what lived there.
5. I described the special features of the land form or body of water.

Personal Application

Teacher Comment: **When is it important to describe all the important characteristics of a land form or body of water?**

Student Response: I need to know how to describe all the important characteristics of a land form or body of water to understand what plants and animals live there or how people need or change it.

© 2016 The Critical Thinking Co.™ • www.CriticalThinking.com • 800-458-4849

CHAPTER EIGHT – THINKING ABOUT LIVING AND NON-LIVING THINGS (Pages 95-117)

GENERAL INTRODUCTION

CURRICULUM APPLICATIONS

Language Arts: Identify the properties of various animals as they appear in myths and stories. Discuss grade two topics and texts with peers and adults in large and small groups. Compare and contrast the most important points in describing two concepts. Produce complete sentences in order to provide adequate detail and clarification. Use appropriate adjectives, adverbs, and verbs to describe key concepts. Describe the connections between a series of events, concepts, or steps. Write sentences and paragraphs that show comparison, contrast, sequences, classification, and analogy.

Science: Identify the properties of living and non-living things. Identify plants and animals. State what animals need to live and grow. Recognize types of animals (insects, fish, birds, amphibians, reptiles, mammals). Identify key characteristics of common types of animals (appearance, habitat, food, reproduction and protection). Understand animal life cycles. Identify how organisms differ from or are similar to their parents.

Social Studies: Identify how people in various cultures use animals for food, clothing, or shelter.

Enrichment: Create student art in which non-living things seem to have living properties. Create student art that shows the properties of various animals.

TEACHING SUGGESTIONS

- After classification lessons, ask students to draw a picture of any three animals from the animal list and label the drawing to describe how the three animals are alike (insects, birds, fish, mammals, reptiles, and amphibians). Students may classify animals by other characteristics, such as habitat, location on the globe, or how they protect themselves. Create an animal bulletin board display of students' drawings.
- After classification exercises, have students create a group display. Each group of four students will use a large sheet of newsprint, pictures of animals, or index cards labeled with the names of various animals. Using a large branching diagram as a background, students will sort the pictures or labels to create a display.
- Create a chart or bulletin board display of different kinds of animals. Discuss how each animal reproduces, whether it warm- or cold-blooded, and other special characteristics.
    1. Birds: egg-laying, with feathers and wings
    2. Fish: egg-laying animals that swim and have scales and gills
    3. Reptiles: egg-laying animals that crawl and have scales
    4. Amphibians: egg-laying animals that crawl and have moist skin
    5. Mammals: animals whose babies grow inside mother's body, run, and have hair
- Teachers may use the graphic organizer at the right for bulletin board displays, student art work, or as an end-of-unit summary lesson.

MENTAL MODEL

A mental model is a framework for understanding a concept. It outlines the characteristics that one must state to describe or define a concept. After completing this chapter, each student will have applied this mental model to animals in the lessons. A mental model helps a student:

- anticipate what he or she needs to know to understand a new animal.
- remember the characteristics of an animal.
- state a clear definition or write an adequate description of an animal.
- explain an animal to someone else.

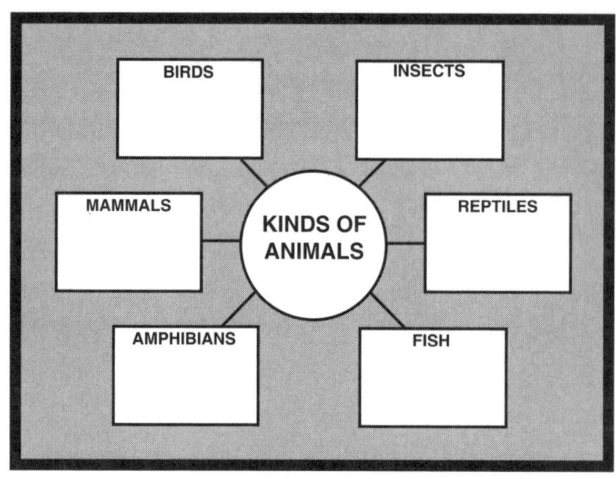

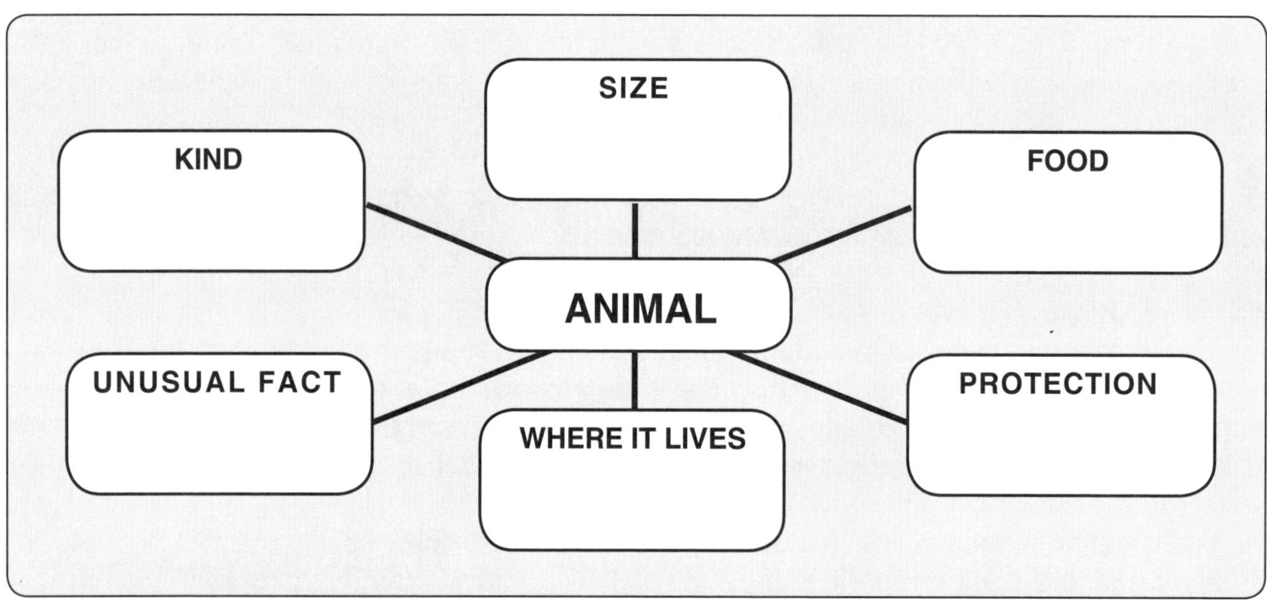

Page 96: DESCRIBING LIVING OR NON-LIVING THINGS

LESSON

- Second-grade students generally understand the difference between living and non-living things. However, they may be confused distinguishing between organic growth and increase in size. For example, clouds and rivers increase in size and seem to grow much like a plant does. When discussing growth, clarify the difference between fluctuations in size and growth in the life cycle.
- Second-grade students may not distinguish between food and fuel. A child may think that gasoline is "food" for an automobile or that electricity is "food" for a microwave oven. Clarify the difference between energy sources and intake of nutrients.
- Reproduction may not be clearly understood. Clouds may seem to reproduce by appearing spontaneously or from nearby clouds. When discussing reproduction, clarify the difference between irregular changes and the pattern of birth and growth in the life cycle.

© 2016 The Critical Thinking Co.™ • www.CriticalThinking.com • 800-458-4849

Introduction

Teacher Comment: **Animals are living things. Living things grow, need food, air and water, and reproduce. Some things appear to be alive because they seem to grow or move.**

Explaining the Objective

Teacher Comment: **In this lesson you will check whether each of these objects has all the important characteristics of living things.**

DESCRIBING LIVING AND NON-LIVING THINGS

Living things grow, need food, air and water, and can reproduce. Write "YES" or "NO" to show whether each thing grows, needs food, needs air and water, or reproduces itself. In the last box write "L" to show it is living, or write "N" to show that it is non-living.

LIVING OR NON-LIVING?	Grows	Needs Food	Needs Air & Water	Reproduces	Living or Non-Living
cactus	YES	YES	YES	YES	L
cell phone	NO	NO	NO	NO	N
fire	NO	NO	NO	NO	N
cloud	NO	NO	NO	NO	N
lemons	YES	YES	YES	YES	L
potatoes	YES	YES	YES	YES	L
sun	NO	NO	NO	NO	N
turtle	YES	YES	YES	YES	L

Conducting the Lesson

Teacher Comment: **Look at the object in each line. Write "YES" or "NO" to show whether each thing grows, needs food, reproduces itself, or needs air and water. In the last box write "N" or "L" to show whether it is non-living or living.**

Teacher Comment: **The first picture shows a cactus. Does a cactus grow?**

Student Response: Yes, a cactus grows.

Teacher Comment: **Write "YES" in the first box.**

- Continue this line of questioning for "Needs Food," "Needs Air & Water,"and "Reproduces."

Teacher Comment: **A cactus has all the characteristics of a living thing. Write an "L" in the last box to show that a cactus is a living thing.**

- Check students' work. Continue this dialog to discuss students' answers. After the first few items, students may complete the lesson independently.

Thinking About Thinking

Teacher Comment: **What did you pay attention to when you decided the difference between non-living and living things?**

Student Response:

1. I thought about whether the object grows, needs food, needs air and water, and reproduces itself.
2. If it has all these characteristics, I know that it is alive.
3. If it does not have all these characteristics, I know that it is not alive.

Personal Application

Teacher Comment: **When is it important to know whether or not something is alive?**

Student Response: I need to know whether or not something is alive to understand how to take care of it and to avoid being frightened about it.

© 2016 The Critical Thinking Co.™ • www.CriticalThinking.com • 800-458-4849

Page 97: COMPARING PLANTS AND ANIMALS

LESSON

- Students in second grade begin to use the term "reproduces," rather than "make babies."
- Encourage students to use as many verbs as they know to discuss the movement of animals shown in the pictures, i.e. (scampers, crawls, runs, creeps, etc.). You may introduce the term "locomotion" to describe animal movement.

COMPARING PLANTS AND ANIMALS

Plants grow in one place and make their food from sunlight and water. Some plants make new ones from seeds. Animals move by themselves and eat plants or other animals. They make baby animals from eggs or from inside their bodies.

In each box write "YES" or "NO." Decide whether each living thing is a plant or an animal. In the last box write "P" for plant or "A" for animal.

LIVING THINGS	Makes its food from air, water, and light?	Must stay where it is planted?	Gets its food from plants and animals	Moves itself?	Plant or Animal?
alligator	NO	NO	YES	YES	A
butterfly	NO	NO	YES	YES	A
palm trees	YES	YES	NO	NO	P
peaches	YES	YES	NO	NO	P
roses	YES	YES	NO	NO	P
rabbit	NO	NO	YES	YES	A
whale	NO	NO	YES	YES	A

Introduction

Teacher Comment: **We have learned that living things grow, need air and water, need food, and reproduce themselves.**

Explaining the Objective

Teacher Comment: **In this lesson you will show whether these living things are a plant or an animal.**

Conducting the Lesson

Teacher Comment: **Plants grow in one place and make their food from sunlight and water. Animals move by themselves and eat plants or other animals. The first picture shows an alligator. Does the alligator make its own food or stay where it is planted?**

Student Response: An alligator does not make its own food or stay where it is planted.

Teacher Comment: **"NO" is written in the first two boxes. Does the alligator get its food from plants and animals and move itself?**

Student Response: An alligator gets its food from other plants and animals and can move itself.

Teacher Comment: **"YES" is written in the next two boxes. Is the alligator a plant or an animal?**

Student Response: An alligator is an animal.

Teacher Comment: **An "A" is written in the last box to tell that the alligator is an animal. In each box write "YES" or "NO." Decide whether each living thing is a plant or an animal. In the last box write "P" for plant or "A" for animal.**

- Check students' work. Continue this dialog to discuss students' answers.

Thinking About Thinking

Teacher Comment: **What did you pay attention to when you decided whether a living thing is a plant or an animal?**

Student Response:

1. I remembered whether it makes its own food or eats plants or other animals.
2. I remembered whether it stays in one place or can move around by itself.
3. I decided whether it was a plant or an animal.

© 2016 The Critical Thinking Co.™ • www.CriticalThinking.com • 800-458-4849

Personal Application

Teacher Comment: **When do you need to think about to decide whether a living thing is a plant or an animal?**

Student Response: I need to know whether or not something is a plant or an animal to know what it needs to survive.

Page 98: DESCRIBING ANIMALS

LESSON

Introduction

Teacher Comment: **To understand what animals need to survive, we need to know whether it is warm- or cold-blooded. Warm-blooded animals make heat inside their bodies, can huddle together to stay warm, and have a better chance to survive in cold weather. Cold-blooded animals must get heat from their surroundings.**

Whether or not an animal has a backbone will tell how large an animal can grow. The backbone supports the weight of the animal. Only tiny animals have bodies that are supported by a stiff skin instead of a backbone.

Explaining the Objective

Teacher Comment: **In this lesson you will circle the picture of the animal I describe.**

Conducting the Lesson

Teacher Comment: **Look at the top row. Name these animals.**

Student Response: These animals are a beaver, a prairie dog, and a rabbit.

Teacher Comment: **Listen to the clues and name the animal that I describe. Since this animal is a mammal, it is warm-blooded and has a backbone. It is larger than a prairie dog. It builds its home, called a lodge, in rivers and streams that run through woods. It uses strong, sharp teeth to cut trees to build its home. It eats wood and other plants. It has a large, broad tail and webbed feet for easy swimming. It slaps its tail loudly on the surface of the water to warn others of danger.**

- Ask students to decide with their partners which animal has been described.

DESCRIBING ANIMALS

Circle the picture of the animal that your teacher describes.*

beaver prairie dog rabbit

salmon shark tuna

duck blue jay bat

lizard snake alligator

butterfly mosquito bee

*Descriptions are available on page 19 of the free answer guide.

Teacher Comment: **Which animal did I describe?**

Student Response: That animal is a beaver.

Teacher Comment: **Circle the picture of the beaver.**

Teacher Comment: **What clues let you know that the animal is a beaver?**

Student Response: I saw its large, flat tail, it's larger than the prairie dog, and it climbs out of the river to get wood to make its home.

© 2016 The Critical Thinking Co.™ • www.CriticalThinking.com • 800-458-4849

Teacher Comment: **Why don't the prairie dog or the rabbit fit the description?**
Student Response: The beaver is larger than either a prairie dog or a rabbit. The prairie dog lives on the plains and digs a hole for a home. The rabbit lives in woodlands and on plains and also digs a hole for a home.

Teacher Comment: **Look at the second row. Name these animals.**
Student Response: These animals are salmon, a shark, and a tuna.
Teacher Comment: **Listen to the clues and name the animal that I describe. Since this animal is a fish, it is cold-blooded and has a backbone. It lives in the ocean. It is a very large fish and eats small fish. Its meat is a popular food in both large pieces and in sandwiches. Fishing and canning this fish are large industries.**

- Ask students to decide with their partners which animal has been described.

Teacher Comment: **Which animal did I describe?**
Student Response: That animal is a tuna.
Teacher Comment: **Circle the picture of the tuna.**

Teacher Comment: **What clues let you know that the animal is a tuna?**
Student Response: I saw its large body in the ocean.
Teacher Comment: **Why don't the salmon or the shark fit the description?**
Student Response: The salmon lives in a river part of its life. The shark is not a popular food.
Teacher Comment: **Look at the third row. Name these animals.**
Student Response: These animals are a duck, a blue jay, and a bat.
Teacher Comment: **Listen to the clues and name the animal that I describe. Since this animal is a bird, it is warm-blooded and has a backbone. It builds its nest near water and has webbed feet for swimming. Its wide bill scoops small plants and animals from the water.**

- Ask students to decide with their partners which animal has been described.

Teacher Comment: **Which animal did I describe?**
Student Response: That animal is a duck.
Teacher Comment: **Circle the picture of the duck.**

Teacher Comment: **What clues let you know that the animal is a duck?**
Student Response: I saw its webbed feet and its flat bill. It swims easily on water.
Teacher Comment: **Why don't the blue jay or the bat fit the description?**
Student Response: The blue jay lives in trees. It has a claw on each foot to hold on to the branches. It has a sharp beak, not a flat bill. The bat is a mammal, not a bird. It lives in trees, not in the water.

Teacher Comment: **Look at the fourth row. Name these animals.**
Student Response: These animals are lizard, a snake, and an alligator.
Teacher Comment: **Listen to the clues and name the animal that I describe. Since this animal is a reptile, it is cold-blooded and has a backbone. It is the largest reptile and lives in warm areas near rivers and marshes. It can swim very fast with its webbed feet. It has long claws to catch fish and other animals. Its bumpy skin is made of hardened**

© 2016 The Critical Thinking Co.™ • www.CriticalThinking.com • 800-458-4849

scales. It is hunted for its meat and skin.

• Ask students to decide with their partners which animal has been described.

Teacher Comment: **Which animal did I describe?**
Student Response: That animal is an alligator.
Teacher Comment: **Circle the picture of the alligator.**

Teacher Comment: **What clues let you know that the animal is an alligator?**
Student Response: I saw its bumpy, thick skin and that it lives near water.
Teacher Comment: **Why don't the lizard or the snake fit the description?**
Student Response: The lizard is small and does not live near water. The snake has no legs and has thin, shiny scales.

Teacher Comment: **Look at the last row. Name these animals.**
Student Response: These animals are a butterfly, a mosquito, and a bee.
Teacher Comment: **Listen to the clues and name the animal that I describe. Since this animal is an insect, it is cold-blooded and does not have a backbone. It is found in large numbers all over the world, except in very cold areas. This tiny insect lays many eggs in still water. It sucks blood through a tube that it sticks through the skin of other animals and people. Because of the way it feeds, it transmits many diseases that infect millions of people and other animals.**

• Ask students to decide with their partners which animal has been described.

Teacher Comment: **Which animal did I describe?**
Student Response: That animal is a mosquito.
Teacher Comment: **Circle the picture of the mosquito.**

Teacher Comment: **What clues let you know that the animal is a mosquito?**
Student Response: I saw its long feeding tube. I see that it is tiny compared to the hairs on the skin of the person that it is biting.
Teacher Comment: **Why don't the butterfly or the bee fit the description?**
Student Response: The butterfly is a large insect compared to the flower that it feeds on. The bee is smaller than the butterfly, but larger than the mosquito. The bee and butterfly don't feed on blood.

Thinking About Thinking

Teacher Comment: **What did you pay attention to when you decided which animal was described?**
Student Response:
1. I recalled the important characteristics of the animal: its size, where it lives, what it eats, unusual facts about its body, what kind of animal it is.
2. I found clues in the pictures for those important characteristics.
3. I checked that pictures of the other animals did not show those important characteristics.

Personal Application

Teacher Comment: **When is it important to identify an animal from its description?**
Student Response: I need to know how to identify an animal from its description to understand stories about animals.

© 2016 The Critical Thinking Co.™ • www.CriticalThinking.com • 800-458-4849

Page 99: DESCRIBING ANIMALS

Introduction

Teacher Comment: **We have identified some important characteristics of different animals. We should also understand whether the animal lays eggs or develops its babies inside the mother's body. When the mother animal lays an egg, the new animal is not yet formed. Its body parts develop inside the egg.**

When the baby animal grows inside its mother's body, it is born with its body parts already developed. It looks similar to the adult animal. This way of reproducing is called "live birth."

To understand what animals need to survive, we need to know whether it is warm- or cold-blooded. Warm-blooded animals make heat inside their bodies, can huddle together to stay warm, and have a better chance to survive in cold weather. Cold-blooded animals must get heat from their surroundings.

Whether or not an animal has a backbone will tell how large an animal can grow. The backbone supports the weight of the animal. Only tiny animals have bodies that have stiff skin to support it instead of a backbone.

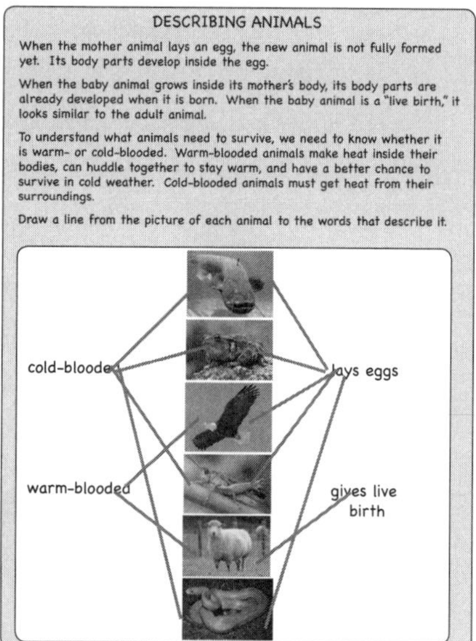
DESCRIBING ANIMALS

When the mother animal lays an egg, the new animal is not fully formed yet. Its body parts develop inside the egg.

When the baby animal grows inside its mother's body, its body parts are already developed when it is born. When the baby animal is a "live birth," it looks similar to the adult animal.

To understand what animals need to survive, we need to know whether it is warm- or cold-blooded. Warm-blooded animals make heat inside their bodies, can huddle together to stay warm, and have a better chance to survive in cold weather. Cold-blooded animals must get heat from their surroundings.

Draw a line from the picture of each animal to the words that describe it.

Explaining the Objective

Teacher Comment: **In this lesson you will match the picture of each animal to the words that describe it.**

Conducting the Lesson

Teacher Comment: **Is a catfish warm- or cold-blooded?**
  Student Response: Fish are cold-blooded animals.
Teacher Comment: **Draw a line from the picture of the fish to "cold-blooded."**

Teacher Comment: **How do fish reproduce?**
  Student Response: Fish reproduce by laying eggs.
Teacher Comment: **Draw a line from the picture of the fish to "lays eggs."**

- Check students' work. Continue this dialog to discuss students' answers.

Thinking About Thinking

Teacher Comment: **What did you think about to tell what kind of animal it is?**
  Student Response:
  1. I named the animal.
  2. I remembered whether it was warm- or cold-blooded.
  3. I remembered how it reproduces.

Personal Application

Teacher Comment: **When is it important to know kinds of animals?**
  Student Response: I need to know kinds of an animals to describe them and to understand what they need to survive.

© 2016 The Critical Thinking Co.™ • www.CriticalThinking.com • 800-458-4849

Pages 100-101: DESCRIBING ANIMALS

Introduction

Teacher Comment: **We have identified some important characteristics of different animals. We know whether it is warm- or cold-blooded and whether it has a backbone. We also understand whether the animal lays eggs or develops its babies inside the mother's body.**

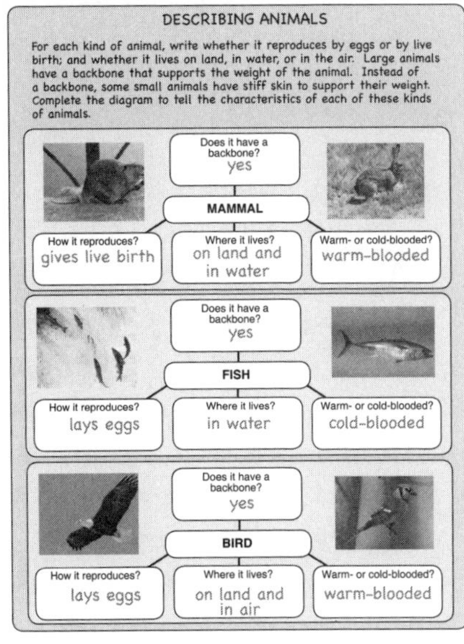
DESCRIBING ANIMALS

For each kind of animal, write whether it reproduces by eggs or by live birth; and whether it lives on land, in water, or in the air. Large animals have a backbone that supports the weight of the animal. Instead of a backbone, some small animals have stiff skin to support their weight. Complete the diagram to tell the characteristics of each of these kinds of animals.

	Does it have a backbone?	How it reproduces?	Where it lives?	Warm- or cold-blooded?
MAMMAL	yes	gives live birth	on land and in water	warm-blooded
FISH	yes	lays eggs	in water	cold-blooded
BIRD	yes	lays eggs	on land and in air	warm-blooded

Explaining the Objective

Teacher Comment: **In this lesson you will write the characteristics of different kinds of animals.**

Conducting the Lesson

Teacher Comment: **Whether or not an animal has a backbone will tell how large an animal can grow. The backbone supports the weight of the animal. Only tiny animals have bodies that have stiff skin to support it instead of a backbone. Do mammals have backbones?**

Student Response: Mammals have backbones.

Teacher Comment: **Write "yes" in the top box.**

Teacher Comment: **How do mammals reproduce?**

Student Response: Mammals reproduce by giving live birth.

Teacher Comment: **Write "gives live birth" in the next box.**

Teacher Comment: **Where do mammals live?**

Student Response: Most mammals live on land, but some spend a lot of time in water.

Teacher Comment: **Write "on land" in the next box.**

Teacher Comment: **Are mammals warm- or cold-blooded?**

Student Response: Mammals are warm-blooded.

Teacher Comment: **Write "warm-blooded" in the next box.**

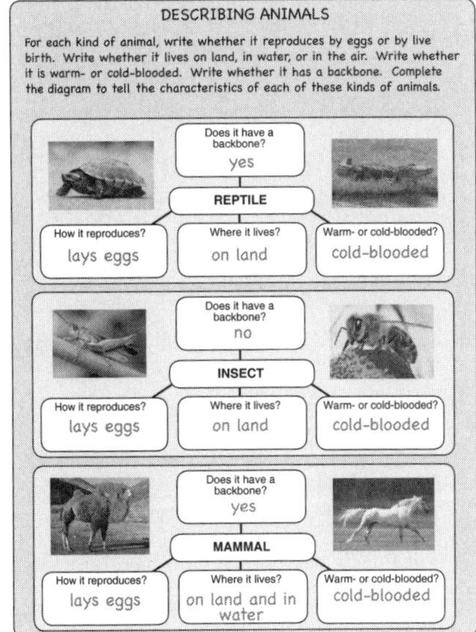
DESCRIBING ANIMALS

For each kind of animal, write whether it reproduces by eggs or by live birth. Write whether it lives on land, in water, or in the air. Write whether it is warm- or cold-blooded. Write whether it has a backbone. Complete the diagram to tell the characteristics of each of these kinds of animals.

	Does it have a backbone?	How it reproduces?	Where it lives?	Warm- or cold-blooded?
REPTILE	yes	lays eggs	on land	cold-blooded
INSECT	no	lays eggs	on land	cold-blooded
MAMMAL	yes	lays eggs	on land and in water	cold-blooded

- Check students' work. Continue this dialog to discuss students' answers.

Teacher Comment: **Remember that when you use the one word to tell what kind of animal it is, you are telling four things about it: whether it has a backbone, how it reproduces, where it lives, and whether it is warm- or cold-blooded.**

Thinking About Thinking

Teacher Comment: **What did you think about to describe each kind of animal?**

Student Response:

1. I named the animal.
2. I looked at its skin, its body parts, and its surroundings.
3. I remembered how it reproduces.
4. I learned the word for that kind of animal.

© 2016 The Critical Thinking Co.™ • www.CriticalThinking.com • 800-458-4849

Personal Application

Teacher Comment: **When is it important to know kinds of animals?**

Student Response: I need to know kinds of animals to describe them and to understand what they need to survive.

Page 102: KINDS OF ANIMALS

LESSON

Introduction

Teacher Comment: **We studied different kinds of animals. Birds lay eggs and have feathers and wings. Fish are animals that lay eggs and live in water. Insects are tiny animals that lay eggs and have at least six legs and antennae. Mammals have hair. Mammal mothers carry their babies inside their bodies and make milk to feed them. Reptiles are animals that lay eggs, have scaly skin, and move by crawling.**

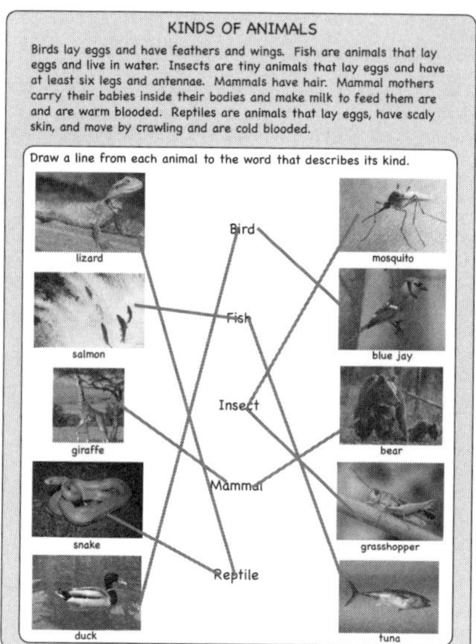
KINDS OF ANIMALS

Birds lay eggs and have feathers and wings. Fish are animals that lay eggs and live in water. Insects are tiny animals that lay eggs and have at least six legs and antennae. Mammals have hair. Mammal mothers carry their babies inside their bodies and make milk to feed them are and are warm blooded. Reptiles are animals that lay eggs, have scaly skin, and move by crawling and are cold blooded.

Draw a line from each animal to the word that describes its kind.

Explaining the Objective

Teacher Comment: **In this lesson you will match animals to the words that describe its kind.**

Conducting the Lesson

Teacher Comment: **Name the animal in the first picture.**

Student Response: That animal is a lizard.

Teacher Comment: **What kind of animal is a lizard?**

Student Response: A lizard is a reptile.

Teacher Comment: **Draw line from the picture of the lizard to "reptile."**

- Check students' work. Continue this dialog to discuss students' answers.

Thinking About Thinking

Teacher Comment: **What did you think about to tell what kind of animal it is?**

Student Response:

1. I named the animal.
2. I looked at its skin, its body parts, and its surroundings.
3. I remembered how it reproduces.
4. I found the word for that kind of animal.

Personal Application

Teacher Comment: **When is it important to know kinds of animals?**

Student Response: I need to know kinds of animals to describe them and to understand what they need to survive.

© 2016 The Critical Thinking Co.™ • www.CriticalThinking.com • 800-458-4849

Page 103: UNUSUAL ANIMALS

LESSON

Introduction

Teacher Comment: **We have learned about many kinds of animals. Some animals have characteristics that are unusual for animals of that kind.**

Explaining the Objective

Teacher Comment: **In this lesson you will match the descriptions of unusual animals to their pictures.**

Conducting the Lesson

Teacher Comment: **Read the first description.**
Student Response: This animal lives in the ocean and is the largest mammal on Earth.
Teacher Comment: **What large mammal lives in the ocean?**
Student Response: The blue whale is the world's largest mammal and it lives in the ocean.
Teacher Comment: **Draw a line from the description to the picture of the whale.**

Teacher Comment: **Read the second description.**
Student Response: This insect works with others to carry objects that are heavier than its own weight.
Teacher Comment: **What animal can carry heavy objects?**
Student Response: The ant is a very strong insect.
Teacher Comment: **Draw a line from the description to the picture of the ant.**

• Continue this dialog to discuss students' answers.

Thinking About Thinking

Teacher Comment: **What did you pay attention to when you matched a description to an animal?**
Student Response:
1. I looked at the details in the picture of the animal.
2. I remembered what kind of animal each picture showed.
3. I named that animal and matched it to the description.

Personal Application

Teacher Comment: **When do you need to know what kind of animal it is?**
Student Response: I need to know what kind of animal it is to understand what it needs to survive and to write about it.

Page 104 : ANIMAL HABITATS

LESSON

Introduction

Teacher Comment: **In the previous lesson we identified an animal from a description.**

Explaining the Objective

Teacher Comment: **In this lesson you will draw a line from each animal to its habitat.**

Conducting the Lesson

Teacher Comment: **Some animals live on the land–dry deserts, grassy plains, or shady woodlands. Some animals live in large, salty oceans or freshwater rivers. The land form or body of water where animals live is their HABITAT. The animal in the first picture is a beaver. What is the habitat of a beaver?**

Student Response: The beaver lives in a river.

Teacher Comment: **Draw a line from "beaver" to "river."**

Teacher Comment: **What is the habitat of the deer?**

Student Response: The deer lives in the woodlands.

Teacher Comment: **Draw a line from "deer" to "woodlands."**

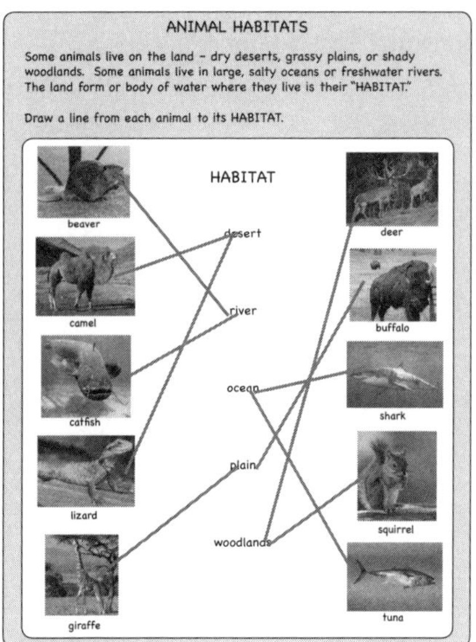

- Check students' work. Continue this dialog to discuss students' answers.

Thinking About Thinking

Teacher Comment: **What did you think about to match an animal to its habitat?**

Student Response:

1. I named the animal.
2. I looked at the land or water around it.
3. I remembered whether the place where it lives is wet or dry, small or open.

Personal Application

Teacher Comment: **When is it important to know where an animal lives?**

Student Response: I need to know where an animal lives to understand what it needs to survive.

© 2016 The Critical Thinking Co.™ • www.CriticalThinking.com • 800-458-4849

Pages 105: DESCRIBING PARTS OF AN ANT

LESSON

Introduction

Teacher Comment: **To describe animals, we sometimes need to know how parts of its body are important for the animal to be healthy and to survive.**

Explaining the Objective

Teacher Comment: **In this lesson you will tell what each part does and what would happen to the ant if that part was missing or damaged.**

Conducting the Lesson

Teacher Comment: **Listen to this description as I read it. An ant is an insect, a tiny animal that has six legs. The outside of the ant's body is a hard shell for protection. On its head it has two long feelers called antennae that it uses to find food. Its mouth has a strong jaw that it uses to carry food, construct its nest, and to defend itself. Why is the ant's hard shell needed?**

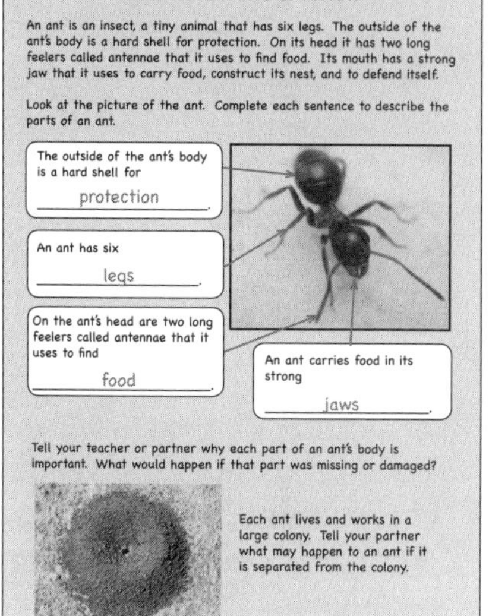

DESCRIBING PARTS OF AN ANT

An ant is an insect, a tiny animal that has six legs. The outside of the ant's body is a hard shell for protection. On its head it has two long feelers called antennae that it uses to find food. Its mouth has a strong jaw that it uses to carry food, construct its nest, and to defend itself.

Look at the picture of the ant. Complete each sentence to describe the parts of an ant.

The outside of the ant's body is a hard shell for protection.

An ant has six legs.

On the ant's head are two long feelers called antennae that it uses to find food.

An ant carries food in its strong jaws.

Tell your teacher or partner why each part of an ant's body is important. What would happen if that part was missing or damaged?

Each ant lives and works in a large colony. Tell your partner what may happen to an ant if it is separated from the colony.

Student Response: The ant's hard shell protects the inside of its body.

Teacher Comment: **What would happen if the ant's hard shell was missing or damaged?**

Student Response: If the ant's hard shell was missing or damaged, the insides of the ant's body could be damaged.

Teacher Comment: **Write "protection" in the first box.**

Teacher Comment: **How does the ant move?**

Student Response: The ant moves on six legs.

Teacher Comment: **What would happen if one or more of the ant's six legs was missing or damaged?**

Student Response: If any of the ant's six legs was missing or damaged, it could not move fast enough to get out of the way of danger.

Teacher Comment: **Write "legs" in the second box.**

Teacher Comment: **Why are the ant's antennae needed?**

Student Response: The ant needs its antennae to find food.

Teacher Comment: **What would happen if an ant's antennae were missing or damaged?**

Student Response: If any of the ant's antennae were missing or damaged, it could not find food for itself or the colony.

Teacher Comment: **Write "food" in the third box.**

Teacher Comment: **How does the ant carry its food?**

Student Response: The ant carries its food in its strong jaw.

Teacher Comment: **What would happen if an ant's jaw was missing or damaged?**

© 2016 The Critical Thinking Co.™ • www.CriticalThinking.com • 800-458-4849

Student Response: If an ant's jaw was missing or damaged, it could not pick up food for itself or the colony.

Teacher Comment: **Write "jaw" in the last box.**

Teacher Comment: **Each ant lives and works in a large colony. What would happen to the ant if it was separated from the colony?**

Student Response: The ant may not be able to find enough food, it would lose its shelter, it would not have the protection of the large group.

Thinking About Thinking

Teacher Comment: **What did you think about to describe parts of an animal?**

Student Response:

1. I looked at each part and named it.
2. I remembered what each part does.
3. I thought about what each part did to help the animal be healthy and safe.

Personal Application

Teacher Comment: **When is it important to describe the parts of an animal?**

Student Response: I need to know how to describe the parts of an animal correctly to tell a story about it.

Pages 106: THE LIFE CYCLE OF A FROG

LESSON

Introduction

Teacher Comment: **We learned that animals are born or hatched, grow, reproduce themselves, and die. For many animals the newborn baby looks similar to the adult. However some amphibians and insects go through big changes in their shape and how they live.**

Explaining the Objective

Teacher Comment: **In this lesson you will tell how a frog changes from birth to becoming an adult.**

Conducting the Lesson

Teacher Comment: **The first sentence tells what kind of animal a frog is. Find the word in the WORD BOX that describes that kind of animal.**

Student Response: That animal is an amphibian.

Teacher Comment: **Write "amphibian" on the first line.**

Teacher Comment: **What makes an amphibian different from other animals?**

Student Response: An amphibian lives first in water and then on land.

Teacher Comment: **Write "water" and "land" on the next two blanks.**

Teacher Comment: **A frog lays eggs that hatch into an animal that looks like a fish.**

© 2016 The Critical Thinking Co.™ • www.CriticalThinking.com • 800-458-4849

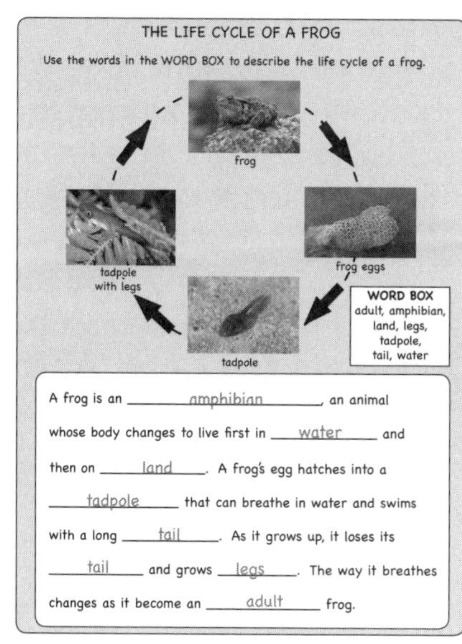

What is it called?
Student Response: The egg hatches into a tadpole.
Teacher Comment: **Write "tadpole" on the next blank.**

Teacher Comment: **How does the tadpole move?**
Student Response: A tadpole swims with a long tail.
Teacher Comment: **Write "tail" on the next blank.**

Teacher Comment: **As it grows up, it loses one part of its body and grows another. How does the tadpole's body change?**
Student Response: A tadpoles loses its tail and grows legs.
Teacher Comment: **Write "tail" and "legs" on the next two blanks.**

Teacher Comment: **The way it breathes changes as it grows up. What do we call a grown-up animal?**
Student Response: A grown-up animal is an adult.
Teacher Comment: **Write "adult" on the next blank.**

Thinking About Thinking
Teacher Comment: **What did you pay attention to when you explained how the frog changes form as it grows up?**
Student Response:
1. I described its body when it hatched.
2. I described how its body changed.
3. I described how it looked and survived as an adult.

Personal Application
Teacher Comment: **When do you need to describe the life cycle of an animal?**
Student Response: I need to describe the life cycle of an animal to explain how they look and what they need to survive.

Page 107: THE LIFE CYCLE OF A BUTTERFLY

LESSON

Introduction
Teacher Comment: **In the previous lesson we learned how a frog changes form as it grows.**

Explaining the Objective
Teacher Comment: **In this lesson you will describe how a butterfly's body changes as it grows.**

Conducting the Lesson

Teacher Comment: **Use the words in the WORD BOX to describe the life cycle of a butterfly. What kind of animal is a butterfly?**

Student Response: A butterfly is an insect.

Teacher Comment: **Write "insect" on the first blank.**

Teacher Comment: **The butterfly's egg hatches into an animal that looks very different from the butterfly. It has no wings and looks like a worm that moves slowly on tiny legs. What do we call this form of the butterfly?**

Student Response: The egg hatches into a caterpillar.

Teacher Comment: **Write "caterpillar" on the second blank.**

THE LIFE CYCLE OF A BUTTERFLY

Use the words in the WORD BOX to describe the life cycle of a butterfly.

adult butterfly

butterfly eggs

caterpillar

cocoon

WORD BOX
adult, cocoon, caterpillar, insect, skin, wings

A butterfly is an insect. Its egg hatches into a caterpillar that looks like a worm that moves slowly on tiny legs. It sheds its fuzzy skin that becomes harder each time it sheds. It sticks itself to a branch and its thick skin becomes a cocoon. Inside the cocoon it develops wings. The cocoon breaks open and an adult butterfly comes out.

Teacher Comment: **What does the caterpillar shed as it grows?**

Student Response: The caterpillar sheds its skin.

Teacher Comment: **Write "skin" on the third blank.**

Teacher Comment: **Each time the caterpillar sheds, its skin becomes harder until it sticks itself to a branch. What does its thick skin become?**

Student Response: The caterpillar's skin becomes a cocoon.

Teacher Comment: **Write "cocoon" on the fourth blank.**

Teacher Comment: **Inside the cocoon the caterpillar begins to grow a new body part. How does the caterpillar change?**

Student Response: Inside the cocoon the caterpillar develops wings.

Teacher Comment: **Write "wings" on the next blank.**

Teacher Comment: **When the cocoon breaks open, the grown-up butterfly comes out. What do we call a grown-up form of an animal?**

Student Response: The word for grown-up is adult.

Teacher Comment: **Write "adult" on the last blank.**

Thinking About Thinking

Teacher Comment: **What did you pay attention to when you explained how an animal changes form as it grows up?**

Student Response:

1. I described its body when it hatched.
2. I described how its body changed.
3. I described how it looked and survived as an adult.

Personal Application

Teacher Comment: **When do you need to describe the life cycle of an animal?**

Student Response: I need to describe the life cycle of an animal to explain how they look and what they need to survive.

© 2016 The Critical Thinking Co.™ • www.CriticalThinking.com • 800-458-4849

Page 108: SIMILAR ANIMALS

LESSON

Introduction

Teacher Comment: **We have described different kinds of animals.**

Explaining the Objective

Teacher Comment: **In this lesson you will find an animal most like another one.**

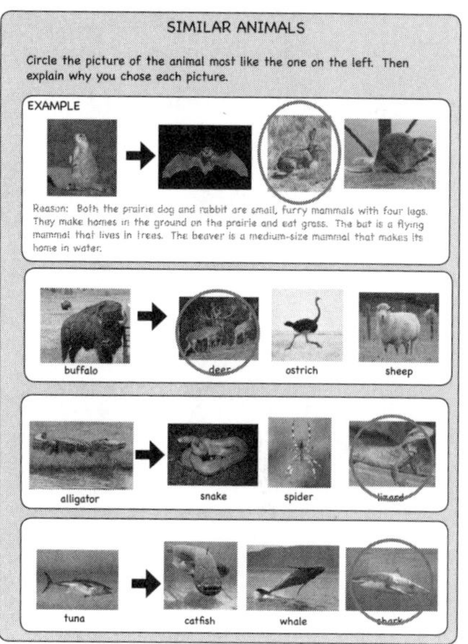

Conducting the Lesson

Teacher Comment: **In the example we see four animals: a prairie dog, a bat, a rabbit, and a beaver. We will decide which animal is most like the prairie dog. The rabbit is most like the prairie dog. Both the prairie dog and rabbit are small, furry mammals with four legs. They make homes in the ground on the prairie and eat grass. The bat is a flying mammal that lives in trees. The beaver is a medium-size mammal that makes its home in water.**

Teacher Comment: **Name the animals in the second box.**
Student Response: The animals are a buffalo, deer, an ostrich, and a sheep.
Teacher Comment: **Which animal is most like a buffalo?**
Student Response: The deer is most like a buffalo. They are both mammals that have horns and live in the wild.
Teacher Comment: **Circle the picture of the deer.**

Teacher Comment: **How are an ostrich and a sheep different from a buffalo?**
Student Response: An ostrich is a bird, not a mammal. A sheep is a farm animal.
Teacher Comment: **Name the animals in the third box.**
Student Response: The animals are an alligator, a snake, a spider, and a lizard.
Teacher Comment: **Which animal is most like an alligator?**
Student Response: The lizard is most like an alligator. They are both reptiles with short legs.

Teacher Comment: **How are a snake and spider different from the alligator?**
Student Response: A snake has no legs. A spider is not a reptile.
Teacher Comment: **Circle the picture of the lizard.**

Teacher Comment: **Name the animals in the bottom box.**
Student Response: The animals are a tuna, a catfish, a whale, and a shark.
Teacher Comment: **Which animal is most like a tuna?**
Student Response: The shark is most like a tuna. They are both large fish that live in the ocean.
Teacher Comment: **How are a catfish and a whale different from a tuna?**

© 2016 The Critical Thinking Co.™ • www.CriticalThinking.com • 800-458-4849

Student Response: The catfish is a medium sized fish that lives in rivers or lakes. The whale is a mammal, not a fish.

Teacher Comment: **Circle the picture of the shark.**

- Remind students that "both" is a signal word that tells how two things are alike.

Thinking About Thinking

Teacher Comment: **What did you pay attention to when you described the animals?**

Student Response:

1. I named the animals.
2. I thought about the type of animals (mammal, reptile, bird, etc.).
3. I thought about where the animal lived.
4. I found the animal that was the same kind and was in similar surroundings.
5. I checked that the other animals were not similar.

Personal Application

Teacher Comment: **When do you need to know how animals are alike?**

Student Response: I need to know how animals are alike to understand what they need to survive and to write about them.

Page 109: HOW ARE THESE ANIMALS ALIKE?

LESSON

- Remind students that when we tell how two things are alike we compare them. "Both" is the signal word that tells that two things are alike.

Introduction

Teacher Comment: **We have identified an animal most like another.**

Explaining the Objective

Teacher Comment: **In this lesson you will explain how pairs of animals are alike.**

Conducting the Lesson

Teacher Comment: **Name the animals in the first box.**

Student Response: The animals are an elephant and a giraffe.

Teacher Comment: **What kind are they?**

Student Response: The elephant and the giraffe are large mammals.

Teacher Comment: **Write "large mammals" on the first two lines.**

Teacher Comment: **Use the words in the WORD BOX to explain how the elephant and giraffe are alike.**

- Check students' work. Continue this dialog to discuss students' answers.

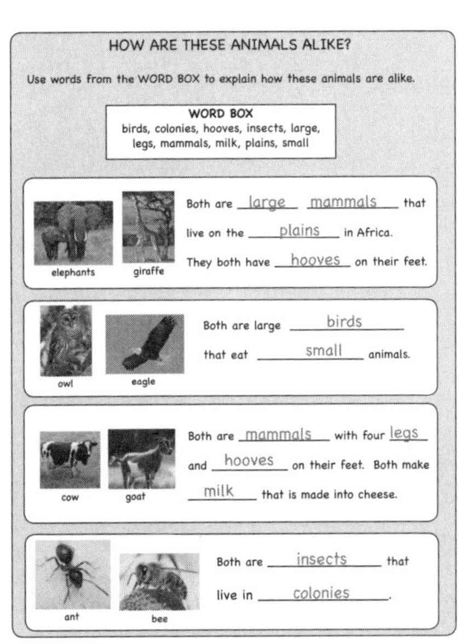
HOW ARE THESE ANIMALS ALIKE?

Use words from the WORD BOX to explain how these animals are alike.

WORD BOX
birds, colonies, hooves, insects, large, legs, mammals, milk, plains, small

elephants giraffe
Both are large mammals that live on the plains in Africa. They both have hooves on their feet.

owl eagle
Both are large birds that eat small animals.

cow goat
Both are mammals with four legs and hooves on their feet. Both make milk that is made into cheese.

ant bee
Both are insects that live in colonies.

© 2016 The Critical Thinking Co.™ • www.CriticalThinking.com • 800-458-4849

Thinking About Thinking

Teacher Comment: **What did you pay attention to when you described the animals?**

Student Response:

1. I named the animals.
2. I thought about the type of animals (mammal, reptile, bird, etc.).
3. I thought about where the animal lived.
4. I chose the words that completed the sentence.

Personal Application

Teacher Comment: **When do you need to know how animals are alike?**

Student Response: I need to know how animals are alike to understand what they need to survive and to write about them.

Page 110: HOW ARE THESE ANIMALS DIFFERENT?

LESSON

- Remind students that when we tell how two things are different, we contrast. "But" is a signal word that tells that two things are different.

Introduction

Teacher Comment: **We have explained how animals were alike.**

Explaining the Objective

Teacher Comment: In this lesson you will explain how two animals are different.

Conducting the Lesson

Teacher Comment: **Name the animals in the first box.**

Student Response: The animals are a spider and a mosquito.

Teacher Comment: **Count the legs on each animal. Which as eight legs?**

Student Response: The spider has eight legs.

Teacher Comment: **Write "spider" on the first line and "mosquito" on the second line.**

What kind of animal is a mosquito?

Student Response: The mosquito is an insect.

Teacher Comment: **Write "insect" on the next line.**

Teacher Comment: **How many legs does a mosquito have?**

Student Response: A mosquito has six legs.

Teacher Comment: **Write "six" on the last line.**

- You may want to explain that a spider is an arachnid, not an insect.

- Check students' work. Continue this dialog to discuss students' answers.

HOW ARE THESE ANIMALS DIFFERENT?

Use words from the WORD BOX to explain how these animals are different.

WORD BOX
eagle, fly, goat, insect, mammal, mosquito, milk, ostrich, sheep, six, spider, tuna, whale

spider mosquito

The spider has eight legs, but the mosquito is an insect that has six legs.

sheep goat

People get wool from the sheep but they get milk from the goat.

tuna whale

The tuna is a large fish. The whale is a large mammal that lives in the ocean.

eagle ostrich

The eagle can fly high for long distances, but the ostrich cannot.

© 2016 The Critical Thinking Co.™ • www.CriticalThinking.com • 800-458-4849

Thinking About Thinking

Teacher Comment: **What did you pay attention to when you described the animals?**

Student Response:

1. I named the animals.
2. I thought about the type of animals (mammal, reptile, bird, etc.).
3. I thought about where the animal lived.
4. I chose the words that completed the sentence.

Personal Application

Teacher Comment: **When do you need to know how animals are different?**

Student Response: I need to know how animals are different to understand what they need to survive and to write about them.

Page 111: DESCRIBING SIMILARITIES AND DIFFERENCES

LESSON

- Remind students that "both" is a signal word that tells that things are alike. "But" is a signal word that tells that things are different.

Introduction

Teacher Comment: **When we explain how two animals are alike, we compare them. When we explain how two animals are different, we contrast them.**

Explaining the Objective

Teacher Comment: You will explain how two animals are alike <u>and</u> how they are different.

Conducting the Lesson

Teacher Comment: **Name the animals in the first box.**

Student Response: The animals are an owl and a bat.

Teacher Comment: **Write "owl" and "bat" in the first two blanks.**

Teacher Comment: **When are bat and the owl active?**

Student Response: The bat and the owl are active at night.

Teacher Comment: **Write "night" on the next line.**

Teacher Comment: **What do the bat and the owl eat?**

Student Response: These animals eat insects.

Teacher Comment: **Write "insects" on the next line.**

Teacher Comment: **Which animal is a bird?**

Student Response: The owl is a bird.

Teacher Comment: **Write "owl" on the next line.**

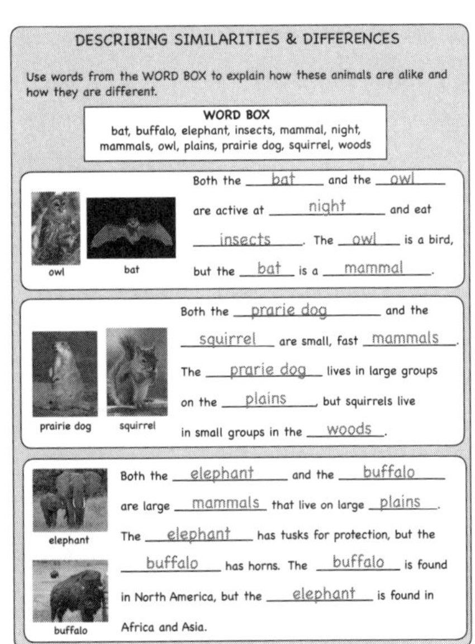

DESCRIBING SIMILARITIES & DIFFERENCES

Use words from the WORD BOX to explain how these animals are alike and how they are different.

WORD BOX
bat, buffalo, elephant, insects, mammal, night, mammals, owl, plains, prairie dog, squirrel, woods

owl bat

Both the bat and the owl are active at night and eat insects. The owl is a bird, but the bat is a mammal.

prairie dog squirrel

Both the prarie dog and the squirrel are small, fast mammals. The prarie dog lives in large groups on the plains, but squirrels live in small groups in the woods.

elephant buffalo

Both the elephant and the buffalo are large mammals that live on large plains. The elephant has tusks for protection, but the buffalo has horns. The buffalo is found in North America, but the elephant is found in Africa and Asia.

© 2016 The Critical Thinking Co.™ • www.CriticalThinking.com • 800-458-4849

Teacher Comment: **The word "but" tells that the rest of the sentence will tell something different about the other animal, the bat. What kind of animal is a bat?**

Student Response: The bat is a flying mammal.

Teacher Comment: **Write "bat" and "mammal" on the last two lines.**

- Check students' work. Continue this dialog to discuss students' answers.

Thinking About Thinking

Teacher Comment: **What did you think about to compare and contrast animals?**

Student Response:

1. I remembered the important characteristics of each animal (appearance, body structure, how it gives birth).
2. I thought about how the animals were alike.
3. I thought about how the animals were different.

Personal Application

Teacher Comment: **When is it important to understand how animals are alike and different?**

Student Response: I need to understand how animals are alike and different to tell or write about them.

Page 112: DESCRIBING SIMILARITIES AND DIFFERENCES

LESSON

Introduction

Teacher Comment: **We have described how two animals are alike and how they are different. We can show similarities and differences on a diagram.**

Explaining the Objective

Teacher Comment: **In this lesson you use a diagram to compare and contrast an ant and a bee.**

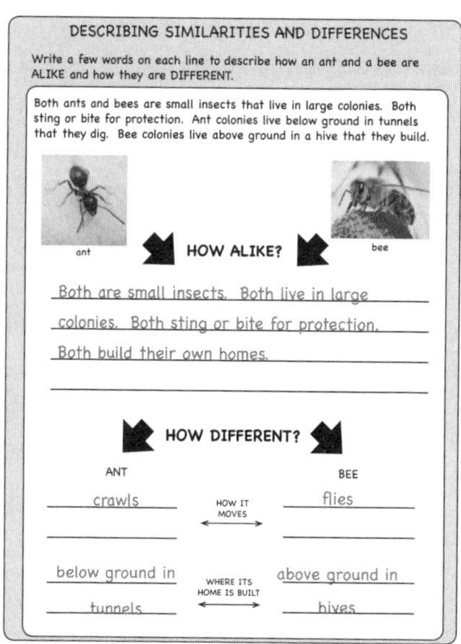

DESCRIBING SIMILARITIES AND DIFFERENCES

Write a few words on each line to describe how an ant and a bee are ALIKE and how they are DIFFERENT.

Both ants and bees are small insects that live in large colonies. Both sting or bite for protection. Ant colonies live below ground in tunnels that they dig. Bee colonies live above ground in a hive that they build.

ant

bee

HOW ALIKE?

Both are small insects. Both live in large colonies. Both sting or bite for protection. Both build their own homes.

HOW DIFFERENT?

ANT		BEE
crawls	HOW IT MOVES	flies
below ground in tunnels	WHERE ITS HOME IS BUILT	above ground in hives

Conducting the Lesson

Teacher Comment: **Both ants and bees are small insects that live in large colonies. Both sting or bite for protection. Ant colonies live underground in tunnels that they dig. Bee colonies live above ground in a hive that they build. How are these animals alike?**

Student Response: Both are small insects. Both live in large colonies. Both sting or bite for protection. Both build their homes.

Teacher Comment: **On the "how alike" lines, write a few short sentences to describe how an ant and a bee are alike.**

© 2016 The Critical Thinking Co.™ • www.CriticalThinking.com • 800-458-4849

Teacher Comment: **How are these insects different?**

Student Response: Ants crawl, but bees fly. Ants build a colony underground, but bees live above ground in a hive.

Teacher Comment: **Write your answers on the "how different" lines.**

Thinking About Thinking

Teacher Comment: **What did you think about to compare and contrast animals?**

Student Response:

1. I remembered the important characteristics of each animal (appearance, body structure, how it gave birth).
2. I thought about how the animals were alike.
3. I thought about how the animals were different.

Personal Application

Teacher Comment: **When is it important to understand how animals are alike or different?**

Student Response: I need to understand how animals are alike or different to tell or write about them.

Page 113: A DIFFERENT KIND OF ANIMAL

LESSON

Introduction

Teacher Comment: **We have described how two animals are different.**

Explaining the Objective

Teacher Comment: **In this lesson you will show which animal is different from the others.**

Conducting the Lesson

Teacher Comment: **Three of these animals are the same kind. Circle the animal that is different. Explain your answer to your partner. In the example; a butterfly, an ant, and a bee are insects. The spider is not an insect and has been circled*. Name the animals in the second box.**

Student Response: The animals are a bat, an eagle, an owl, and an ostrich.

Teacher Comment: **How are three of the animals alike?**

Student Response: The eagle, the owl, and the ostrich are birds. The bat is a flying mammal.

Teacher Comment: **Circle the bat.**

- Check students' work. Continue this dialog to discuss students' answers.

*A spider is an arachnid, not an insect.

© 2016 The Critical Thinking Co.™ • www.CriticalThinking.com • 800-458-4849

Thinking About Thinking

Teacher Comment: **What did you think about to decide which animal is not the same kind?**

Student Response:

1. I looked at the picture of each animal and identified whether it was a bird, insect, mammal, or reptile.
2. I found three animals that were the same kind.
3. I identified the animal that did not fit that group and explained why.

Personal Application

Teacher Comment: **When is it important to understand how an animal is different from others?**

Student Response: I need to know how an animal is different from others to understand how its body and needs are different.

Page 114: CLASSIFYING ANIMALS

LESSON

Introduction

Teacher Comment: **We have identified kinds of animals. When we identify the same kinds of animals, we are classifying them.**

Explaining the Objective

Teacher Comment: **In this lesson you will name the class and list examples of that class of animals.**

Conducting the Lesson

Teacher Comment: **Name the animals in the first box.**

Student Response: The animals are a lizard, a snake, and a turtle.

Teacher Comment: **What kind of animals are they?**

Student Response: These animals are reptiles.

Teacher Comment: **What can we say about an animal when we call it a reptile?**

Student Response: A reptile is a cold-blooded, egg-laying animal that has scaly skin and moves on land by crawling.

Teacher Comment: **Use the words in the WORD BOX to write the class of animals and examples of animals in that class. Write "reptiles" on the top line. Write the names of the three reptiles on the next three lines.**

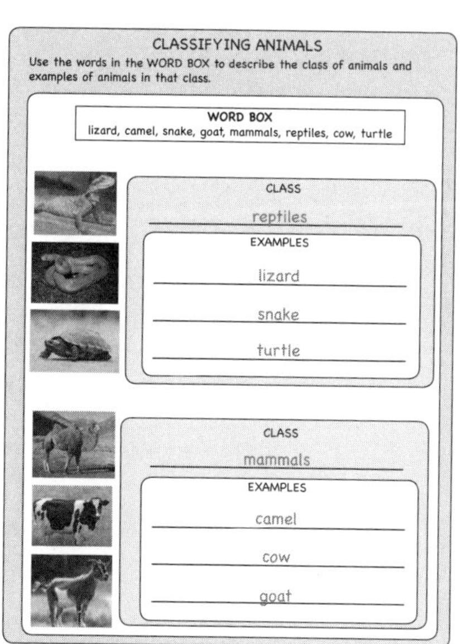

Teacher Comment: **Name the animals in the second box.**

Student Response: The animals are a camel, a cow, and a goat.

Teacher Comment: **What kind of animals are they?**

Student Response: These animals are mammals.

© 2016 The Critical Thinking Co.™ • www.CriticalThinking.com • 800-458-4849

Teacher Comment: **What can we say about an animal when we call it a mammal?**

Student Response: A mammal is an animal that carries its babies inside its body and makes milk to feed their babies. Mammals have hair and are warm-blooded. Most mammals live on land.

Teacher Comment: **Write "mammals" on the top line. Write the names of the three mammals on the next three lines.**

Thinking About Thinking

Teacher Comment: **What did you think about to classify an animal?**

Student Response:

1. I remembered whether it laid eggs or carried babies inside their bodies.
2. I looked at its skin, its body parts, and its surroundings.
3. I remembered whether its habitat was wet or dry.
4. I wrote the name for it in its class.

Personal Application

Teacher Comment: **When is it important to classify animals?**

Student Response: I need to know the class of an animal to describe it and to understand what it needs to survive.

Page 115: CLASSIFYING ANIMALS – PROTECTION

LESSON

Introduction

Teacher Comment: **We have classified animals by their type. We can classify animals another way so that we can understand something important about them. In this lesson we will classify animals by how they protect themselves. Some animals have stingers or horns to protect themselves. Some animals can hide because their colors blend into their environment. Some animals can move very fast to stay safe.**

Explaining the Objective

Teacher Comment: **In this lesson you classify the animals by how they protect themselves.**

Conducting the Lesson

Teacher Comment: **Name the first animal.**

Student Response: The first animal is an ant.

Teacher Comment: **How does the ant protect itself?**

Student Response: The ant protects itself with stingers.

Teacher Comment: **Write "ant" on a line in the stinger box.**

- Check students' work. Continue this dialog to discuss students' answers. Note that the term "camouflage" may be used instead of color.

© 2016 The Critical Thinking Co.™ • www.CriticalThinking.com • 800-458-4849

Thinking About Thinking

Teacher Comment: **What did you think about to classify animals by how they protect themselves?**

Student Response:

1. I remembered the parts of the animal's body.
2. I remembered how it looked in its surroundings.
3. I remembered how it moved.
4. I thought about how its body parts, its color, or its speed protected it.

Personal Application

Teacher Comment: **When do you need to know how an animal protects itself?**

Student Response: I need to know how an animal protects itself to understand what it needs to survive, to write or tell about it, and to stay safe around it.

Page 116: ANIMAL ANALOGIES

LESSON

Introduction

Teacher Comment: **We have discussed how different animals are alike.**

Explaining the Objective

Teacher Comment: **In this lesson you describe how two animals are similar in the same way.**

Conducting the Lesson

Teacher Comment: **An analogy is a comparison of two pairs of things. We describe how the first pair are related. The prairie dog lives on a plain. The word "LIKE" signals that we will say where the beaver lives. Where does a beaver live?**

Student Response: The beaver lives in a stream.

Teacher Comment: **Circle the picture of the stream.**

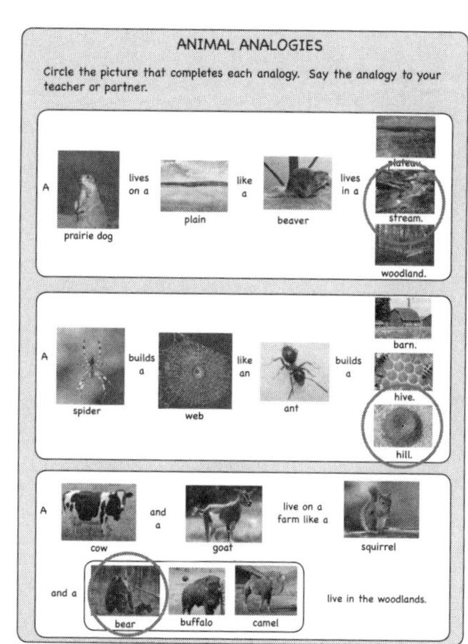

Teacher Comment: **Say the analogy.**

Student Response: A prairie dog lives on a plain like a beaver lives in a stream.

Teacher Comment: **In the second analogy we see that a spider builds a web for its home. What does the ant build for its home?**

Student Response: The ant builds an ant hill.

Teacher Comment: **Circle the picture of the ant hill.**

Teacher Comment: **Say the analogy.**

Student Response: A spider builds a web like an ant builds an ant hill.

Teacher Comment: **In the third analogy we see that both a cow and a goat live on a farm like a squirrel lives in the woodlands. What other animal lives in the woodlands?**

Student Response: The bear also lives in the woodlands.

Teacher Comment: **Circle the picture of the bears.**

Teacher Comment: **Say the analogy.**

Student Response: A cow and a goat live on a farm like a squirrel and a bear live in the woodlands.

Thinking About Thinking

Teacher Comment: **What did you think about to complete analogies about animals?**

Student Response:

1. I thought about how the first two pictures were connected.
2. I decided which picture showed that same connection for the second animal.
3. I said the analogy to be sure.

Personal Application

Teacher Comment: **When do you need to explain the same thing about two animals?**

Student Response: I need to explain the same thing about two animals when I need to tell something important about both of them.

Page 117: WRITING A DESCRIPTION OF AN ANIMAL

LESSON

- To remind students about the significant characteristics of a deer, read aloud a picture book that describes these details.

Introduction

Teacher Comment: **To describe animals we need to explain all the important characteristics that make the animal different from others.**

Explaining the Objective

Teacher Comment: **In this lesson you will recall the details of the important characteristics needed to describe any animal and put those characteristics together to write a description.**

Conducting the Lesson

Teacher Comment: **The diagram shows the six characteristics that we need to say to describe any animal: What kind of animal it is, its size compared to other animals of that kind, where it lives, what it eats, how it protects itself, and unusual facts that make it different from other animals of that kind.**

The example shows that a mosquito is an insect. It is tiny compared to other insects, it lives anywhere on Earth where the climate is warm. It eats by sucking blood from other animals and people. It protects itself with a stinger. It carries diseases to humans and animals.

© 2016 The Critical Thinking Co.™ • www.CriticalThinking.com • 800-458-4849

When we put all these characteristics together, we can write a description of the mosquito that tells how it is different from other insects. Notice that the color of the answer in each box is the same as the words in the description. That way we can see that the description includes all we need to say about the mosquito.

"A mosquito is a tiny insect that sucks blood for food. It protects itself with a stinger. It lives anywhere that is warm and carries diseases to humans and animals.

To organize what we need to say to describe a deer, we begin by telling what kind of animal it is. That will tell the reader whether a deer is warm- or cold-blooded, whether it lays eggs or gives live birth, whether or not it has a backbone, and whether it is a land, water, or air animal.

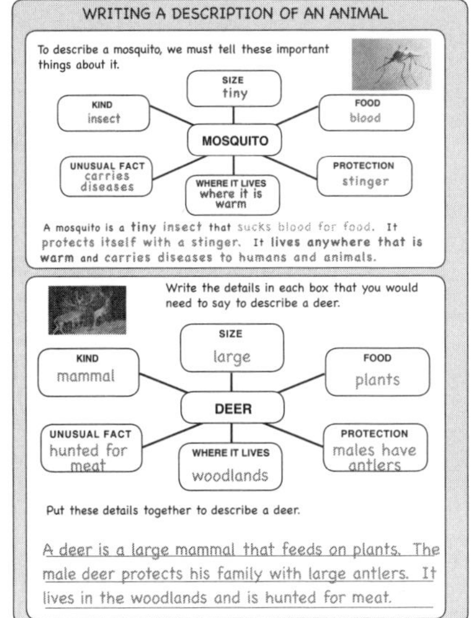

Teacher Comment: **What kind of animal is the deer?**
Student Response: A deer is a mammal.
Teacher Comment: **Write "mammal" in the "kind" box.**

Teacher Comment: **How does the size of a deer compare to other mammals?**
Student Response: A deer is a large mammal.
Teacher Comment: **Write "large" in the "size" box.**

Teacher Comment: **What does a deer eat?**
Student Response: A deer eats plants.
Teacher Comment: **Write "plants" in the food box.**

Teacher Comment: **How does a deer protect itself?**
Student Response: A male deer has long horns called antlers to protect itself.
Teacher Comment: **Write "males have antlers" in the protection box.**

Teacher Comment: **Where does the deer live?**
Student Response: A deer lives in the woodlands.

Teacher Comment: **Write "woodlands" in the box that tells where it lives.**

Teacher Comment: **What unusual facts about a deer tell us that a deer is different from other mammals?**
Student Response: A deer is hunted for its meat.
Teacher Comment: **Write "hunted for meat" in the box that tells unusual facts about a deer.**

Teacher Comment: **Put these details together to describe a deer.**

Thinking About Thinking

Teacher Comment: **What did you think about to describe an animal?**

Student Response:

1. I remembered what kind of animal it was.
2. I remembered how large it was compared to other animals of that kind.
3. I remembered what it ate.
4. I remembered how it protected itself.
5. I remembered where it lived.
6. I remembered unusual facts that made it different from other animals of that kind.

Personal Application

Teacher Comment: **Why is it important to know how to describe the important characteristics of an animal?**

Student Response: I need to know how to describe all the important characteristics of an animal to correctly tell a story about it.

© 2016 The Critical Thinking Co.™ • www.CriticalThinking.com • 800-458-4849

CHAPTER NINE – THINKING ABOUT COMMUNITIES - Pages 118-139
GENERAL INTRODUCTION

CURRICULUM APPLICATIONS

Language Arts: Identify the jobs of various characters in stories and the descriptions and actions that explain what that worker does. Identify how various stories explain how jobs and communities change over time. Compare and contrast how similar jobs are described in different stories to show differences in cultures and change across time. Discuss grade two topics and texts with peers and adults in large and small groups. Compare and contrast the most important points in describing two concepts. Produce complete sentences in order to provide adequate detail and clarification. Use appropriate adjectives, adverbs, and verbs to describe key concepts.
Health: Identify people who produce and distribute food. Identify health and emergency workers.
Social Studies: Define consumer as a user of goods and services. Identify how a family depends upon products and services to meet its needs. Cite examples of community needs and services. Recognize the differences between producing and selling goods. Understand how community helpers are an example of interdependence. Understand the purpose of government. Give examples of ways in which businesses in the community meet the needs and wants of consumers. Explain the roles and impact that producers and consumers have on the economy. Explain how money is used for saving, spending, and borrowing. Summarize the role of financial institutions. Interpret map symbols and cardinal directions. Give examples of ways in which people depend on the physical environment and natural resources to meet basic needs.

TEACHING SUGGESTIONS

- **Drawing:** Each student may use a mental model to describe a person's job. Label the mental model with a description of that job.
- **Telling:** Select a common story about a job, such as "The Shoemaker and the Elves." Ask students to retell the story using another job such as a construction worker instead of a shoemaker. Discuss how the revised story is different from the original. For example, how might the elves help the construction worker and what might the construction worker make for the elves in return?
- Encourage students to identify individuals in their local community who provide the goods and services described in this chapter.
- Use common synonyms for jobs–occupation, livelihood, career, work, etc.

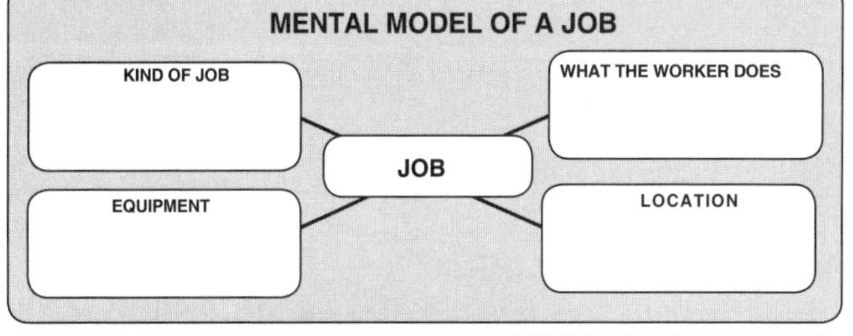

MENTAL MODEL

A mental model outlines the important characteristics to describe or define a concept. After completing this chapter, each student will have used these mental models. A mental model helps a student:

- anticipate what he or she needs to know to understand these concepts.
- remember the characteristics of these concepts.
- state a clear definition or write an adequate description of these concepts.
- explain these concepts to someone else.

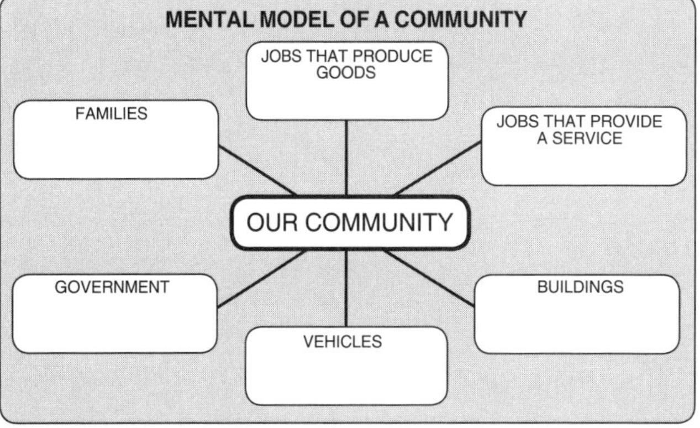

© 2016 The Critical Thinking Co.™ • www.CriticalThinking.com • 800-458-4849

Page 119: WHAT A FAMILY NEEDS

LESSON

Introduction

Teacher Comment: **Each community is a group of families that live in the same place and help each other get the goods and services that people need.**

Explaining the Objective

Teacher Comment: **In this lesson you will identify what a family needs.**

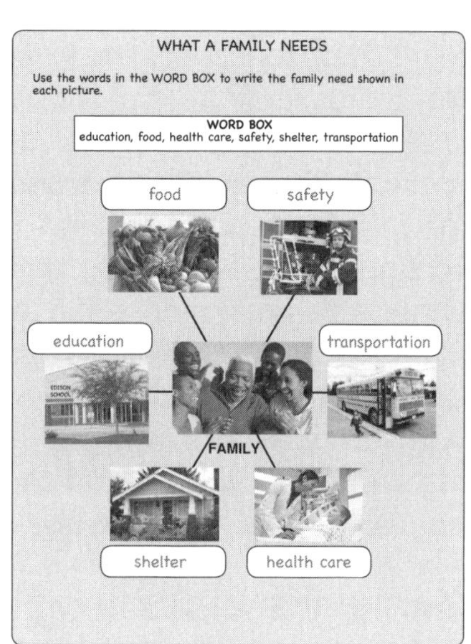

Conducting the Lesson

Teacher Comment: **Each picture shows what a family needs. Use the words in the WORD BOX to write the family need shown in the picture. The first picture shows food. Why does a family need food?**

Student Response: A family needs food for their bodies to be strong and healthy.

Teacher Comment: **Write "food" in the first box.**

Teacher Comment: **The next picture shows a firefighter. Why do families need firefighters?**

Student Response: Firefighters make sure that our homes are safe.

Teacher Comment: **Write "safety" in the blank above the picture of the firefighter.**

• Check students' work. Continue this dialog to discuss students' answers.

Thinking About Thinking

Teacher Comment: **What did you pay attention to when you identified what a family needs?**

Student Response:

1. I looked at the worker or object in the picture.
2. I thought about why we need that worker or object.
3. I matched the family's need to the word in the word box.

Personal Application

Teacher Comment: **When do you need to understand what families need?**

Student Response: I need to understand what families need so I can know what help people may need if they do not have these things.

© 2016 The Critical Thinking Co.™ • www.CriticalThinking.com • 800-458-4849

Page 120: NEEDS AND WANTS

LESSON

NEEDS AND WANTS

People must have some things to live. Families also buy things that they want, but do not need, to live. In the boxes, write what families need and what they want.

NEEDS AND WANTS

THINGS FAMILIES NEED	THINGS FAMILIES WANT
shelter	basketball
food	bicycle
shoes	teddy bear
water	television

Introduction

Teacher Comment: **Families buy what they need to live and what they want to make their lives more comfortable and enjoyable.**

Explaining the Objective

Teacher Comment: **In this lesson you will sort objects into two groups; "needs," things people must have to live, and "wants," things that people would like to have.**

Conducting the Lesson

Teacher Comment: **The first picture shows shelter. Is shelter a "need" or a "want"?**

Student Response: Shelter is something people need.

Teacher Comment: **Write "shelter" in the box for "things families need."**

Teacher Comment: **The second picture shows a basketball. Is a basketball a "need" or a "want"?**

Student Response: A basketball is something people want.

Teacher Comment: **Write "basketball" in the box for "things families want."**

• Check students' work. Continue this dialog to discuss students' answers.

Thinking About Thinking

Teacher Comment: **What did you pay attention to when you decided which things are needs or wants?**

Student Response:

1. I looked at each picture and decided whether people need it to survive.
2. If people need it to survive, I wrote the word in the "need" box.
3. If people do not need it to survive, I knew that the object was nice to have to be more comfortable or to entertain our family.
4. I wrote the word for things that we did not need to survive in the "want" box.

Personal Application

Teacher Comment: **When do you need to know the difference between needs and wants?**

Student Response: I need to now the difference between needs and wants to understand how families spend their money and to know which things we buy are really necessary.

© 2016 The Critical Thinking Co.™ • www.CriticalThinking.com • 800-458-4849

Page 121: DESCRIBING JOBS

LESSON

• Explain that a lawyer is also called an attorney.

Introduction

Teacher Comment: **We have thought about family members and their needs and wants. Some adults in each family have jobs to earn money so that they can buy what their families need and want. In a community, families rely on other workers to provide each others' needs and wants.**

Explaining the Objective

Teacher Comment: **In this lesson I will describe a worker's job and you will circle the picture of the job I describe.**

Conducting the Lesson

Teacher Comment: **Look at the top row. Name these workers.**

Student Response: These workers are an architect, an artist, and a plumber.

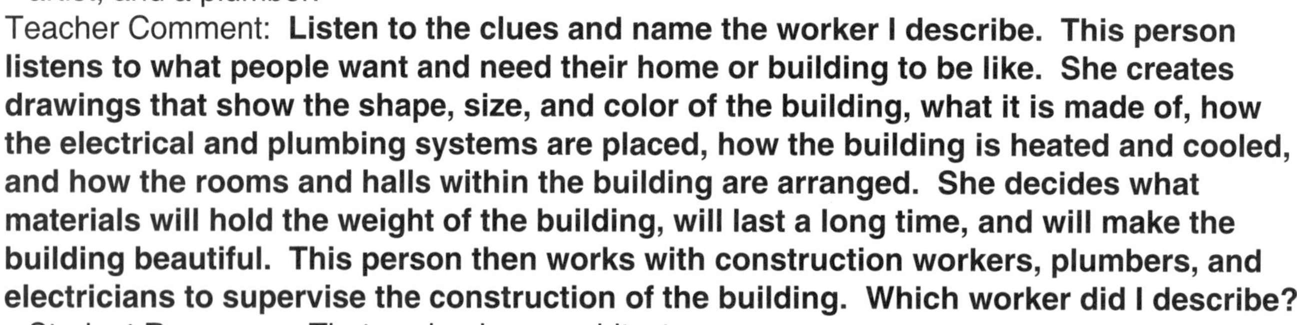

Teacher Comment: **Listen to the clues and name the worker I describe. This person listens to what people want and need their home or building to be like. She creates drawings that show the shape, size, and color of the building, what it is made of, how the electrical and plumbing systems are placed, how the building is heated and cooled, and how the rooms and halls within the building are arranged. She decides what materials will hold the weight of the building, will last a long time, and will make the building beautiful. This person then works with construction workers, plumbers, and electricians to supervise the construction of the building. Which worker did I describe?**

Student Response: That worker is an architect.

Teacher Comment: **Circle the picture of the architect.**

Teacher Comment: **What clues let you know that the worker is an architect?**

Student Response: The picture shows her showing drawings to the construction workers, electricians, and plumbers who will build the building.

Teacher Comment: **Why doesn't the artist or the plumber fit the description?**

Student Response: The artist also draws, but does not build. The plumber only works on part of the building, he does not design the building.

Teacher Comment: **Look at the second row. Name these workers.**

Student Response: These workers are a lawyer, a librarian, and a firefighter.

Teacher Comment: **Listen to the clues and name the worker I describe. This person helps to prove whether or not a person has committed a crime or is being treated fairly in a legal argument. She may speak in court for a person who is accused of a crime or for the person who was the victim of a crime. Sometimes she speaks for the government. She must study a long time to learn the laws and understand the facts of**

© 2016 The Critical Thinking Co.™ • www.CriticalThinking.com • 800-458-4849

the crime or argument. She must ask the questions that a judge or a group of citizens need to know to decide the truth. Which worker did I describe?

Student Response: That worker is a lawyer.

Teacher Comment: **Circle the picture of the lawyer.**

Teacher Comment: **What clues let you know that the worker is a lawyer?**

Student Response: I see the flag and judge in a courtroom. The lawyer talks with the person for whom she speaks.

Teacher Comment: **Why doesn't the librarian or the firefighter fit the description?**

Student Response: The librarian helps people get books and does not work in a courtroom. The firefighter puts out fires and helps people to prevent them.

Teacher Comment: **Look at the third row. Name these workers.**

Student Response: These workers are a doctor, a dentist, and a pharmacist.

Teacher Comment: **Listen to the clues and name the worker I describe. This person works in a pharmacy (a store or part of a store where medicines are sold). He fills prescriptions, which are notes from a doctor that tell which medicine a person needs. He has studied how our bodies work so that he understands how each medicine helps our bodies heal. He often wears a white coat to show that the medicines are kept in clean surroundings. Which worker did I describe?**

Student Response: That worker is a pharmacist.

Teacher Comment: **Circle the picture of the pharmacist.**

Teacher Comment: **What clues let you know that the worker is a pharmacist?**

Student Response: I see the shelves of medicine behind him. He wears a white coat.

Teacher Comment: **Why don't the other jobs fit the description?**

Student Response: The doctor and the dentist tell the pharmacist what medicine to give, but they do not provide medicine.

Teacher Comment: **Look at the fourth row. Name these workers.**

Student Response: These workers are a teller, a barber and a teacher.

Teacher Comment: **Listen to the clues and name the worker I describe. This person helps people to save and to receive their money. He gives the customer money for checks that have been given to her. A check is a note that tells the bank that the person who signs the check wants the bank to give the customer money from the signers account. An account is the amount of money that a person has put in the bank for saving or writing checks. What worker did I describe?**

Student Response: That worker is a teller.

Teacher Comment: **Circle the picture of the teller.**

Teacher Comment: **What clues let you know that the worker is a teller?**

Student Response: I see that the teller used a computer that tells how much money the customer has in his account. I see the customer receiving money or information about his account.

Teacher Comment: **Why don't the other jobs fit the description?**

Student Response: The barber cuts hair. The teacher does not help people with their money.

Teacher Comment: **Look at the last row. Name these workers.**

© 2016 The Critical Thinking Co.™ • www.CriticalThinking.com • 800-458-4849

Student Response: These workers are a construction worker, a carpenter, and a sanitation worker.

Teacher Comment: **Listen to the clues and name the worker I describe. This person works to keep the community clean and safe. He is paid by city government to take away trash and garbage. He puts what people throw away into a large truck that takes it to a large area where it is buried or burned. Which worker did I describe?**

Student Response: That worker is a sanitation worker.

Teacher Comment: **Circle the picture of the sanitation worker.**

Teacher Comment: **What clues let you know that the worker is a sanitation worker?**

Student Response: I see the sanitation worker rolling a large trash can from the sidewalk to the street.

Teacher Comment: **Why don't the other jobs fit the description?**

Student Response: A construction worker and the carpenter build buildings, they do not remove trash.

Thinking About Thinking

Teacher Comment: **What did you pay attention to when you picked out the job that was described?**

Student Response:

1. I listened for the important characteristics of the job.
2. I found the important characteristics in the pictures (activities, goods or services, or surroundings).
3. I named the job.
4. I checked that the other photographs of jobs didn't show those important characteristics.

Personal Application

Teacher Comment: When do you need to describe what workers do in their jobs?

Student Response: I need to describe what workers do when I explain what friends or family members do for a living, when I tell about commercials, businesses, and so I can understand how important jobs are to the community.

Page 122: DESCRIBING JOBS

LESSON

Introduction

Teacher Comment: **We have identified workers from descriptions of their jobs.**

Explaining the Objective

Teacher Comment: **In this lesson you will match a picture of a worker to the word or phrase that describes what that worker does.**

Conducting the Lesson

Teacher Comment: **Name the first worker.**

Student Response: The first worker is a lawyer.

Teacher Comment: **What details show that the worker in the picture is a lawyer?**

© 2016 The Critical Thinking Co.™ • www.CriticalThinking.com • 800-458-4849

Student Response: I see the flag and judge in a courtroom. The lawyer talks with the person she speaks for.

Teacher Comment: **What does a lawyer do?**

Student Response: A lawyer helps to prove whether or not a person has committed a crime or is being treated fairly in a legal argument.

Teacher Comment: **Draw a line from the picture of the lawyer to the phrase "enforces the law."**

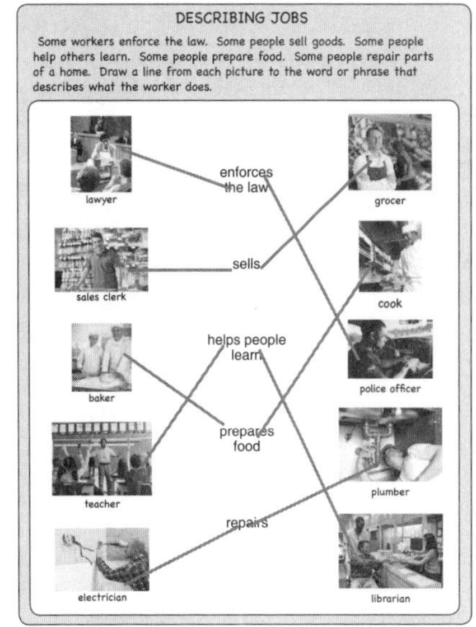

Teacher Comment: **Name the second worker.**

Student Response: The second worker is a sales clerk .

Teacher Comment: **What details show that the worker in the picture is a sales clerk?**

Student Response: He is standing in front of shelves of paint.

Teacher Comment: **What does a sales clerk do?**

Student Response: A sales clerk sells products.

Teacher Comment: **Draw a line from the picture of the sales clerk to the word "sells."**

• Check students' work. Continue this dialog to discuss students' answers.

Thinking About Thinking

Teacher Comment: **How did you decide which phrase belonged with each picture?**

Student Response:

1. I saw what the person was doing.
2. I looked at the clothes, equipment, and surroundings.
3. I looked for the words that described the job.

Personal Application

Teacher Comment: **When is it important to know the words for a job?**

Student Response: I need to know the words for a job in order to write about them.

Page 123: MATCHING WORKERS TO THEIR VEHICLES

LESSON

Introduction

Teacher Comment: **Families need vehicles to go to their jobs, to buy what they need, and to go to school. Some workers need vehicles to carry out their jobs. Businesses need vehicles to deliver what they sell. All these vehicles travel on our streets and highways and make up our transportation system. Our communities rely on vehicles to get what families need.**

Explaining the Objective

Teacher Comment: **In this lesson you will match each worker to the vehicle used in that job.**

Conducting the Lesson

Teacher Comment: **The first picture shows a construction worker. He needs a large vehicle to bring building materials to the building site and to take away trash from it. Name that vehicle.**

Student Response: The construction worker needs a dump truck to bring in building materials and take away trash.

Teacher Comment: **Draw a line from the construction worker to the dump truck.**

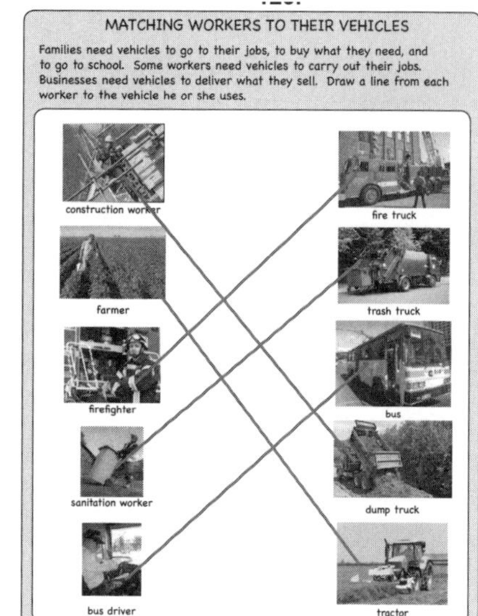

MATCHING WORKERS TO THEIR VEHICLES

Families need vehicles to go to their jobs, to buy what they need, and to go to school. Some workers need vehicles to carry out their jobs. Businesses need vehicles to deliver what they sell. Draw a line from each worker to the vehicle he or she uses.

construction worker
farmer
firefighter
sanitation worker
bus driver

fire truck
trash truck
bus
dump truck
tractor

Teacher Comment: **Why do people in the community need this worker and his vehicle?**

Student Response: The community needs the construction worker and dump truck in order to build homes and buildings.

- Check students' work. Continue this dialog to discuss students' answers.

Thinking About Thinking

Teacher Comment: **What did you think about in order to match a person's job to the vehicle used in that occupation?**

Student Response:

1. I looked at the details of the driver in the picture.
2. I named that driver.
3. I found the vehicle that he drove.
4. I drew a line from the driver to the vehicle.

Personal Application

Teacher Comment: **When is it important to know what vehicle a worker needs?**

Student Response: It's important to know what vehicle a worker needs when I'm telling others about jobs, traffic, or public transportation.

Page 124: DESCRIBING BUILDINGS

LESSON

Introduction

Teacher Comment: **Our communities are made up of buildings where people work and where people go to get what they need.**

Explaining the Objective

Teacher Comment: **In this lesson you match a description of a building to its picture and to the worker who works there.**

Conducting the Lesson

Teacher Comment: **The first description is, "A government building where people borrow books and movies." Name that building.**

© 2016 The Critical Thinking Co.™ • www.CriticalThinking.com • 800-458-4849

Student Response: People borrow books and movies at a library.

Teacher Comment: **Draw line from the description to the picture of the library.**

DESCRIBING BUILDINGS

A community is made up of buildings where people work and go to get what they need. Draw a line from each description to the picture of that building and to the picture of the person who works there.

DESCRIPTION

A government building where people borrow books and movies.

A business where people deposit or borrow money.

A government building where people buy stamps and mail letters and packages.

A building where doctors and nurses treat sick or injured people.

A building and a large area where airplanes take off and land.

airport, bank, hospital, library, post office, mail carrier, librarian, doctor, pilot, bank teller

Teacher Comment: **Who works in a library?**

Student Response: A librarian works in a library.

Teacher Comment: **Draw line from the description to the picture of the librarian.**

- Check students' work. Continue this dialog to discuss students' answers.

Thinking About Thinking

Teacher Comment: **What did you look for when you picked the building that was described?**

Student Response:

1. I listened for and remembered the important characteristics of the building.
2. I found the important characteristics in the pictures.
3. I remembered the workers that worked in that building.
4. I found the picture of the worker that worked in that building.

Personal Application

Teacher Comment: **When is it important to know what workers work in certain buildings?**

Student Response: It is important to know what workers work in certain buildings in order to know where to go to get the things a family needs.

Page 125: KINDS OF JOBS – PRODUCERS OR SERVICE PROVIDERS

LESSON

Introduction

Teacher Comment: **We have described what various workers do. Some workers grow things that families need. The things that they produce are called "goods." Other workers do something that people need. They provide a "service."**

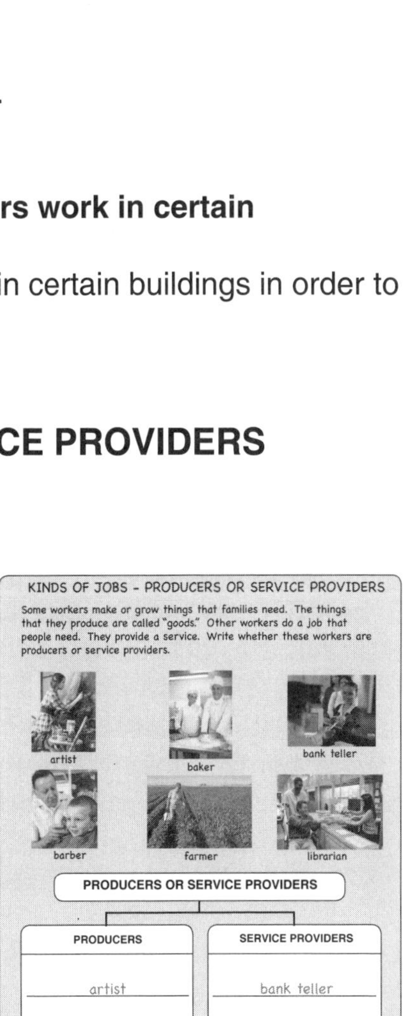
KINDS OF JOBS - PRODUCERS OR SERVICE PROVIDERS

Some workers make or grow things that families need. The things that they produce are called "goods." Other workers do a job that people need. They provide a service. Write whether these workers are producers or service providers.

artist, baker, bank teller, barber, farmer, librarian

PRODUCERS OR SERVICE PROVIDERS

PRODUCERS	SERVICE PROVIDERS
artist	bank teller
baker	barber
farmer	librarian

Explaining the Objective

Teacher Comment: **In this lesson you will decide whether a worker is a "producer" or a "service provider."**

Conducting the Lesson

Teacher Comment: **The first picture shows an artist painting a picture. She is creating something new that people will buy. Is the artist a "producer" or a "service provider?"**

© 2016 The Critical Thinking Co.™ • www.CriticalThinking.com • 800-458-4849

Student Response: The artist is painting a picture that people will buy. She is a producer.
Teacher Comment: **Write "artist" on the first line of the producer box.**

• Check students' work. Continue this dialog to discuss students' answers.

Thinking About Thinking

Teacher Comment: **How did you decide what kind of job the worker did?**

Student Response:

1. I looked at the details of the worker in the picture.
2. I named that kind of job.
3. I decided whether the person was making something new or was doing a service that someone needs.
4. I found the word that described what kind of job the worker did.

Personal Application

Teacher Comment: **When is it important to know what kind of job a worker does?**

Student Response: I need to know what kind of job a worker does to understand how they can help customers and to write or tell about them.

Page 126: WORKERS WHO PROVIDE SERVICES

LESSON

Introduction

Teacher Comment: **Families depend on services to get help that they need. Some workers help people stay healthy or treat them when they are sick. Some workers are paid by the government to provide a service that people need. Some workers sell a product that people need.**

Explaining the Objective

Teacher Comment: **In this lesson you will sort service workers into three groups: "workers who give health care" or "workers who provide government services," or "workers who sell a product."**

Conducting the Lesson

Teacher Comment: **The first picture shows a dentist. The dentist is working on a person's teeth. What service is the dentist providing?**

Student Response: The dentist is making a person's teeth healthy. She is a health care worker.

Teacher Comment: **Write "dentist" on the first line of the health care box.**

• Check students' work. Continue this dialog to discuss students' answers.

© 2016 The Critical Thinking Co.™ • www.CriticalThinking.com • 800-458-4849

Thinking About Thinking

Teacher Comment: **How did you decide what kind of service the worker provided?**

Student Response:

1. I looked at the details of the worker in the picture.
2. I named that kind of job.
3. I found the word that described what kind of service the worker gave.

Personal Application

Teacher Comment: **When is it important to know what kind of job a worker does?**

Student Response: I need to know what kind of job a worker does to understand how he or she can help customers and to write or tell about them.

Page 127: SIMILAR JOBS

LESSON

Introduction

Teacher Comment: **We have described many kinds of workers.**

Explaining the Objective

Teacher Comment: **In this lesson you will find the job that is most like another one.**

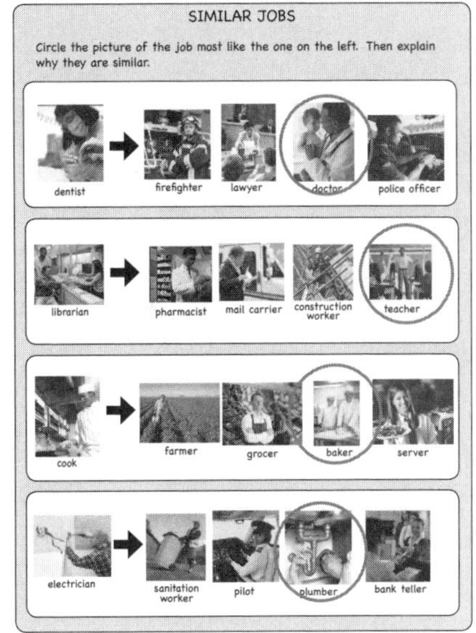

Conducting the Lesson

Teacher Comment: **Name the jobs in the first box.**

Student Response: The jobs are a dentist, a firefighter, a lawyer, a doctor, and a police officer.

Teacher Comment: **Select the job that is most like a dentist. Tell your partner all the important things you know about a dentist.**

Student Response: A dentist helps people have healthy teeth. She must study a long time to learn how people's bodies work. She fixes teeth that cause people pain and removes teeth that can't be saved. She often wears a white coat and works in a very clean office.

Teacher Comment: **Which job is most like a dentist?**

Student Response: The doctor is most like a dentist because they both help people stay healthy. They both must study a long time to learn how people's bodies work. They both often wear white coats and work in very clean offices. They are both called "doctor."

Teacher Comment: **How are the other jobs different from the dentist and the doctor?**

Student Response: The lawyer and police officer are law enforcement workers, the firefighter is an emergency worker.

Teacher Comment: **Circle the doctor.**

Teacher Comment: **Name the jobs in the second row.**

Student Response: The jobs are a librarian, a pharmacist, a mail carrier, a construction worker, and a teacher.

© 2016 The Critical Thinking Co.™ • www.CriticalThinking.com • 800-458-4849

Teacher Comment: **Select the job that is most like a librarian. Tell your partner all the important things you know about an librarian.**

Student Response: A librarian helps people find books and information in a library. She uses a computer to keep track of the books. When people borrow a book or film, they bring the book to her desk, and she tells them when to bring the book back. She helps people use computers to find information that they need.

Teacher Comment: **Which job is most like a librarian?**

Student Response: A teacher is most like a librarian. They both help people to learn and to get information that they need. They both use books and computers to find what people need to know.

Teacher Comment: **How are the other jobs different from the librarian and the teacher?**

Student Response: The pharmacist sells people medicines that a doctor has ordered. The mail carrier delivers letters and packages. The construction worker build new buildings.

Teacher Comment: **Circle the teacher.**

Teacher Comment: **Name the jobs in the third row.**

Student Response: The jobs are a cook, a farmer, a grocer, a baker, and a server.

Teacher Comment: **Select the job that is most like a cook. Tell your partner all the important things you know about a cook.**

Student Response: A cook prepares meals in a restaurant. He needs to know how to mix different foods to make a meal that tastes good. He needs to know how hot and how long to properly cook food. He often wears a white shirt and cap.

Teacher Comment: **Which job is most like a cook?**

Student Response: The baker is most like a cook because they both make food that people buy. He needs to know how to mix different foods to make bread and desserts. He needs to know how hot and how long to properly bake bread. He often wears a white shirt and cap.

Teacher Comment: **How are the other jobs different from the cook and the baker?**

Student Response: The farmer grows food. The grocer sells food that other people will cook. The server delivers meals to customers.

Teacher Comment: **Circle the baker.**

Teacher Comment: **Name the jobs in the last row.**

Student Response: The jobs are an electrician, a sanitation worker, a pilot, a plumber, and a bank teller.

Teacher Comment: **Select the job that is most like a electrician. Tell your partner all the important things you know about an electrician.**

Student Response: An electrician puts electrical wires and lights in a house. He repairs or replaces them when they don't work.

Teacher Comment: **Which job is most like an electrician?**

Student Response: The plumber is most like an electrician because he puts pipes, sinks, and toilets in a house. He repairs or replaces them when they don't work.

Teacher Comment: **How are the other jobs different from the electrician and the plumber?**

Student Response: The sanitation worker takes away trash. The pilot flies an airplane. The bank teller helps people save or receive their money.

Teacher Comment: **Circle the plumber.**

© 2016 The Critical Thinking Co.™ • www.CriticalThinking.com • 800-458-4849

Thinking About Thinking

Teacher Comment: **What kind of characteristics did you pay attention to when you described the jobs?**

Student Response:

1. I recalled the important characteristics of the first job (whether the job provided a service or produced a product, whether the worker built things, or sold things.)
2. I looked for similar characteristics in the other jobs.
3. I selected the job that had most of the same characteristics.
4. I checked to see that other jobs did not fit the important characteristics better than the one I selected.

Personal Application

Teacher Comment: **When is it important to understand how different jobs are alike?**

Student Response: I need to understand how jobs are similar to write or tell about them.

Page 128: DESCRIBING SIMILARITIES AND DIFFERENCES – JOBS

LESSON

Introduction

Teacher Comment: **We have described how two jobs are alike. When we tell how jobs are alike, we are comparing them. It is also important to know how they are different. When we tell how two jobs are different, we are contrasting them.**

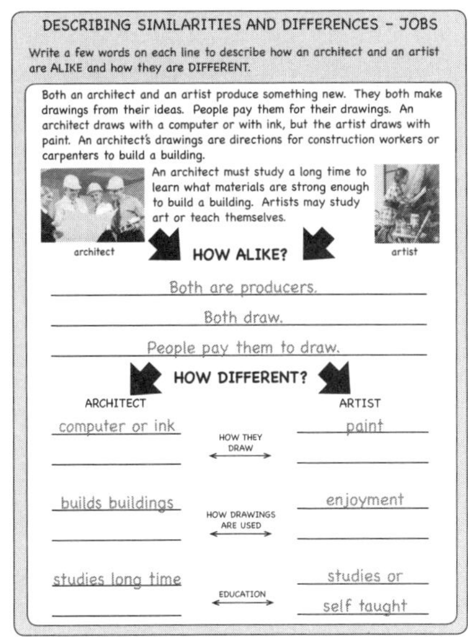

DESCRIBING SIMILARITIES AND DIFFERENCES – JOBS

Write a few words on each line to describe how an architect and an artist are ALIKE and how they are DIFFERENT.

Both an architect and an artist produce something new. They both make drawings from their ideas. People pay them for their drawings. An architect draws with a computer or with ink, but the artist draws with paint. An architect's drawings are directions for construction workers or carpenters to build a building. An architect must study a long time to learn what materials are strong enough to build a building. Artists may study art or teach themselves.

architect artist

HOW ALIKE?

Both are producers.

Both draw.

People pay them to draw.

HOW DIFFERENT?

ARCHITECT		ARTIST
computer or ink	HOW THEY DRAW	paint
builds buildings	HOW DRAWINGS ARE USED	enjoyment
studies long time	EDUCATION	studies or self taught

Explaining the Objective

Teacher Comment: **In this lesson you will compare and contrast an architect and an artist.**

Conducting the Lesson

Teacher Comment: **Both an architect and an artist produce something new. They both make drawings from their ideas. People pay them for their drawings. On the "how alike" lines, write a few words to describe how an architect and an artist are alike.**

Teacher Comment: **An architect draws with a computer or with ink, but the artist draws with paint. An architect's drawings are directions for construction workers or carpenters to build a building. An architect must study a long time to learn what materials are strong enough to build a building. Artists may study art or teach themselves. On the "how different" lines, write a few words to describe how an architect and an artist are different.**

© 2016 The Critical Thinking Co.™ • www.CriticalThinking.com • 800-458-4849

Thinking About Thinking

Teacher Comment: **What did you pay attention to when you compared and contrasted jobs?**

Student Response:

1. I remembered the important characteristics of each job (whether the worker produced something new or provided a service, their equipment, what they did, their education).
2. I thought about how the jobs were alike.
3. I thought about how the jobs were different.

Personal Application

Teacher Comment: **When is it important to understand how jobs are alike or different?**

Student Response: I need to understand how jobs are alike or different to tell or write about them.

Page 129: A DIFFERENT KIND OF JOB

LESSON

Introduction

Teacher Comment: **We have compared and contrasted jobs.**

Explaining the Objective

Teacher Comment: **In this lesson you will identify a job that is not like the others.**

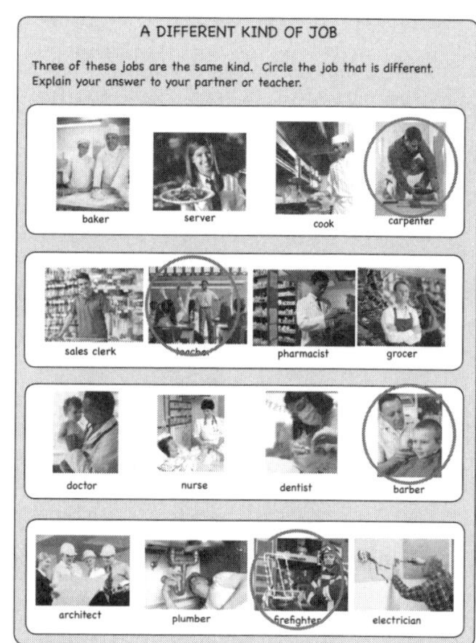
A DIFFERENT KIND OF JOB

Three of these jobs are the same kind. Circle the job that is different. Explain your answer to your partner or teacher.

Conducting the Lesson

Teacher Comment: **Name the jobs shown in the pictures in the first row.**

Student Response: The workers are a baker, a server, a cook, and a carpenter.

Teacher Comment: **Discuss with your partner how three of these jobs are alike.**

Student Response: The baker, the server, and the cook are food workers.

Teacher Comment: **Which worker is not a food worker?**

Student Response: The carpenter is a builder, not a food worker.

Teacher Comment: **Draw a circle around the picture of the carpenter.**

• Check students' work. Continue this dialog to discuss students' answers.

© 2016 The Critical Thinking Co.™ • www.CriticalThinking.com • 800-458-4849

Thinking About Thinking

Teacher Comment: **What do you think about when you decide which job was not like the others?**

Student Response:

1. I looked at the picture of each worker and identified what kind of job it was.
2. I found three jobs that were the same kind.
3. I identified the job that did not fit that group and explained why.

Personal Application

Teacher Comment. **When is it important to understand how a job may be different from others?**

Student Response. I need to know how a job may be different from others in order to understand what the worker does for the customer, and what kind of training, equipment, or clothing that the job requires.

Page 130: A SEQUENCE OF JOBS

LESSON

Introduction

Teacher Comment: **One way to describe jobs is to compare them to other jobs. Sometimes we compare jobs by describing the order in which workers produce something that we need.**

Explaining the Objective

Teacher Comment: **When your family goes to a restaurant, many people have worked to get food to the table. List these workers in the order in which their work helps get food to your family.**

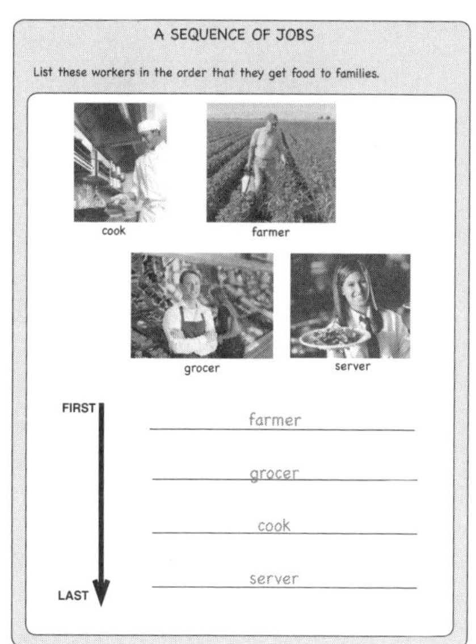

Conducting the Lesson

Teacher Comment: **Name the jobs in the pictures.**

Student Response: They are a cook, a farmer, a grocer, and a server.

Teacher Comment: **Which job comes first in getting food to your family?**

Student Response: A farmer must first plant and care for plants and animals that are grown for food.

Teacher Comment: **Write "farmer" on the first line.**

Teacher Comment: **Which job comes next in helping your family get food?**

Student Response: The farmer sells food to the grocer.

Teacher Comment: **Write "grocer" on the second line.**

• Check students' work. Continue this dialog to discuss students' answers.

© 2016 The Critical Thinking Co.™ • www.CriticalThinking.com • 800-458-4849

Thinking About Thinking

Teacher Comment: **What did you think about to put jobs in a particular order?**

Student Response: I thought about what the workers did at each step to provide the food our families need.

Personal Application

Teacher Comment: **When is it important to understand how to arrange jobs in order?**

Student Response: I need to understand how we often need other people's work in order to understand how much we depend on the goods or services that people offer our families.

Page 131: HOW WORKERS MAKE THEIR MONEY

LESSON

Introduction

Teacher Comment: **In the sequence of food workers there is a beginning and an end. In this lesson the sequence is a cycle that repeats itself. In this lesson we will describe a cycle that shows how money goes around in a community. When a worker receives money, he or she can buy what the family needs, providing income for other workers.**

Explaining the Objective

Teacher Comment: **In this lesson you will show how workers get their money in a community.**

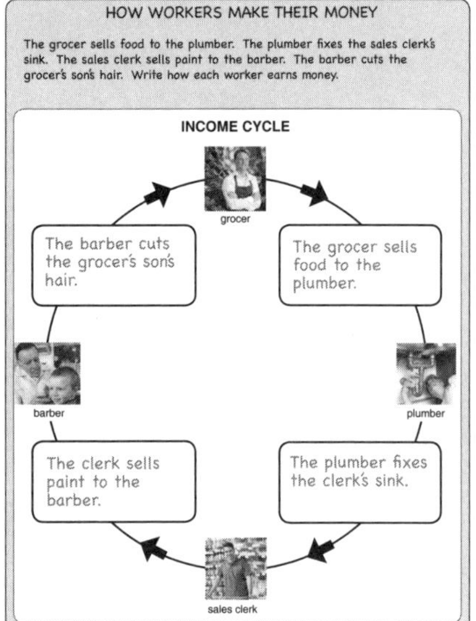

Conducting the Lesson

Teacher Comment: **People in the community earn their money by what they do for each other. The grocer sells food to the plumber. The plumber is paid to fix the sales clerk's sink. The sales clerk sells paint to the barber. The barber cuts the hair of the grocer's son. Because each worker earns his money and spends it, money moves in a cycle through the community. How does the grocer earn money?**

Student Response: The grocer sells food to earn money.

Teacher Comment: **In the first box write a few words to tell how the grocer makes money.**

Teacher Comment: **How does the plumber earn money?**

Student Response: The plumber fixes the sales clerk's sink.

Teacher Comment: **In the first box write a few words to tell how the plumber makes money.**

• Check students' work. Continue this dialog to discuss students' answers.

Thinking About Thinking

Teacher Comment: **What did you think about to understand how a worker's income provided income for other workers?**

 © 2016 The Critical Thinking Co.™ • www.CriticalThinking.com • 800-458-4849

Student Response:

1. I thought about what the workers did to earn money.
2. I showed that workers' incomes moved through the community to help each other.

Personal Application

Teacher Comment: **Why is it important to understand how workers earn their money?**

Student Response: It's important to understand how workers earn their money so I can understand how communities work together to help each other.

Page 132: HOW WORKERS SPEND THEIR MONEY

LESSON

Introduction

Teacher Comment: **We learned that the income that workers earn becomes an "income cycle" in the community.**

Explaining the Objective

Teacher Comment: **In this lesson you will complete a cycle of how workers spend their money. This is a "spending cycle."**

Conducting the Lesson

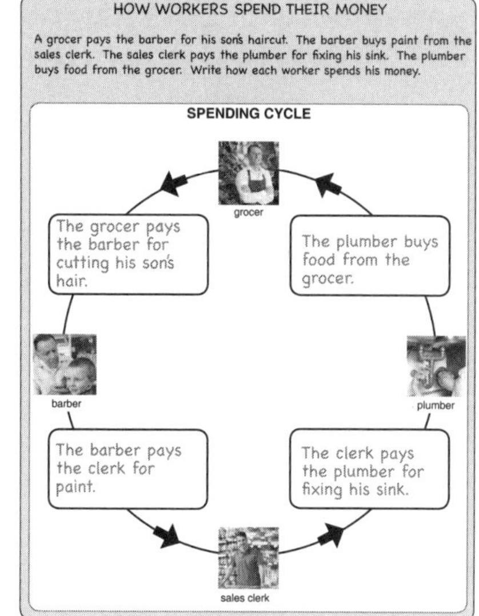

Teacher Comment: **A grocer pays the barber for his son's haircut. The barber buys paint from the sales clerk. The sales clerk pays the plumber for fixing his sink. The plumber buys food from the grocer. How does the grocer spend money?**

Student Response: The grocer pays the barber for cutting his son's hair.

Teacher Comment: **In the first box write a few words to tell how the grocer spends his money.**

Teacher Comment: **How does the barber spend his money?**

Student Response: The barber buys paint from the sales clerk.

Teacher Comment: **In the second box write a few words to tell how the barber spends his money.**

• Check students' work. Continue this dialog to discuss students' answers.

Thinking About Thinking

Teacher Comment: **What did you think about to understand how money that workers spend provides money for other workers in the community to spend for their families?**

Student Response:

1. I thought about how the workers spent money.
2. I showed how money spent by workers provided income for other workers in the community.

Personal Application

Teacher Comment: **Why is it important to understand how workers spend their money?**

Student Response: It's important to understand how workers earn their money so I can understand how communities work together to help each other.

Page 133: WHAT A FAMILY NEEDS

LESSON

• Encourage students to identify additional workers in each category.

Introduction

Teacher Comment: **We have identified the difference between wants and needs.**

Explaining the Objective

Teacher Comment: **In this lesson you will identify the worker that provides the goods or services that a family needs.**

Conducting the Lesson

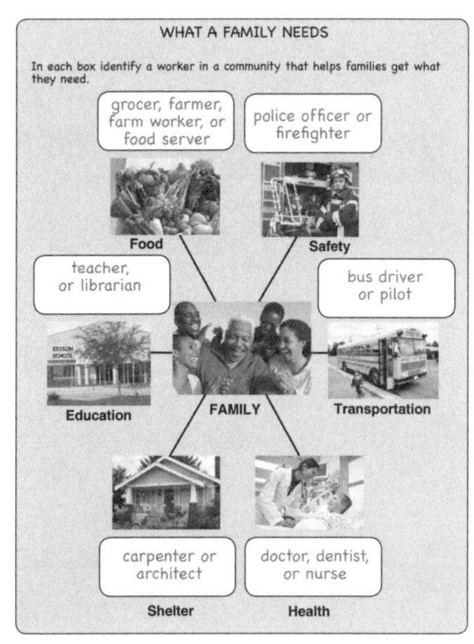

Teacher Comment: **Each picture shows what a family needs. Look at each picture and name a worker that fills that need. The first picture shows food. Name a worker that helps people get food.**

Student Response: A family gets food at a supermarket from a grocer.

Teacher Comment: **Write "grocer" in the first box.**

Teacher Comment: **The next picture shows a firefighter who provides safety. What other worker also provides safety?**

Student Response: Police officers help keep people safe.

Teacher Comment: **Write "police officer" in the blank above the picture of the firefighter.**

• Check students' work. Continue this dialog to discuss students' answers.

Thinking About Thinking

Teacher Comment: **What did you pay attention to when you identified a worker that provides a family need?**

Student Response:

1. I looked at the worker or object in the picture.
2. I thought about the worker that provided that need.
3. I wrote the name of the worker in the box.

Personal Application

Teacher Comment: **When do you need to understand who provides what families need?**

Student Response: I need to understand who provides what families need so I can know who can help people get what they need.

© 2016 The Critical Thinking Co.™ • www.CriticalThinking.com • 800-458-4849

Page 134: ANALOGIES ABOUT JOBS

LESSON

Introduction

Teacher Comment: **We have compared jobs.**

Explaining the Objective

Teacher Comment: **In this lesson you will describe analogies about the vehicles used in various jobs.**

Conducting the Lesson

Teacher Comment: **An analogy is a comparison of two pairs of things. In this lesson you will explain analogies about the vehicles that various workers use in their jobs. First we tell what vehicle the first worker uses. A construction worker uses a dump truck in his work. The word "LIKE" signals that we will tell what vehicle the farmer uses. What does the farmer use to do his farm work?**

Student Response: The farmer uses a tractor in his work.

Student Response: **Say the first analogy.**

Student Response: A construction worker uses a dump truck like a farmer uses a tractor.

Teacher Comment: **Why do the other vehicles not fit the analogy?**

Student Response: The farmer may own a car and a motorcycle, but he does not use them to plow his fields.

Teacher Comment: **Circle the picture of the tractor.**

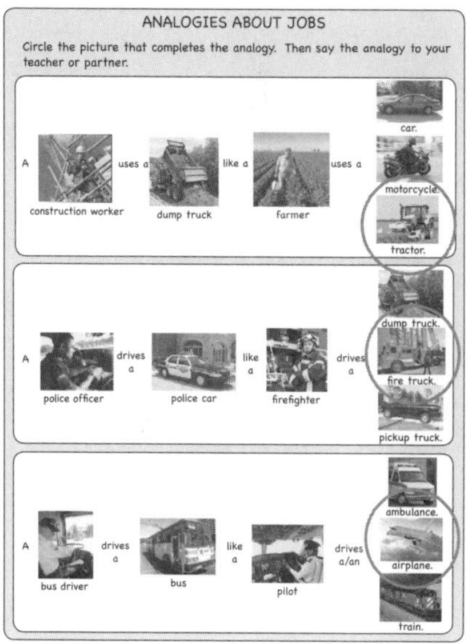

Teacher Comment: **The police officer drives a police car. What vehicle does the firefighter drive for his work?**

Student Response: The firefighter drives a fire truck at his work.

Student Response: **Say the second analogy.**

Student Response: A police office drives a police car like a firefighter drives a fire truck.

Teacher Comment: **Why do the other vehicles not fit the analogy?**

Student Response: The firefighter may own a pickup truck, but does not drive it to a fire. He does not drive a dump truck.

Teacher Comment: **Circle the picture of the fire truck.**

Teacher Comment: **The bus driver drives a bus. What vehicle does the pilot drive?**

Student Response: The pilot drives or flies an airplane.

Teacher Comment: **Say the third analogy.**

Student Response: A bus driver drives a bus like a pilot drives an airplane.

Teacher Comment: **Why do the other vehicles not fit the analogy?**

Student Response: A pilot flies an air vehicle. The ambulance and the train are land vehicles.

Teacher Comment: **Circle the airplane.**

- Check students' work.

Thinking About Thinking

Teacher Comment: **What did you think about when you completed the analogies about jobs?**

Student Response:

1. I thought about how the first two pictures were connected.
2. I decided which vehicle had the same connection for the second job.
3. I said the analogy to be sure.
4. I checked that the other vehicles did not fit the analogy.

Personal Application

Teacher Comment: **When do you need to explain the same thing about two jobs?**

Student Response: I need to explain the same thing about two jobs when I need to tell something important about both of them.

Page 135: ANALOGIES ABOUT JOBS

LESSON

Introduction

Teacher Comment: **We have completed analogies about the vehicles that workers use in their jobs.**

Explaining the Objective

Teacher Comment: **In this lesson you will complete analogies about where a worker works.**

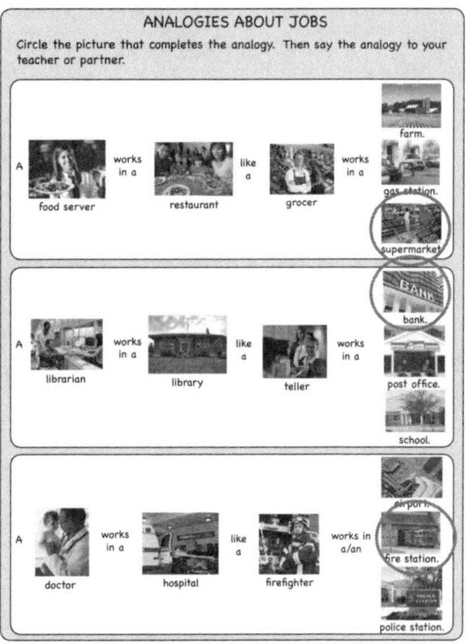

Conducting the Lesson

Teacher Comment: **We have learned that an analogy is a comparison of two pair of things. In this lesson you will explain analogies about where people work. First we tell where the first worker works. A food server works in a restaurant. The word "LIKE" signals that we will tell where the grocer works. Where does a grocer work?**

Student Response: The grocer works in a supermarket.

Teacher Comment: **Say the analogy.**

Student Response: A food server works in a restaurant like a grocer works in a supermarket.

Teacher Comment: **Why do the other buildings not fit the analogy?**

Student Response: A farmer, not a grocer, works on a farm. A clerk, not a grocer, works in a gas station.

Teacher Comment: **Circle the picture of the supermarket.**

Teacher Comment: **In the second analogy we see that a librarian works in a library. The word "LIKE" signals that we will say where the teller works. Where does the teller work?**

Student Response: A teller works in a bank.

Teacher Comment: **Why do the other buildings not fit the analogy?**

 © 2016 The Critical Thinking Co.™ • www.CriticalThinking.com • 800-458-4849

Student Response: A postal clerk, not a bank teller, works in a post office. A teacher, not a bank teller, works in a school.

Teacher Comment: **Circle the picture of the bank.**

Teacher Comment: **In the third analogy we see that a doctor works in a hospital The word"LIKE" signals that we will say where the firefighter works. Where does the firefighter work?**

Student Response: The firefighter works in a fire station.

Teacher Comment: **Why do the other places not fit the analogy?**

Student Response: A pilot, not a firefighter, works in an airport. A police office, not a firefighter, works in a police station.

Teacher Comment: **Circle the picture of the fire station.**

- Check students' work.

Thinking About Thinking

Teacher Comment: **What did you think about when you completed the analogies about jobs?**

Student Response:

1. I thought about how the first two pictures were connected.
2. I decided which picture would show that same connection for the second job.
3. I said the analogy to be sure.
4. I checked that the other buildings did not fit the analogy.

Personal Application

Teacher Comment: **When do you need to explain the same thing about two jobs?**

Student Response: I need to explain the same thing about two jobs when I need to tell something important about both of them.

Page 136: WRITING A DESCRIPTION OF A JOB

LESSON

Introduction

Teacher Comment: **To describe a job we need to explain all the important characteristics that make the job different from others.**

Explaining the Objective

Teacher Comment: **In this lesson you will write a description of a job.**

Conducting the Lesson

Teacher Comment: **To describe a job, we must tell the important characteristics of that job. First we tell what kind of job he has. A doctor is a health care worker.**

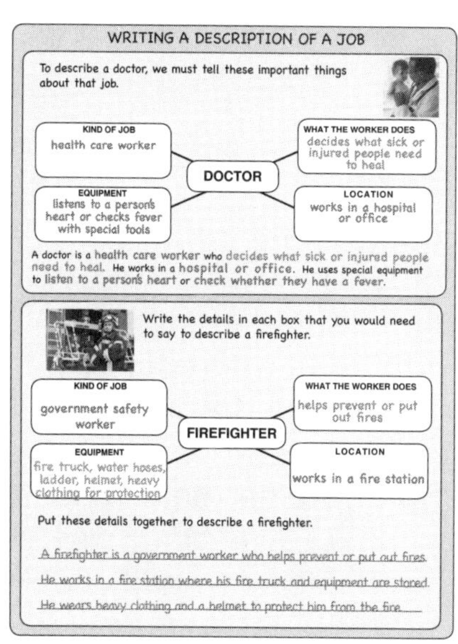

WRITING A DESCRIPTION OF A JOB

To describe a doctor, we must tell these important things about that job.

KIND OF JOB: health care worker

WHAT THE WORKER DOES: decides what sick or injured people need to heal

DOCTOR

EQUIPMENT: listens to a person's heart or checks fever with special tools

LOCATION: works in a hospital or office

A doctor is a health care worker who decides what sick or injured people need to heal. He works in a hospital or office. He uses special equipment to listen to a person's heart or check whether they have a fever.

Write the details in each box that you would need to say to describe a firefighter.

KIND OF JOB: government safety worker

WHAT THE WORKER DOES: helps prevent or put out fires

FIREFIGHTER

EQUIPMENT: fire truck, water hoses, ladder, helmet, heavy clothing for protection

LOCATION: works in a fire station

Put these details together to describe a firefighter.

A firefighter is a government worker who helps prevent or put out fires. He works in a fire station where his fire truck and equipment are stored. He wears heavy clothing and a helmet to protect him from the fire.

© 2016 The Critical Thinking Co.™ • www.CriticalThinking.com • 800-458-4849

Next we tell what he does. A doctor decides what sick or injured people need to heal.

Next we tell where a doctor works. He works in a hospital or office.

Finally we describe the equipment that the doctor uses. He uses special equipment to listen to a person's heart and to check for fever.

When we put all these characteristics together, we can write a description of a doctor that tells how this job is different from other jobs. Notice that the color of the answer in each box is the same as the words in the description. That way we see that the description includes what we need to say about the doctor.

"A doctor is a health care worker who decides what sick or injured people need to heal. He works in a hospital or office. He uses special equipment to listen to a person's heart or to check whether they have a fever."

Teacher Comment: **Use the diagram to describe a firefighter. What kind of worker is a firefighter?**

Student Response: A firefighter is a government safety worker.
Teacher Comment: **Write "government safety worker" in the "kind of job" box.**

Teacher Comment: **What does a firefighter do?**
Student Response: A firefighter helps prevent or put out fires.
Teacher Comment: **Write "helps prevent or put out fires" in the box that tells "what the worker does."**

Teacher Comment: **Where does a firefighter work?**
Student Response: A firefighter works in a fire station.
Teacher Comment: **Write "works in a fire station" in the "location" box.**

Teacher Comment: **What equipment does the firefighter use?**
Student Response: A firefighter uses a fire truck, water hoses, ladders, a helmet, and heavy clothing to protect him from fire.
Teacher Comment: **Write "fire truck, water hoses, ladders, helmet, heavy clothing for protection" in the "equipment" box.**

Teacher Comment: **Put these details together to describe a firefighter.**

• Check students' work.

Thinking About Thinking

Teacher Comment: **What did you think about when you described a job?**
Student Response:
1. I remembered what kind of job it was.
2. I remembered what the worker did.
5. I remembered where worker worked.
6. I remembered what kind of equipment the worker used.

© 2016 The Critical Thinking Co.™ • www.CriticalThinking.com • 800-458-4849

Personal Application

Teacher Comment: **When is it important to describe all the important characteristics of a worker?**

Student Response: I need to know how to describe all the important characteristics of a worker to correctly describe him or her or to tell a story about him or her.

Page 137: DESCRIBING LOCATIONS

LESSON

Introduction

Teacher Comment: **We have learned that families need vehicles to get to work and to buy what they need. These vehicles use the streets in our community. We use maps to find where buildings are located and to understand how to get to various places. A map is a drawing that shows the streets in a town or city.**

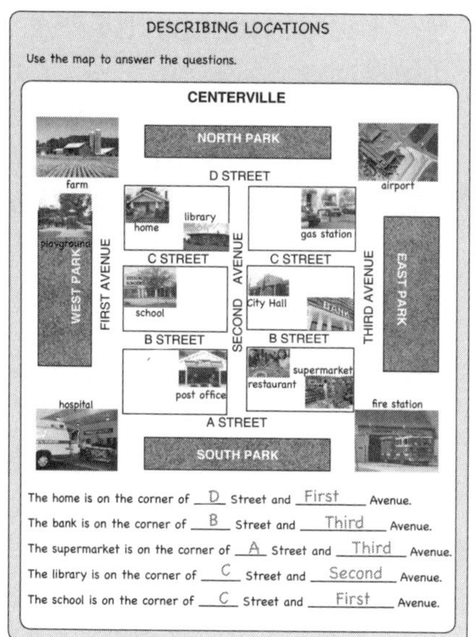

DESCRIBING LOCATIONS

Use the map to answer the questions.

The home is on the corner of D Street and First Avenue.

The bank is on the corner of B Street and Third Avenue.

The supermarket is on the corner of A Street and Third Avenue.

The library is on the corner of C Street and Second Avenue.

The school is on the corner of C Street and First Avenue.

Explaining the Objective

Teacher Comment: **In this lesson you will use a map to locate the position of buildings.**

Conducting the Lesson

Teacher Comment: **Find the home on the map. What street is it on?**

Student Response: The home is on D Street.

Teacher Comment: **What avenue is the home on?**

Student Response: The home is on First Avenue.

Teacher Comment: **Write those answers on the first blanks.**

• Check students' work. Continue this dialog to discuss students' answers.

Thinking About Thinking

Teacher Comment: **What did you think about when you described the location of a building?**

Student Response:

1. I found the picture of the building on the map.
2. I found the street where it was located.
3. I found the avenue where it was located.

Personal Application

Teacher Comment: **When is it important to explain where a building is located?**

Student Response: It's important to explain where a place is located to receive deliveries or to give or understand directions.

© 2016 The Critical Thinking Co.™ • www.CriticalThinking.com • 800-458-4849

Page 138: DESCRIBING DIRECTIONS

LESSON

Introduction

Teacher Comment: **We have used a map to locate the position of places.**

Explaining the Objective

Teacher Comment: **In this lesson you will use the directions north, south, east, and west to describe the position of a place.**

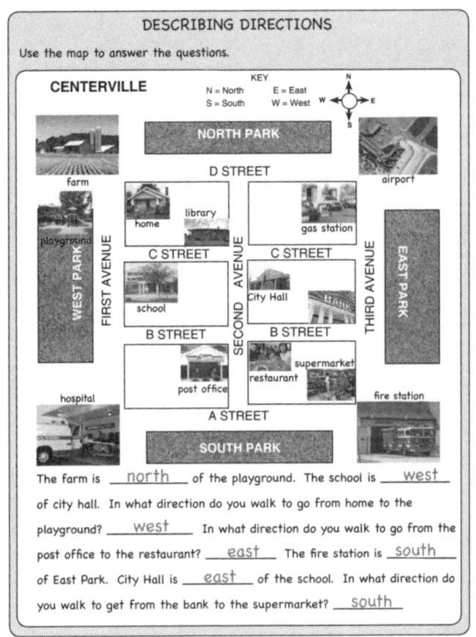
DESCRIBING DIRECTIONS

Use the map to answer the questions.

The farm is <u>north</u> of the playground. The school is <u>west</u> of city hall. In what direction do you walk to go from home to the playground? <u>west</u> In what direction do you walk to go from the post office to the restaurant? <u>east</u> The fire station is <u>south</u> of East Park. City Hall is <u>east</u> of the school. In what direction do you walk to get from the bank to the supermarket? <u>south</u>

Conducting the Lesson

Teacher Comment: **Look at the symbol that shows how directions are shown on a map. North is toward the top of the page; south is toward the bottom of the page; east is toward the right of the page; and west is toward the left of the page. Find the farm and the playground on the map. The farm is above the playground. When one location is above another on a map, how do we describe it?**

Student Response: A location that is above another one is north of it.

Teacher Comment: **Write "north" on the first blank.**

• Check students' work. Continue this dialog to discuss students' answers.

Thinking About Thinking

Teacher Comment: **What did you think about when you described directions on a map?**

Student Response:

1. I found the picture of the building or place on the map.
2. I compared its location to another.
3. I checked the direction symbol to show whether a location was north, south, east, or west of another place.

Personal Application

Teacher Comment: **When do you need to tell whether a place is north, south, east, or west?**

Student Response: I need to explain where a place is located to give or understand directions.

© 2016 The Critical Thinking Co.™ • www.CriticalThinking.com • 800-458-4849

Page 139: DESCRIBING DIRECTIONS

LESSON

Introduction

Teacher Comment: **We have used the directions "north," "south, "east," and "west" to describe locations.**

Explaining the Objective

Teacher Comment: **In this lesson you will add the directions "northwest," "northeast," "southwest," and "southeast" to describe location.**

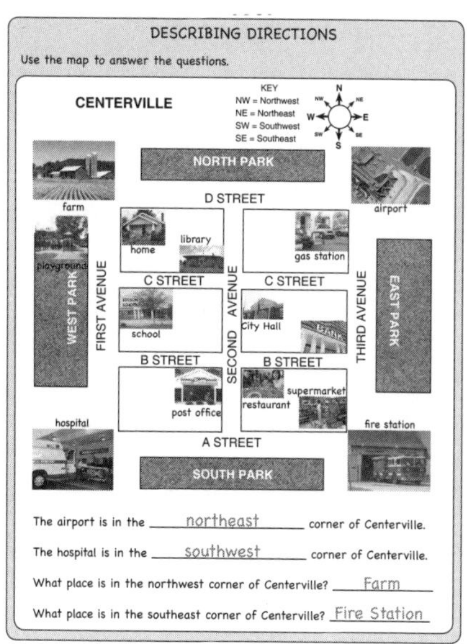

Conducting the Lesson

Teacher Comment: **Name the places near the airport.**

Student Response: The airport is near North Park and East Park.

Teacher Comment: **Use the direction symbol to tell where the airport is located in the city of Centerville.**

Student Response: The symbol shows "NE" which stand for "northeast." The airport is in the northeast corner of Centerville.

Teacher Comment: **Write "northeast"on the first blank.**

• Check students' work. Continue this dialog to discuss students' answers.

Thinking About Thinking

Teacher Comment: **What did you think about when you described directions on a map?**

Student Response:

1. I found the picture of the building or place on the map.
2. I compared its location to another.
3. I checked the direction symbol to decide if the place was northwest, northeast, southwest, or southeast on the map.

Personal Application

Teacher Comment: **When do you need to tell whether a place is northwest, northeast, southwest, or southeast of another place?**

Student Response: I need to explain where a place is located to give or understand directions.

© 2016 The Critical Thinking Co.™ • www.CriticalThinking.com • 800-458-4849

CHAPTER TEN – THINKING ABOUT OUR COUNTRY (Pages 140-154)

GENERAL INTRODUCTION

CURRICULUM APPLICATIONS

Language Arts: Identify how various stories explain how our country has changed over time. Compare and contrast how different cultures change across time. Discuss grade two topics and texts with peers and adults in large and small groups. Compare and contrast the most important points in describing two concepts. Produce complete sentences in order to provide adequate detail and clarification. Use appropriate adjectives, adverbs, and verbs to describe key concepts.
Science: Identify how climate affects plants and animals in a region.
Social Studies: Identify how Native Americans and early colonists relied on their environment to secure basic needs. Interpret maps of the United States that contain symbols and cardinal directions. Identify changes in how Americans have secured their basic needs over time.

TEACHING SUGGESTIONS

- Display globes and maps for the lessons on map reading and Native Americans.
- Read picture books about the importance of maps.
- Prior to lessons about Native Americans, read picture books that show the diversity of cultures among native people, and how they use available resources.

Page 141: DESCRIBING OUR CONTINENT

LESSON

Introduction

Teacher Comment: **We have studied land forms and bodies of water.**

Explaining the Objective

Teacher Comment: **In this lesson you will identify land forms and bodies of water around our country.**

Conducting the Lesson

Teacher Comment: **The largest land forms are continents. Continents are surrounded by oceans. The United States is on the continent of North America.**

On this page we see two photographs that show our country. The first photograph shows the continent of North America on Earth; the second is a photograph of the United States that shows dry, brown deserts, mountains, green plains, and woodlands. At the top of the page is a symbol with N, E, S, and W printed at the ends of arrows. What do these letters show?

Student Response: The letters show the directions north, east, south, and west.

Teacher Comment: **What body of water is south of the United States?**

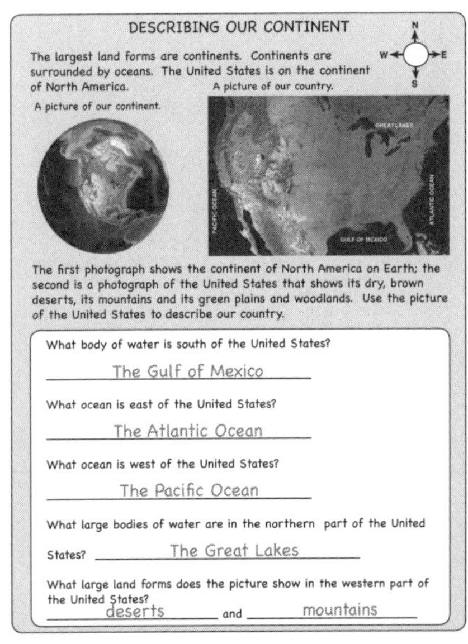

DESCRIBING OUR CONTINENT

The largest land forms are continents. Continents are surrounded by oceans. The United States is on the continent of North America.

A picture of our country.

A picture of our continent.

The first photograph shows the continent of North America on Earth; the second is a photograph of the United States that shows its dry, brown deserts, its mountains and its green plains and woodlands. Use the picture of the United States to describe our country.

What body of water is south of the United States?
The Gulf of Mexico

What ocean is east of the United States?
The Atlantic Ocean

What ocean is west of the United States?
The Pacific Ocean

What large bodies of water are in the northern part of the United States? The Great Lakes

What large land forms does the picture show in the western part of the United States?
deserts and mountains

© 2016 The Critical Thinking Co.™ • www.CriticalThinking.com • 800-458-4849

Student Response: The Gulf of Mexico is south of the United States.

Teacher Comment: **Write "Gulf of Mexico" on the first line.**

- Check students' work. Continue this dialog to discuss students' answers.

Thinking About Thinking

Teacher Comment: **What did you think about when you identified land forms and bodies of water in a photograph?**

Student Response:

1. I looked carefully at the colors to find the brown and green land forms and the blue lakes and oceans.
2. I compared the location of the bodies of water shown in the photograph of our country.
3. I checked the direction symbol showing north, south, east, and west.

Personal Application

Teacher Comment: **When do you need to tell whether a place is north, south, east, or west?**

Student Response: I need to explain where a place is located to describe our country and its land forms and bodies of water.

Page 142: DESCRIBING GLOBES

LESSON

Introduction

Teacher Comment: **We have identified bodies of water and land forms in the United States.**

Explaining the Objective

Teacher Comment: **In this lesson you will identify details on a globe that shows our country.**

Conducting the Lesson

Teacher Comment: **We see a picture of a globe. When a map of Earth is on a sphere, it is called a globe.**

Teacher Comment: **Look at the globe. What country is north of the United States?**

Student Response: I can see on the globe that Canada is north of the United States.

Teacher Comment: **Write "Canada" on the first line.**

- Check students' work. Continue this dialog to discuss students' answers.

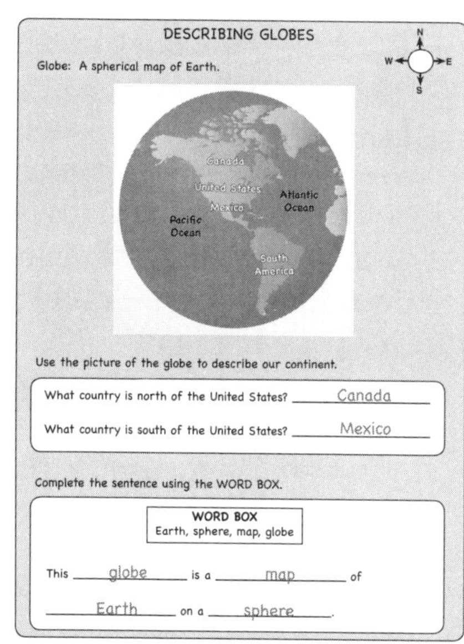

Thinking About Thinking

Teacher Comment: **What did you think about when you identified the locations of countries on our continent?**

Student Response:

1. I looked carefully at the picture of the globe and what places were marked.
2. I used the direction symbol to check if each country was north, south, east, or west on the globe.
3. I used the WORD BOX to complete the sentence about a globe.

Personal Application

Teacher Comment: **When do you need to tell whether a place is north, south, east, or west?**

Student Response: I need to explain where a place is located to describe our country and its land forms and bodies of water.

Page 143: DESCRIBING GLOBES

LESSON

Introduction

Teacher Comment: **We have described out continent and a globe. Globes are a map on a sphere that has lines to show where places on Earth are located.**

Explaining the Objective

Teacher Comment: **In this lesson you will learn how we describe locations on Earth.**

Conducting the Lesson

Teacher Comment: **The imaginary line around the middle of Earth is called the Equator. Places close to the Equator are heated by sunlight all year round, they have a hot climate. Why do places near the Equator have a hot climate?**

Student Response: Places near the Equator are hot because they are heated by sunlight all year round.

Teacher Comment: **The lines on the globe that circle the world east to west are called lines of latitude. These circles look smaller toward the North Pole. These lines show where a place is located north or south of the Equator. Places close to the poles have a cold climate. Because lands near the poles get very little heat from sunlight, they are frozen all year round. Why do places near the poles have a cold climate?**

Student Response: Places near the poles are cold because they get very little heat from sunlight all year round.

Teacher Comment: **The imaginary circles that come together at the North Pole and at the South Pole are called lines of longitude. These lines show where a place is located east or west on the earth. What is the point at the top of Earth called?**

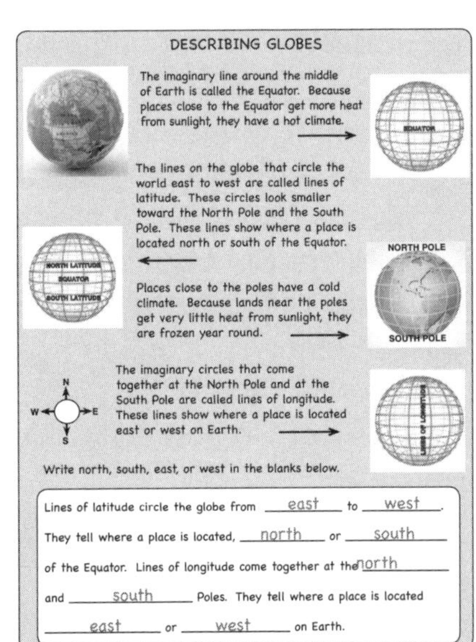

DESCRIBING GLOBES

The imaginary line around the middle of Earth is called the Equator. Because places close to the Equator get more heat from sunlight, they have a hot climate.

The lines on the globe that circle the world east to west are called lines of latitude. These circles look smaller toward the North Pole and the South Pole. These lines show where a place is located north or south of the Equator.

Places close to the poles have a cold climate. Because lands near the poles get very little heat from sunlight, they are frozen year round.

The imaginary circles that come together at the North Pole and at the South Pole are called lines of longitude. These lines show where a place is located east or west on Earth.

Write north, south, east, or west in the blanks below.

Lines of latitude circle the globe from east to west. They tell where a place is located, north or south of the Equator. Lines of longitude come together at the north and south Poles. They tell where a place is located east or west on Earth.

© 2016 The Critical Thinking Co.™ • www.CriticalThinking.com • 800-458-4849

Student Response: The point at the top of Earth is the North Pole.

Teacher Comment: **What is the point at the bottom of Earth called?**

Student Response: The point at the bottom of Earth is the South Pole.

Teacher Comment: **What is the climate like near the poles?**

Student Response: The climate near the poles is cold. Because the land at the poles gets very little heat from sunlight, it is frozen all year long.

Teacher Comment: **Where do lines of longitude come together?**

Student Response: Lines of longitude come together at the North and South Poles.

Teacher Comment: **Write "north," "south," "east" or "west" in the blanks below.**

• Check students' work.

Thinking About Thinking

Teacher Comment: **What did you think about to understand lines on a globe?**

Student Response:

1. I found the equator and saw the lines of latitude.
2. I saw that the lines of latitude show the location north or south of the Equator.
3. I found the poles and saw the lines of longitude.
4. I saw that the lines of longitude show the location east or west on Earth.

Personal Application

Teacher Comment: **When do you need to tell whether a place is north, south, east, or west?**

Student Response: I need to explain where a place is located to describe our country and its land forms and bodies of water.

Page 144: DESCRIBING OUR COUNTRY

LESSON

Introduction

Teacher Comment: **We have learned about latitude and longitude.**

Explaining the Objective

Teacher Comment: **In this lesson you will locate some cities or states in our country and think about the climate in that area.**

Conducting the Lesson

Teacher Comment: **Look at the picture of the globe and find the outline of our country. Our country is between the North Pole and the Equator. Land that is close to the North Pole has a cold climate. Alaska has very long, cold winters and short, cool summers. Why is the climate in Alaska cold?**

Student Response: The climate in Alaska is cold because it is close to the North Pole and gets very little heat from sunlight.

Teacher Comment: **Land that is close to the Equator has a warm climate. Hawaii is warm all the time. Why is the climate in Hawaii warm?**

© 2016 The Critical Thinking Co.™ • www.CriticalThinking.com • 800-458-4849

Student Response: The climate in Hawaii is warm because it is close to the Equator and gets heat from sunlight all year.

Teacher Comment: **Look at the map of the other states. The Northern states have longer, colder winters. The Southern states have longer, hotter summers. Look at the direction symbol to remember how to describe locations. In what part of the United States is Boston located?**

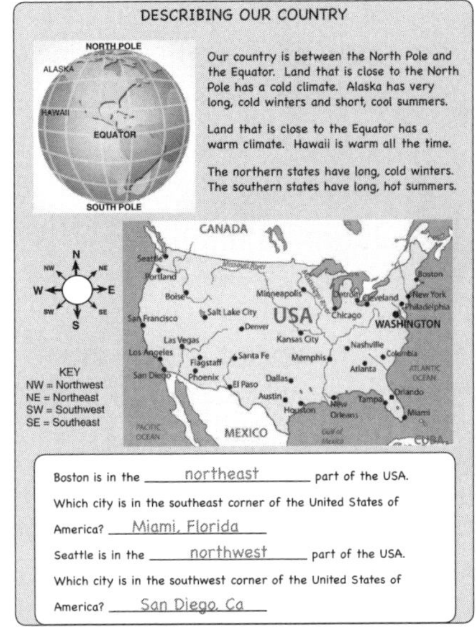
DESCRIBING OUR COUNTRY

Our country is between the North Pole and the Equator. Land that is close to the North Pole has a cold climate. Alaska has very long, cold winters and short, cool summers.

Land that is close to the Equator has a warm climate. Hawaii is warm all the time.

The northern states have long, cold winters. The southern states have long, hot summers.

Boston is in the ___northeast___ part of the USA.

Which city is in the southeast corner of the United States of America? ___Miami, Florida___

Seattle is in the ___northwest___ part of the USA.

Which city is in the southwest corner of the United States of America? ___San Diego, Ca___

Student Response: Boston is in the northeast part of the United States.

Teacher Comment: **What kind of climate does Boston have?**

Student Response: Boston has long, cold winters.

Teacher Comment: **Write "northeast" on the first line.**

Teacher Comment: **Which city is in the southeast corner of the United States?**

Student Response: Miami is in the southeast corner of the United States.

Teacher Comment: **What kind of climate does Miami have?**

Student Response: Miami has long, hot summers.

Teacher Comment: **Write "Miami" on the second line.**

Teacher Comment: **In what part of the United States is Seattle located?**

Student Response: Seattle is in the northwest part of the United States.

Teacher Comment: **Write "northwest" on the next line.**

- Because of the warming effects of the Pacific current, the climate in Seattle is not as cold as the winters in Boston although they are at a similar latitude. Therefore, we don't ask about the climate there.

Teacher Comment: **Which city is in the southwest corner of the United States?**

Student Response: San Diego is in the southwest corner of the United States.

Teacher Comment: **What kind of climate does San Diego have?**

Student Response: San Diego has long, hot summers.

Teacher Comment: **Write "San Diego" on the next line.**

Thinking About Thinking

Teacher Comment: **What did you think about to locate cities on a map?**

Student Response:

1. I found the location of the place on the map.
2. I compared its location to the map of the United States.
3. I checked the direction symbol to decide if the place was north, south, east, or west in our country.

Personal Application

Teacher Comment: **When do you need to tell where a city is located in our country?**

Student Response: I need to tell where a city is located to describe our community, to understand where people travel, and to tell about the plants and animals that live in that area.

© 2016 The Critical Thinking Co.™ • www.CriticalThinking.com • 800-458-4849

Page 145: DESCRIBING OUR COUNTRY

LESSON

- In this lesson each student is asked to name one plant or animal that can grow in specific areas of the United States, based on the climate, land forms, and bodies of water in that region. List or discuss many responses in order to get a general idea of the plants and animals that live there, and how people there use those plants and animals for food, clothing, and shelter.

Introduction

Teacher Comment: **We have thought about the climate in different parts of our country.**

Explaining the Objective

Teacher Comment: **In this lesson you will decide how land, water, and climate are related to the plants or animals that can grow in various parts of our country.**

Conducting the Lesson

Teacher Comment: **The photograph of our country shows brown, dry deserts and mountains and green, moist plains, woodlands, and wetlands. Look at the picture of the northwest corner of our country. What landforms and bodies of water are located there?**

Student Response: Mountains, rivers, and woodlands are located in the northwest corner of our country.

Teacher Comment: **Think about the plants or animals that can live in mountains, rivers, and woodlands in that part of our country. In the first box, name a plant or animal that can grow in this area. Pick one that people can use for food, clothing, or to build their homes.**

Student Response: Answers will vary. They may include, but are not limited to: salmon, deer, bears, tall trees, etc.

Teacher Comment: **Look at the picture of the north-central part of our country. What landforms and bodies of water are located there?**

Student Response: Plains, rivers, and streams are located in the north-central corner of our country.

Teacher Comment: **Think about the plants or animals that can live on the plains and in the rivers and streams in that part of our country. In the second box, name a plant or animal that can grow in this area. Pick one that people can use for food, clothing, or to build their homes.**

Student Response: Answers will vary. They may include, but are not limited to: fish, buffalo, prairie dogs, grass, small trees, corn, etc.

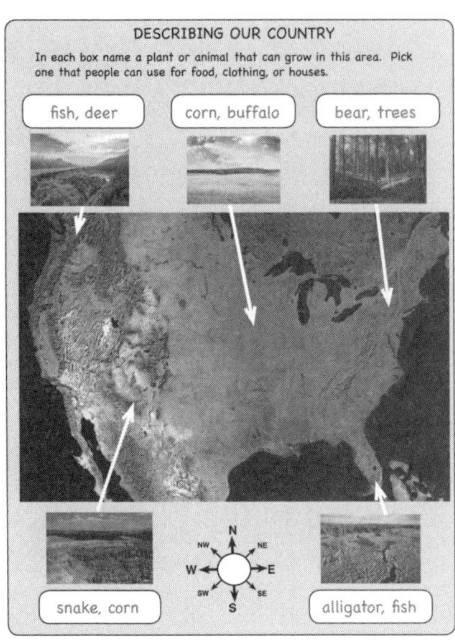

Teacher Comment: **Look at the picture of the northeast part of our country. What landforms and bodies of water are located there?**

Student Response: Mountains, hills, rivers, streams, and woodlands are located in the northeast corner of our country.

Teacher Comment: **Think about the plants or animals that can live in the mountains, the hills, and in the rivers and streams in that part of our country. In the third box, name a plant or animal that can grow in this area. Pick one that people can use for food, clothing, or to build their homes.**

Student Response: Answers will vary. They may include, but are not limited to: deer, bears, squirrels, fish, trees, corn, etc.

Teacher Comment: **Look at the picture of the southwest part of our country. What landforms and bodies of water are located there?**

Student Response: Mountains, plateaus, deserts, small rivers and streams are located in the southwest corner of our country.

Teacher Comment: **Think about the plants or animals that can live on the plateaus, deserts, and in the small rivers and streams in that part of our country. In the box, name a plant or animal that can grow in this area. Pick one that people can use for food, clothing, or to build their homes.**

Student Response: Answers will vary. They may include, but are not limited to: sheep, snakes, lizards, corn, etc.

Teacher Comment: **Look at the picture of the southeast part of our country. What landforms and bodies of water are located there?**

Student Response: Woodlands, wetlands, and many rivers and streams are located in the southeast corner of our country.

Teacher Comment: **Think about the plants or animals that can live in the woodlands and wetlands and in the many rivers and streams in that part of our country. In the box, name a plant or animal that can grow in this area. Pick one that people can use for food or clothing, or to build their homes.**

Student Response: Answers will vary. They may include, but are not limited to: deer, bears, alligators, snakes, fish, frogs, palm trees, pine trees, corn, etc.

Thinking About Thinking

Teacher Comment: **What did you pay attention to when you decided which land forms, bodies of water, plants, and animals are located in different parts of our country?**

Student Response:

1. I looked carefully at the colors to find the brown and green land forms and the blue lakes and oceans.
2. I checked the location shown in the photograph for the land forms and bodies of water in that area.
3. I remembered what the climate was like in that part of our country.
4. I remembered the plants and animals that can live in that kind of land and climate.

Personal Application

Teacher Comment: **When do you need to know how land forms, water, and climate are related to the plants and animals that can live there?**

Student Response: I need to know how land, water, and climate are related to plants and animals in that area to understand how people get food, clothing, and shelter in that part of the country.

© 2016 The Critical Thinking Co.™ • www.CriticalThinking.com • 800-458-4849

Page 146: DESCRIBING NATIVE AMERICANS

LESSON

Introduction

Teacher Comment: **People's food, clothing, and shelter depend on the climate where they live. Climate is the weather in a place for long periods of the time. It can be many months of hot or cold weather. It can be many months of wet or dry weather. Since the climate is different in parts of our country, Native Americans find different plants and animals to meet their needs.**

Explaining the Objective

Teacher Comment: **In this lesson you will tell about the climate and the land where various Native American tribes lived.**

Conducting the Lesson

Teacher Comment: **Native Americans used the plants and animals where they lived for food, clothing, and houses. Plants and animals that live in the north where the winters are long and cold are different from those that live in the south where the summers are long and hot. The plants and animals that live in the desert or on the plains are different from the ones that live along rivers, in the woodlands, or in the wetlands.**

Teacher Comment: **First we will describe the climate and the land where different groups of Native Americans live. What kind of climate do the Northwest tribes have?**

Student Response: The Northwest tribes have a cool climate.

Teacher Comment: **On what kind of land do the Northwest tribes live?**

Student Response: The Northwest tribes live in woodlands, along rivers, and the West coast.

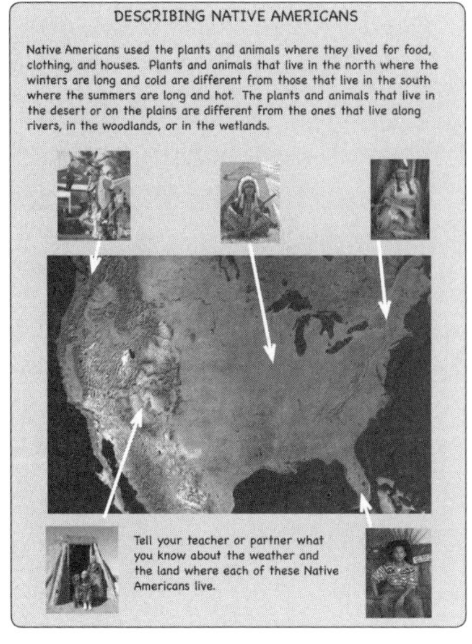
DESCRIBING NATIVE AMERICANS

Native Americans used the plants and animals where they lived for food, clothing, and houses. Plants and animals that live in the north where the winters are long and cold are different from those that live in the south where the summers are long and hot. The plants and animals that live in the desert or on the plains are different from the ones that live along rivers, in the woodlands, or in the wetlands.

Tell your teacher or partner what you know about the weather and the land where each of these Native Americans live.

- Check students' work. Continue this dialog to discuss students' answers.

Answers:
Plains tribes - long, cold winters on grassy plains
Northeast tribes - long, cold winters in the woodlands, along rivers and the East coast
Southeast tribes - hot, moist climate in the wetlands with many rivers, lakes, and streams
Southwest tribes - hot, dry climate in the desert, plateaus, and mountains

Thinking About Thinking

Teacher Comment: **What did you pay attention to when you told about the weather and the land where Native Americans lived?**

Student Response:

1. I looked at the land and water in that part of the country.
2. I remembered that the climate was hot near the equator and cold far away from it.
3. I looked for details in the photograph to tell whether the land was wet or dry.

Personal Application

Teacher Comment: **When do you need to understand how different land, water, and climate are important to learn about the Native Americans that live in different parts of our country?**

Student Response: I need to understand the land, water and climate to understand what plants and animals grow there so that Native Americans can get what they need.

Page 147: NEEDS OF THE NORTHWEST TRIBES

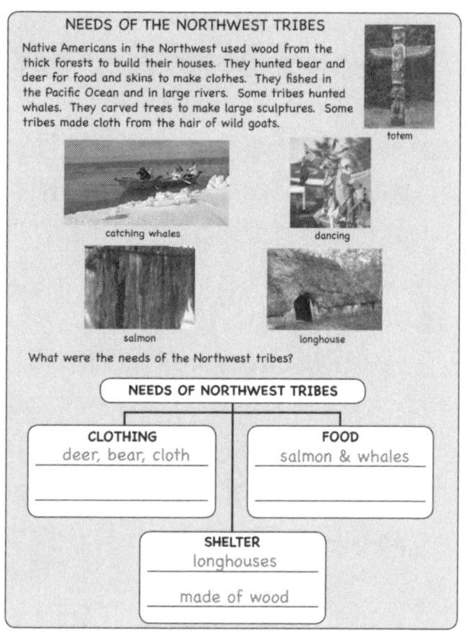

NEEDS OF THE NORTHWEST TRIBES

Native Americans in the Northwest used wood from the thick forests to build their houses. They hunted bear and deer for food and skins to make clothes. They fished in the Pacific Ocean and in large rivers. Some tribes hunted whales. They carved trees to make large sculptures. Some tribes made cloth from the hair of wild goats.

totem

catching whales

dancing

salmon

longhouse

What were the needs of the Northwest tribes?

NEEDS OF NORTHWEST TRIBES

CLOTHING
deer, bear, cloth

FOOD
salmon & whales

SHELTER
longhouses
made of wood

LESSON

Introduction

Teacher Comment: **In the last lessons we thought about how land, water, and climate make a difference in how Native Americans lived.**

Explaining the Objective

Teacher Comment: **In this lesson you will identify the clothing, food, and shelter of the Northwest tribes.**

Conducting the Lesson

Teacher Comment: **Native Americans in the northwest used wood from the thick forests to build their houses. They hunted bear and deer for food and skins. They fished in the Pacific Ocean and in large rivers. Some tribes hunted whales. They carved trees to make large sculptures. Some tribes made cloth from the hair of wild goats.**

Teacher Comment: **What kind of clothing did the Northwest tribes wear?**

Student Response: The Northwest tribes wore made clothing from deer or bear skins and wove cloth from the hair of wild goats.

Teacher Comment: **Write a few words in the "clothing" box to remind you of their clothing.**

Teacher Comment: **What food did the Northwest tribes eat?**

Student Response: The Northwest tribes ate deer, bear, salmon, whales and other fish.

Teacher Comment: **Write a few words in the "food" box to remind you of their food.**

Teacher Comment: **What kind of shelter did the Northwest tribes build?**

Student Response: The Northwest tribes built longhouses out of wood.

Teacher Comment: **Write a few words in the "shelter" box to remind you of their shelter.**

- Check students' work.

© 2016 The Critical Thinking Co.™ • www.CriticalThinking.com • 800-458-4849

Thinking About Thinking

Teacher Comment: **What did you pay attention to when you described how Northwest tribes met their needs?**

Student Response:

1. I listened to the description.
2. I matched the description to the pictures.
3. I wrote a few words about their clothing, food, and shelter.

Personal Application

Teacher Comment: **Why do you need to understand how people use the plants and animals where they live?**

Student Response: I need to understand how people use the plants and animals where they live to understand how they get the food, clothing, and shelter that they need.

Page 148: NEEDS OF THE SOUTHWEST TRIBES

LESSON

Introduction

Teacher Comment: **In the last lessons we thought about the clothing, food, and shelter of the Northwest tribes.**

Explaining the Objective

Teacher Comment: **In this lesson you will think about the clothing, food, and shelter of the Southwest tribes.**

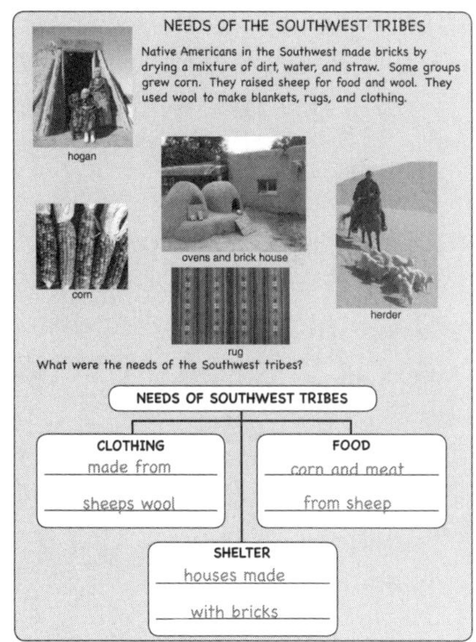

Conducting the Lesson

Teacher Comment: **Native Americans in the southwest made bricks by drying a mixture of dirt, water, and straw. Some groups grew corn. They raised sheep for food and wool. They used wool to make blankets and rugs.**

Teacher Comment: **What kind of clothing did the southwest tribes wear?**

Student Response: The Southwest tribes wore clothing made from sheep's wool.

Teacher Comment: **Write a few words in the "clothing" box to remind you of their clothing.**

Teacher Comment: **What food did the Southwest tribes eat?**

Student Response: The Southwest tribes ate corn and the meat from sheep.

Teacher Comment: **Write a few words in the "food" box to remind you of their food.**

Teacher Comment: **What kind of shelter the Southwest tribes build?**

Student Response: The Southwest tribes built houses made from bricks.

Teacher Comment: **Write a few words in the "shelter" box to remind you of their shelter.**

- Check students' work.

Thinking About Thinking

Teacher Comment: **What did you pay attention to when you described how Southwest tribes met their needs?**

Student Response:
1. I listened to the description.
2. I matched the description to the pictures.
3. I wrote a few words about their clothing, food, and shelter.

Personal Application

Teacher Comment: **Why do you need to understand how people use the plants and animals where they live?**

Student Response: I need to understand how people use the plants and animals where they live to understand how they get the food, clothing, and shelter that they need.

Page 149: NEEDS OF THE PLAINS TRIBES

LESSON

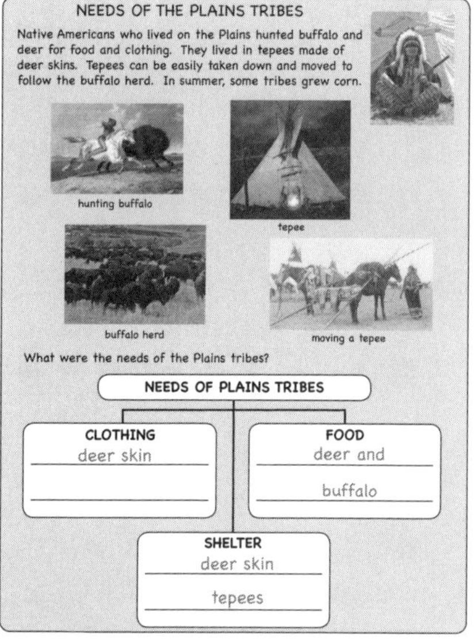
NEEDS OF THE PLAINS TRIBES

Native Americans who lived on the Plains hunted buffalo and deer for food and clothing. They lived in tepees made of deer skins. Tepees can be easily taken down and moved to follow the buffalo herd. In summer, some tribes grew corn.

hunting buffalo

tepee

buffalo herd

moving a tepee

What were the needs of the Plains tribes?

NEEDS OF PLAINS TRIBES

CLOTHING
deer skin

FOOD
deer and
buffalo

SHELTER
deer skin
tepees

Introduction

Teacher Comment: **In the last lesson we thought about the clothing, food, and shelter of the Southwest tribes.**

Explaining the Objective

Teacher Comment: **In this lesson you will think about the clothing, food, and shelter of the Plains tribes.**

Conducting the Lesson

Teacher Comment: **The Plains tribes hunted deer and buffalo for food and clothing. They lived in tepees made of buffalo hides. Tepees can be easily taken down and moved to follow the buffalo herd. In summer, some tribes grew corn.**

Teacher Comment: **What kind of clothing did the Plains tribes wear?**

Student Response: The Plains tribes wore clothing made from deer or buffalo skins.

Teacher Comment: **Write a few words in the "clothing" box to remind you of their clothing.**

Teacher Comment: **What food did the Plains tribes eat?**

Student Response: The Plains tribes ate buffalo, deer, and corn.

Teacher Comment: **Write a few words in the "food" box to remind you of their food.**

Teacher Comment: **What kind of shelter did the Plains tribes build?**

Student Response: The Plains tribes built tepees out of deer skin.

Teacher Comment: **Write a few words in the "shelter" box to remind you of their shelter.**

- Check students' work.

 © 2016 The Critical Thinking Co.™ • www.CriticalThinking.com • 800-458-4849

Thinking About Thinking

Teacher Comment: **What did you pay attention to when you described how Plains tribes met their needs?**

Student Response:

1. I listened to the description.
2. I matched the description to the pictures.
3. I wrote a few words about their clothing, food, and shelter.

Personal Application

Teacher Comment: **Why do you need to understand how people use the plants and animals where they live?**

Student Response: I need to understand how people use the plants and animals where they live to understand how they get the food, clothing, and shelter that they need.

Page 150: NEEDS OF THE NORTHEAST TRIBES

LESSON

Introduction

Teacher Comment: **In the last lesson we thought about the clothing, food, and shelter of the Plains tribes.**

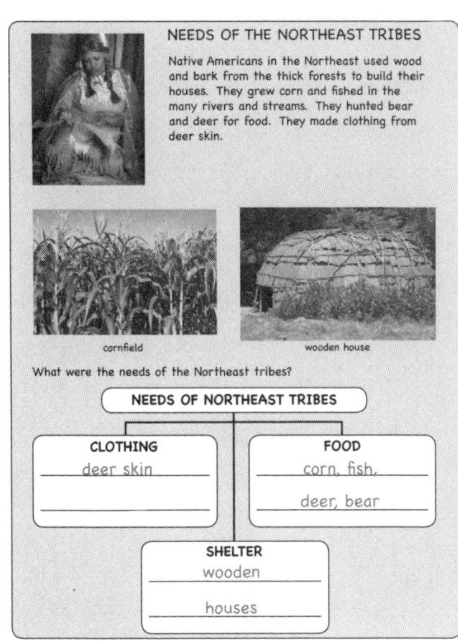

Explaining the Objective

Teacher Comment: **In this lesson you will think about the clothing, food, and shelter of the Northeast tribes.**

Conducting the Lesson

Teacher Comment: **Native Americans in the northeast used wood and bark from the thick forests to build their houses. They grew corn and fished in the many rivers and streams. They hunted bear and deer for food. They made clothing from deer skin. What kind of clothing did the Northeast tribes wear?**

Student Response: The Northeast tribes wore clothing made from deer skins.

Teacher Comment: **Write a few words in the "clothing" box to remind you of their clothing.**

Teacher Comment: **What food did the Northeast tribes eat?**

Student Response: The Northeast tribes ate fish, bear, deer, and corn.

Teacher Comment: **Write a few words in the "food" box to remind you of their food.**

Teacher Comment: **What kind of shelter did the Northeast tribes build?**

Student Response: The Northeast tribes built houses out of wood.

Teacher Comment: **Write a few words in the "shelter" box to remind you of their shelter.**

• Check students' work.

© 2016 The Critical Thinking Co.™ • www.CriticalThinking.com • 800-458-4849

Thinking About Thinking

Teacher Comment: **What did you pay attention to when you described how Northeast tribes met their needs?**

Student Response:

1. I listened to the description.
2. I matched the description to the pictures.
3. I wrote a few words about their clothing, food, and shelter.

Personal Application

Teacher Comment: **Why do you need to understand how people use the plants and animals where they live?**

Student Response: I need to understand how people use the plants and animals where they live to understand how they get the food, clothing, and shelter that they need.

Page 151: NEEDS OF THE SOUTHEAST TRIBES

LESSON

Introduction

Teacher Comment: **In the last lesson we thought about the clothing, food, and shelter of the Northeast tribes.**

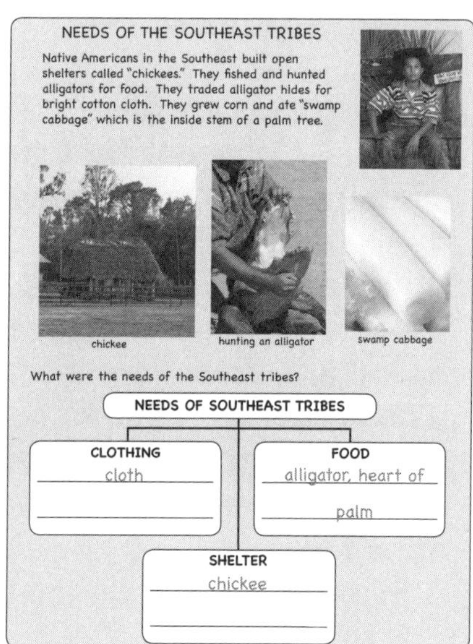

NEEDS OF THE SOUTHEAST TRIBES

Native Americans in the Southeast built open shelters called "chickees." They fished and hunted alligators for food. They traded alligator hides for bright cotton cloth. They grew corn and ate "swamp cabbage" which is the inside stem of a palm tree.

chickee

hunting an alligator

swamp cabbage

What were the needs of the Southeast tribes?

NEEDS OF SOUTHEAST TRIBES

CLOTHING: cloth

FOOD: alligator, heart of palm

SHELTER: chickee

Explaining the Objective

Teacher Comment: **In this lesson you will think about the clothing, food, and shelter of the Southeast tribes.**

Conducting the Lesson

Teacher Comment: **Many Southeast tribes settled in Florida. They built open shelters called "chickees." They fished and hunted alligators for food. They traded alligator hides for bright cotton cloth. They grew corn and ate "swamp cabbage" which is the inside stem of a palm tree.**

Teacher Comment: **What kind of clothing did the Southeast tribes wear?**

Student Response: The Southeast tribes wore colorful clothing made from cloth.

Teacher Comment: **Write "cloth" in the first box.**

Teacher Comment: **What food did the Southeast tribes eat?**

Student Response: The Southeast tribes ate alligator and heart of palm.

Teacher Comment: **Write a few words in the "food" box to remind you of their food.**

Teacher Comment: **What kind of shelter did the Southeast tribes build?**

Student Response: The Southeast tribes built open chickees out of wood.

Teacher Comment: **Write a few words in the "shelter" box to remind you of their shelter.**

© 2016 The Critical Thinking Co.™ • www.CriticalThinking.com • 800-458-4849

• Check students' work.

Thinking About Thinking

Teacher Comment: **What did you pay attention to when you described how Southeast tribes met their needs?**

Student Response:

1. I listened to the description.
2. I matched the description to the pictures.
3. I wrote a few words about their clothing, food, and shelter.

Personal Application

Teacher Comment: **Why do you need to understand how people use the plants and animals where they live?**

Student Response: I need to understand how people use the plants and animals where they live to understand how they get the food, clothing, and shelter that they need.

Page 152: NEEDS OF THE COLONISTS

LESSON

Introduction

Teacher Comment: **We have thought about the needs of Native Americans in different parts of our country. The people from Europe who came to America to build homes and villages were called "colonists." They brought some seeds and animals, but they also had to rely on the plants and animals where they settled.**

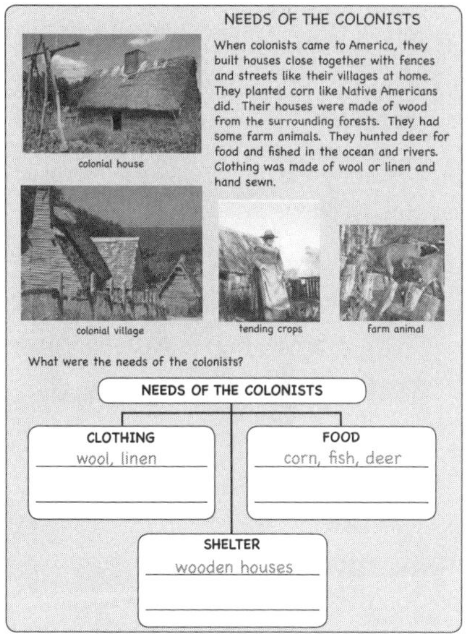

NEEDS OF THE COLONISTS

When colonists came to America, they built houses close together with fences and streets like their villages at home. They planted corn like Native Americans did. Their houses were made of wood from the surrounding forests. They had some farm animals. They hunted deer for food and fished in the ocean and rivers. Clothing was made of wool or linen and hand sewn.

colonial house

colonial village

tending crops

farm animal

What were the needs of the colonists?

NEEDS OF THE COLONISTS

CLOTHING: wool, linen

FOOD: corn, fish, deer

SHELTER: wooden houses

Explaining the Objective

Teacher Comment: **In this lesson you will think about the clothing, food, and shelter of the colonists.**

Conducting the lesson

Teacher Comment: **When colonists came to America, they built houses close together with fences and streets like their villages at home. They planted corn like Native Americans did. Their houses were made of wood from the surrounding forests. They had some farm animals. They hunted deer for food and fished in the ocean and rivers.**

Teacher Comment: **What kind of clothing did the colonists wear?**

Student Response: The colonists wore clothing made from wool and linen.

Teacher Comment: **Write "wool and linen" in the first box.**

Teacher Comment: **What food did the colonists eat?**

Student Response: The colonists ate corn, fish, and deer.

Teacher Comment: **Write a few words in the "food" box to remind you of their food.**

Teacher Comment: **What kind of shelter the colonists build?**

Student Response: The colonists built houses from wood.

Teacher Comment: **Write a few words in the "shelter" box to remind you of their shelter.**

• Check students' work.

Thinking About Thinking

Teacher Comment: **What did you pay attention to when you described how colonists met their needs?**

Student Response:

1. I listened to the description.
2. I matched the description to the pictures.
3. I wrote a few words about their clothing, food, and shelter.

Personal Application

Teacher Comment: **Why do you need to understand how people use the plants and animals where they live?**

Student Response: I need to understand how people use the plants and animals where they live to understand how they get the food, clothing, and shelter that they need.

Page 153: WHAT AMERICANS NEED – THEN AND NOW

LESSON

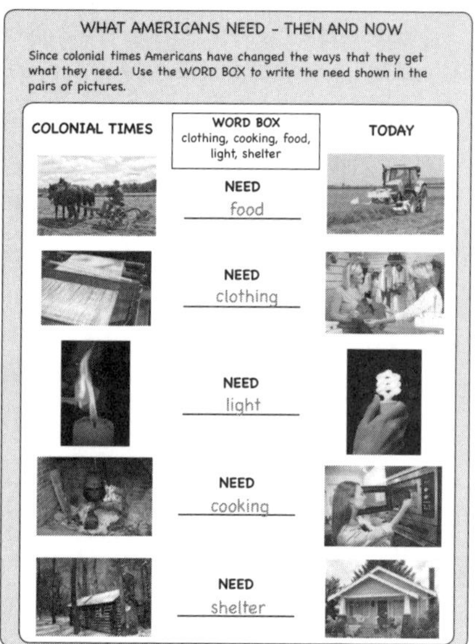
WHAT AMERICANS NEED - THEN AND NOW

Since colonial times Americans have changed the ways that they get what they need. Use the WORD BOX to write the need shown in the pairs of pictures.

COLONIAL TIMES | WORD BOX: clothing, cooking, food, light, shelter | TODAY

NEED food

NEED clothing

NEED light

NEED cooking

NEED shelter

Introduction

Teacher Comment: **In the last lesson we thought about the clothing, food, and shelter of the colonists. People today have the same needs, but have different ways of getting what they need.**

Explaining the Objective

Teacher Comment: **In this lesson you will look at a pair of pictures and tell what need is shown.**

Conducting the Lesson

• Extend this lesson by asking students how the pictures show that people meet these needs differently today than in colonial times.

Teacher Comment: **Look at the first pair of pictures. How do the pictures show people getting what they need?**

Student Response: The farmers are plowing their fields. Plowing is the first step in growing food.

Teacher Comment: **What need does farming fill?**

Student Response: Farming provides food.

Teacher Comment: **How do the pictures show that today people get their food differently than in colonial times?**

© 2016 The Critical Thinking Co.™ • www.CriticalThinking.com • 800-458-4849

Student Response: Colonial farmers plowed with horses to grow a little bit of food. Today farmers plow large fields with a tractor to grow more food.

Teacher Comment: **Write "food" on the first line.**

Teacher Comment: **Look at the second pair of pictures. How do the pictures show people getting what they need?**

Student Response: People are making or buying clothes.

Teacher Comment: **How do the pictures show that today people get their clothes differently than in colonial times?**

Student Response: People in colonial times made their own clothes. People today buy their clothes.

Teacher Comment: **Write "clothing" on the SECOND line.**

Teacher Comment: **Look at the next pair of pictures. How do the pictures show what people use to get what they need?**

Student Response: People use candles or light bulbs to get light.

Teacher Comment: **How do the pictures show that today people get light differently than in colonial times?**

Student Response: People in colonial times used candles to get a little light for a short time. People today use light bulbs that give more light and last a long time.

Teacher Comment: **Write "light" on the line.**

Teacher Comment: **Look at the next pair of pictures. How do the pictures show what people use to get what they need?**

Student Response: People use heat to cook their food.

Teacher Comment: **How do the pictures show that today people cook differently than in colonial times?**

Student Response: People in colonial times used fire to cook their food. People today use stoves or microwave ovens to cook their food.

Teacher Comment: **Write "cooking" on the line.**

Teacher Comment: **Look at the next pair of pictures. How do the pictures show what people use to get what they need?**

Student Response: People build houses for shelter.

Teacher Comment: **How do the pictures show that today people's houses are different than in colonial times?**

Student Response: People in colonial times used wood to build small houses. People today use wood and other materials to build larger houses.

Teacher Comment: **Write "shelter" on the line.**

- Check students' work.

Teacher Comment: **We see that people's needs are the same, but how they get what they need has changed since colonial times. Tell your partner why you think that people today can get what they need more easily.**

- Second grade students are just beginning to learn about technology, the significance of divisions of labor, or details of colonial life. The following discussion helps them develop a simplified understanding that the way people meet their basic needs today is easier than in colonial times.

Teacher Comment: **Why do you think that people today can get what they need more easily?**

Student Response: Answers will vary, but should include that machines and electricity make it easier and faster to get what we need. Students may explain that today people buy most of what they need, that many people in the community have special skills to help them, and that transportation today lets families buy things that are produced far away. Students may realize that the many people who provide services today help us to have or do what families in colonial times had to do for themselves.

Thinking About Thinking

Teacher Comment: **What did you think about when you told how the things people use today to get what they need are different from colonial times?**

Student Response:

1. I decided what need was shown in picture of colonial times.
2. I checked that the same need in today's family was shown in the second picture.
3. I looked at the details to tell how today's families get what they need much more easily than in colonial times.

Personal Application

Teacher Comment: **When do you need to tell the difference in the way people meet their needs?**

Student Response: I need to tell the difference in how people meet their needs to explain how different groups of people use what they have and work together. I need to understand how the way people meet their needs has changed since colonial times.

Page 154: ANALOGIES ABOUT OUR COUNTRY

LESSON

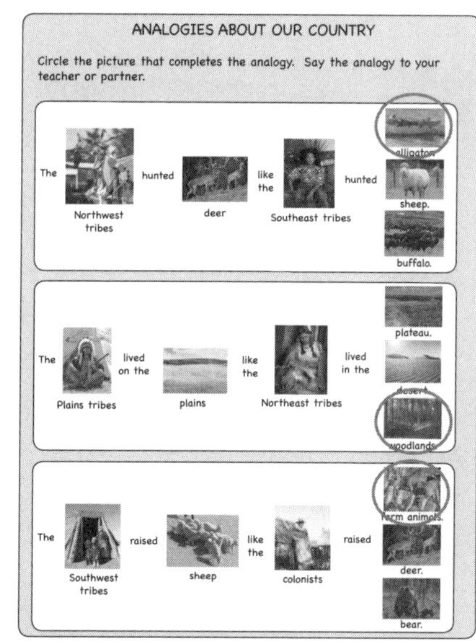

Introduction

Teacher Comment: **We have discussed how people get what they need.**

Explaining the Objective

Teacher Comment: **In this lesson you will compare how different groups get what they need by showing analogies.**

Conducting the Lesson

Teacher Comment: **An analogy is a comparison of two pairs of things. In the first box you see that Northwest tribes hunted deer. The word "LIKE" signals that you will tell the same thing about Southeast tribes. What did Southeast tribes hunt?**

Student Response: The Southeast tribes hunted alligators.

© 2016 The Critical Thinking Co.™ • www.CriticalThinking.com • 800-458-4849

Teacher Comment: **Say the first analogy.**

Student Response: The Northwest tribes hunted deer like the Southeast tribes hunted alligators.

Teacher Comment: **Why do the other animals not fit the analogy?**

Student Response: Southeast tribes didn't raise sheep. Buffaloes lived in the plains, not in the wetlands.

Teacher Comment: **Circle the picture of the alligator.**

Teacher Comment: **In the next box you see that Plains tribes lived on the plains. The word "LIKE" signals that you will tell the same thing about Northeast tribes. Where did Northeast tribes live?**

Student Response: The Northeast tribes lived in the woodlands.

Teacher Comment: **Say the analogy.**

Student Response: The Plains tribes lived on the plains like the Northeast tribes lived in the woodlands.

Teacher Comment: **Why do the other land forms not fit the analogy?**

Student Response: The northeast has woodlands, not plateaus or deserts.

Teacher Comment: **Circle the picture of the woodlands.**

Teacher Comment: **In the next box you see that Southwest tribes raised sheep. The word "LIKE" signals that you will tell the same thing about the colonists. What did the colonists raise?**

Student Response: The colonists raised farm animals.

Teacher Comment: **Say the analogy.**

Student Response: The Southwest tribes raised sheep like the colonists raised farm animals.

Teacher Comment: **Why do the other animals not fit the analogy?**

Student Response: Bear and deer are wild animals that live in the woodlands.

Teacher Comment: **Circle the picture of the farm animal.**

- Check students' work.

Thinking About Thinking

Teacher Comment: **What did you think about to explain analogies?**

Student Response:

1. I thought about how the first two pictures were connected.
2. I decided which picture would show that same connection.
3. I said the analogy to be sure.
4. I checked that the other two pictures did not fit.

Personal Application

Teacher Comment: **When do you need to explain the same thing about two groups of people?**

Student Response: I need to explain the same thing about two groups of people when I need to tell something important about both of them.

APPENDIX

GRAPHIC MASTERS

The following graphics may be used to produce transparencies. They also may be photocopied for distribution to your class.

© 2016 The Critical Thinking Co.™ • www.CriticalThinking.com • 800-458-4849

GRAPHIC MASTER 1 - Pattern of a Cube

Use with lesson on solids - page 23

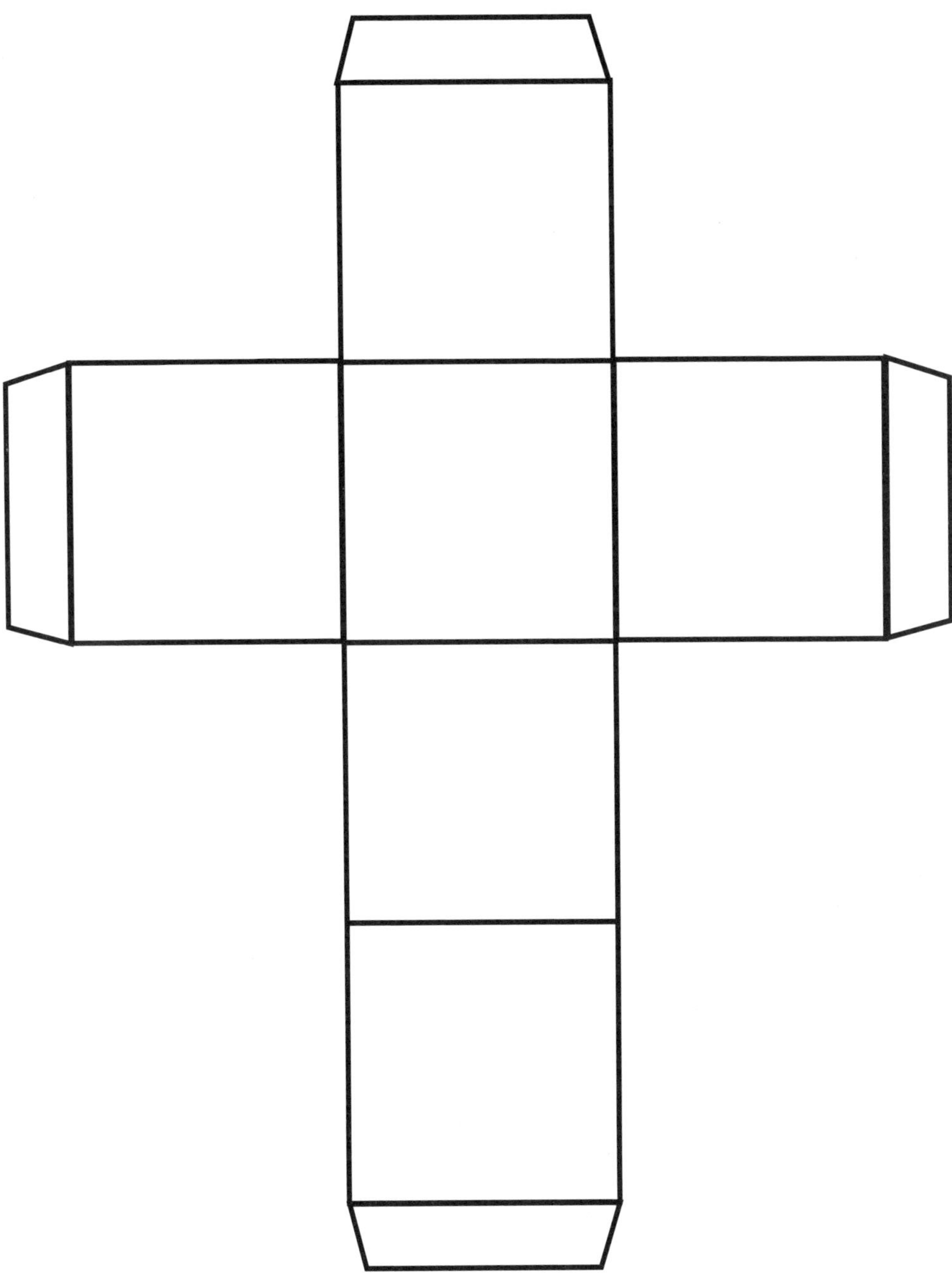

© 2016 The Critical Thinking Co.™ • www.CriticalThinking.com • 800-458-4849

GRAPHIC MASTER 2 - Pattern of a Rectangular Prism
Use with lesson on solids - page 23

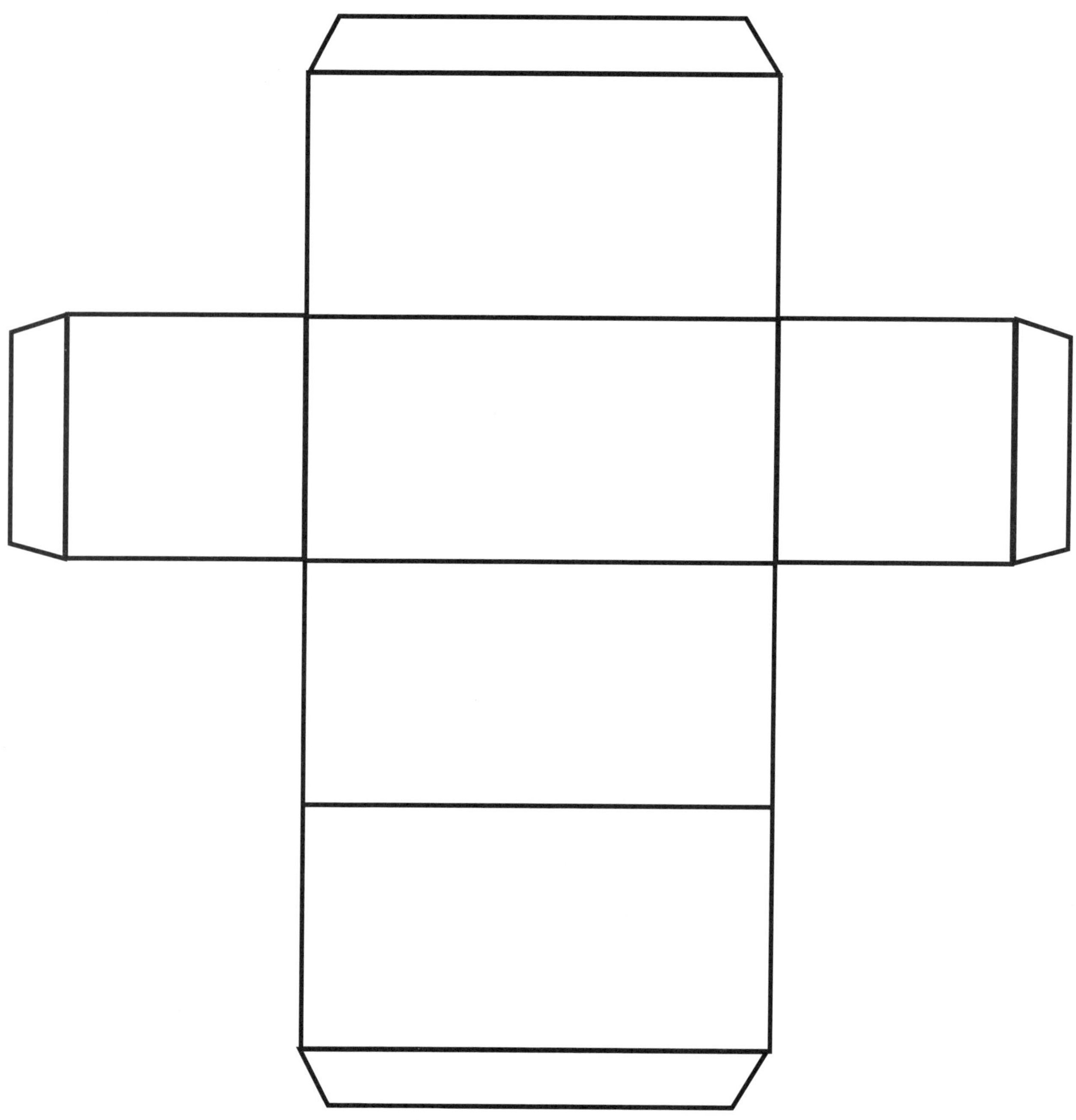

© 2016 The Critical Thinking Co.™ • www.CriticalThinking.com • 800-458-4849

GRAPHIC MASTER 3 - Pattern of a Pyramid
Use with lesson on solids - page 23

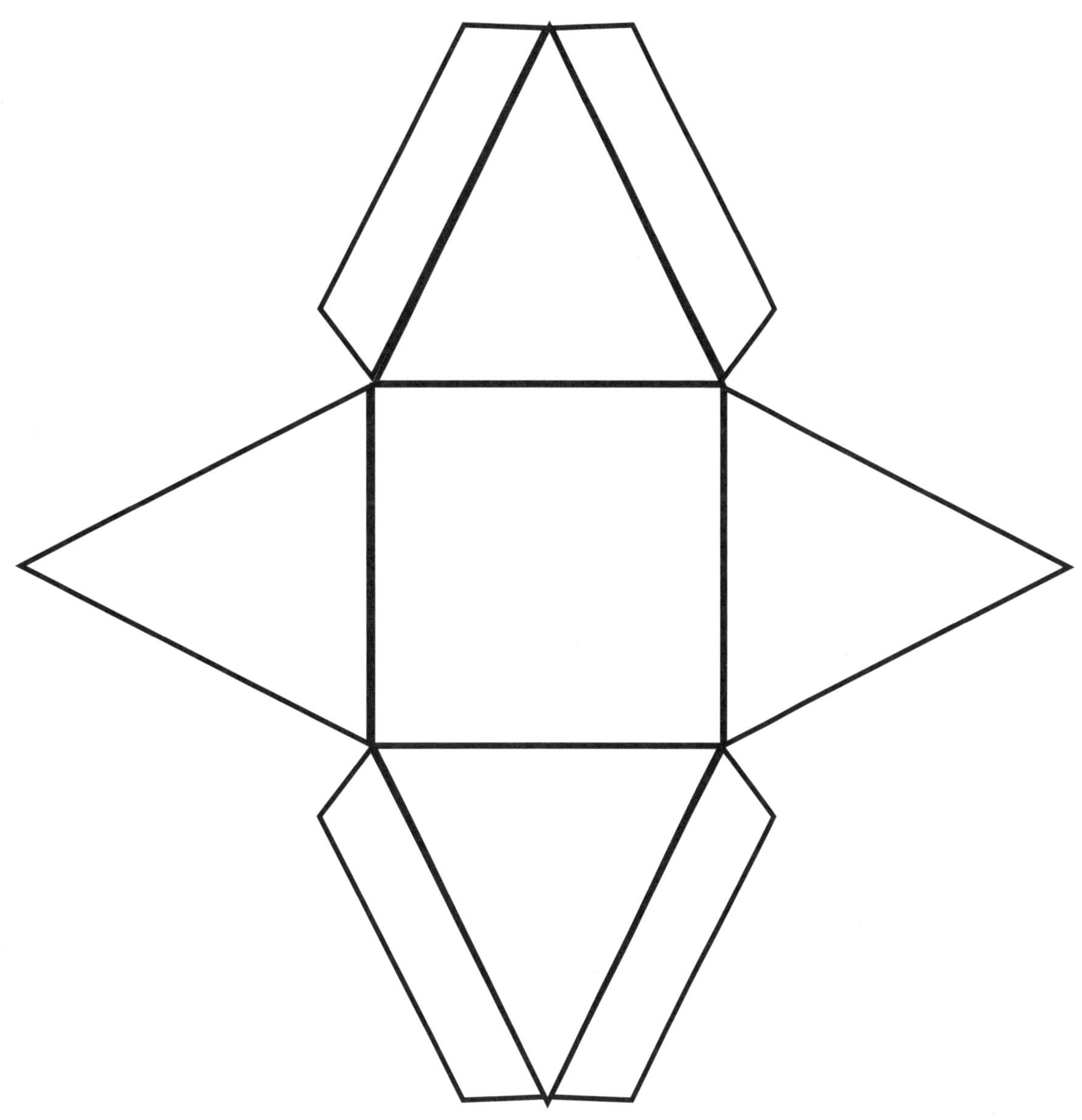

© 2016 The Critical Thinking Co.™ • www.CriticalThinking.com • 800-458-4849

GRAPHIC MASTER 4 - Animal List

ANIMALS

alligator
ant
bat
bear
beaver
bee
blue jay
butterfly
camel
caterpillar
catfish
chicken
cow
deer
duck
eagle
elephant
fish
frog
giraffe
goat
goldfish
grasshopper
horse
lizard
ostrich
owl
prairie dog
rabbit
salmon
shark
sheep
snake
spider
squirrel
tadpole
tuna
turkey
turtle
whale
zebra

© 2016 The Critical Thinking Co.™ • www.CriticalThinking.com • 800-458-4849

GRAPHIC MASTER 5 - Jobs List

JOBS

architect
artist
baker
bank teller
bus driver
carpenter
construction worker
cook
dentist
doctor
electrician
farmer
firefighter
grocer
lawyer
librarian
mail carrier
nurse
pharmacist
pilot
plumber
police officer
sales clerk
sanitation worker
server
teacher

© 2016 The Critical Thinking Co.™ • www.CriticalThinking.com • 800-458-4849

GRAPHIC MASTER 6 - Compare Graphic
Use to show how two family members, foods, animals, occupations, vehicles or buildings are alike.

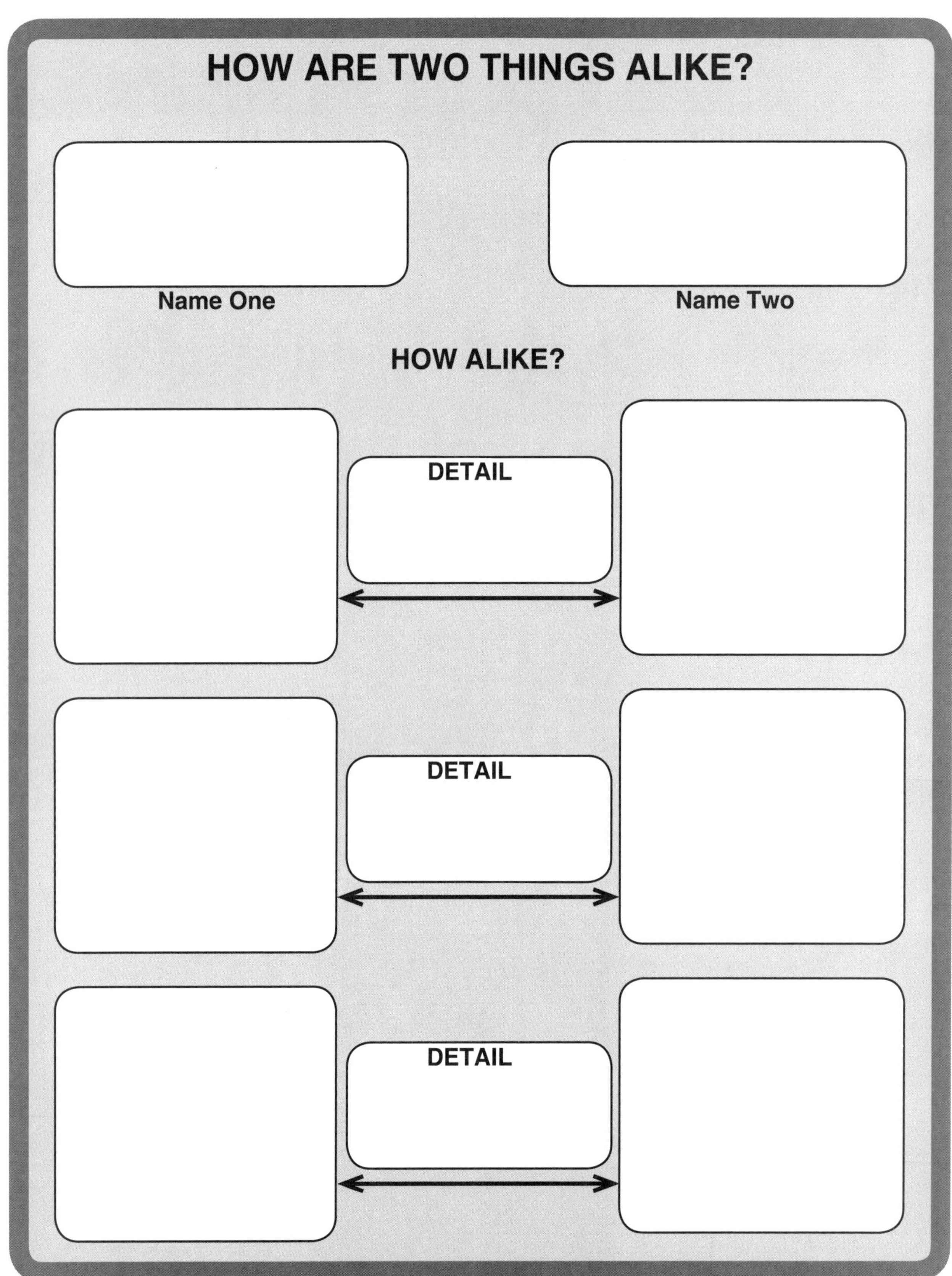

© 2016 The Critical Thinking Co.™ • www.CriticalThinking.com • 800-458-4849

GRAPHIC MASTER 7 - Contrast Graphic

Use to show how two family members, foods, animals, occupations, vehicles or buildings are different.

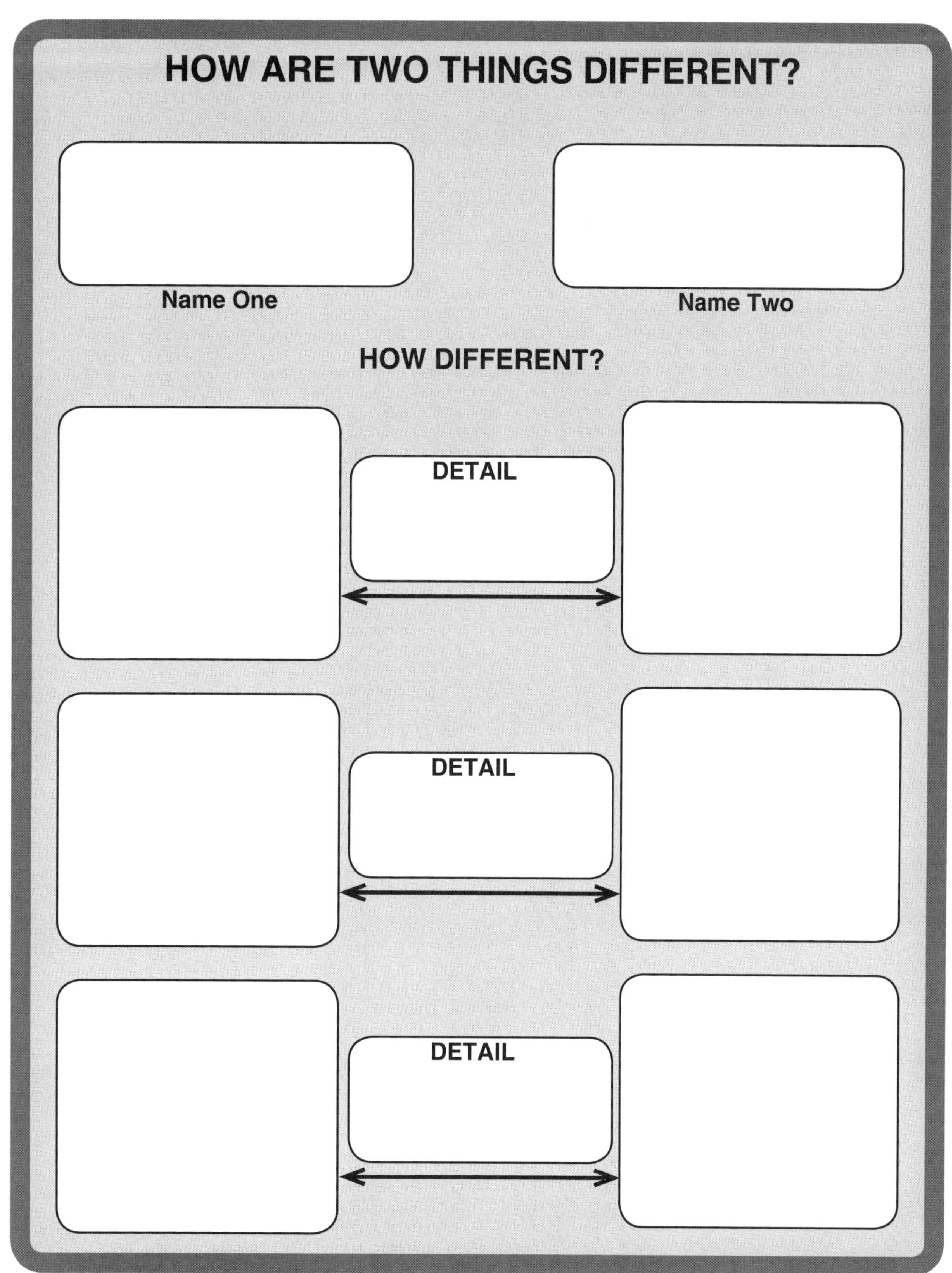

GRAPHIC MASTER 8 - Compare and Contrast Graphic

Use to show how two family members, foods, animals, occupations, vehicles or buildings are alike and different.

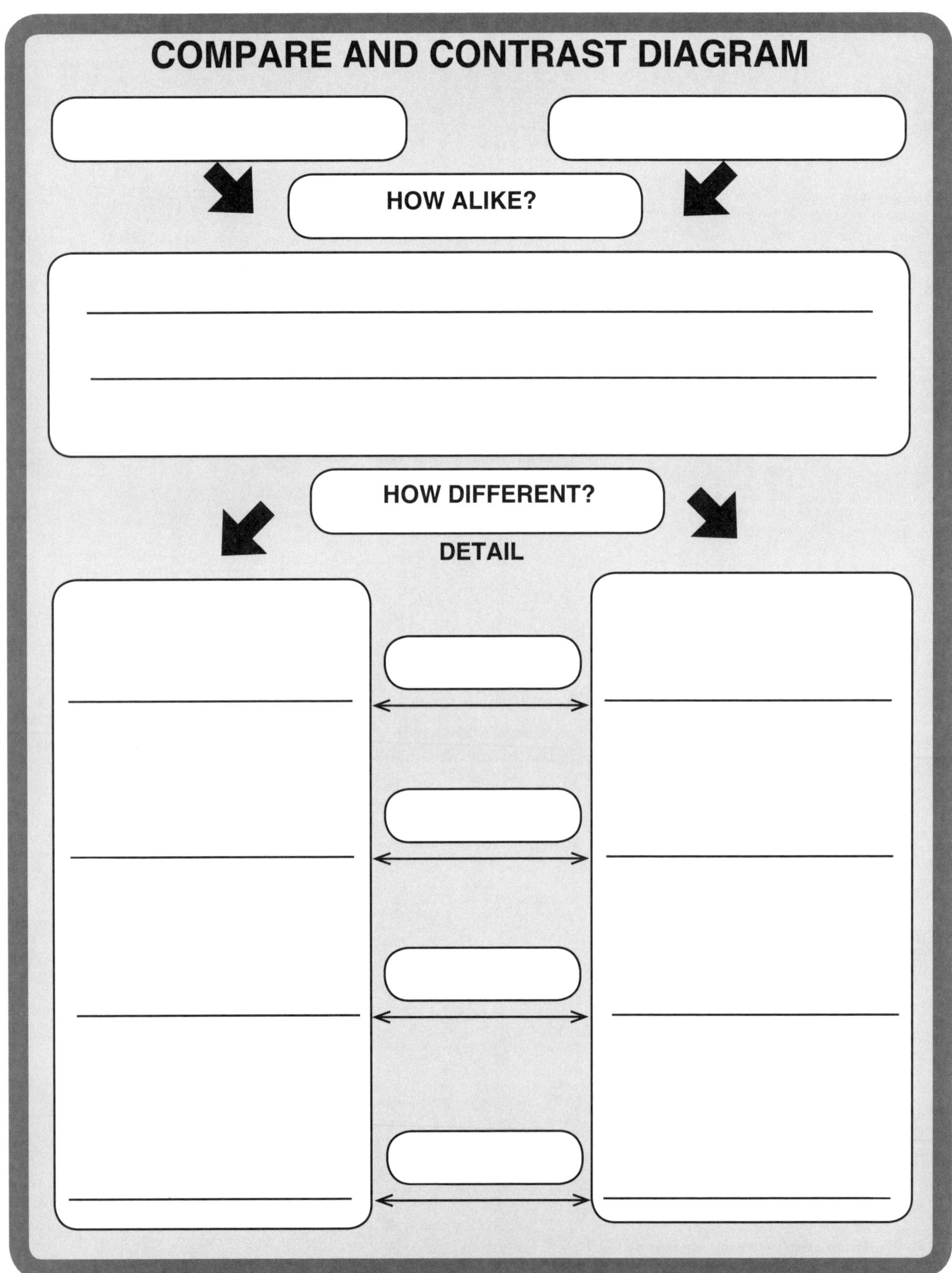

© 2016 The Critical Thinking Co.™ • www.CriticalThinking.com • 800-458-4849

GRAPHIC MASTER 9 - Central Idea Graphic

Use to show a examples of land forms, bodies of water, food, animals, occupations, vehicles or buildings.

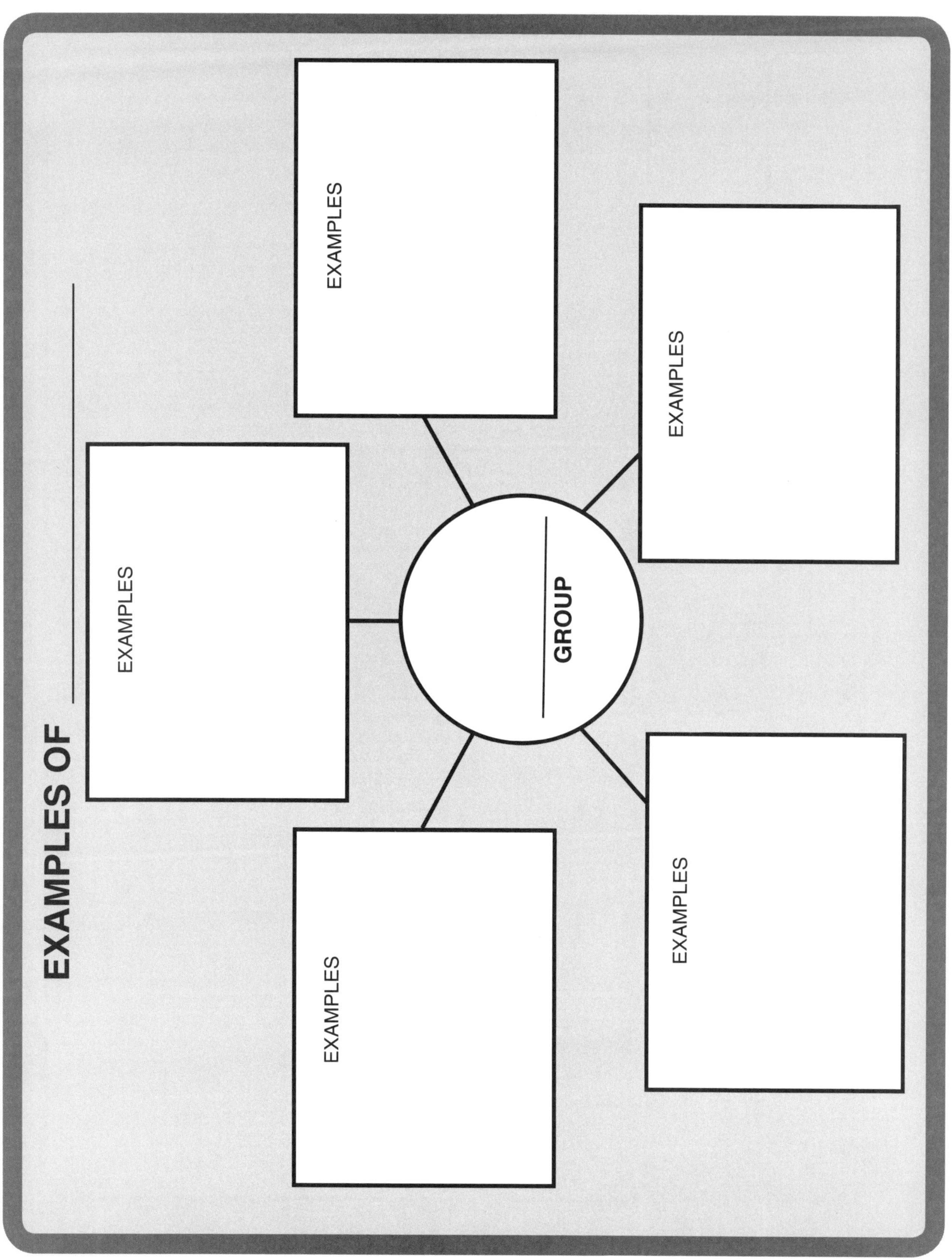

GRAPHIC MASTER 10 - Branching Diagram
Use to sort a group into two classes.

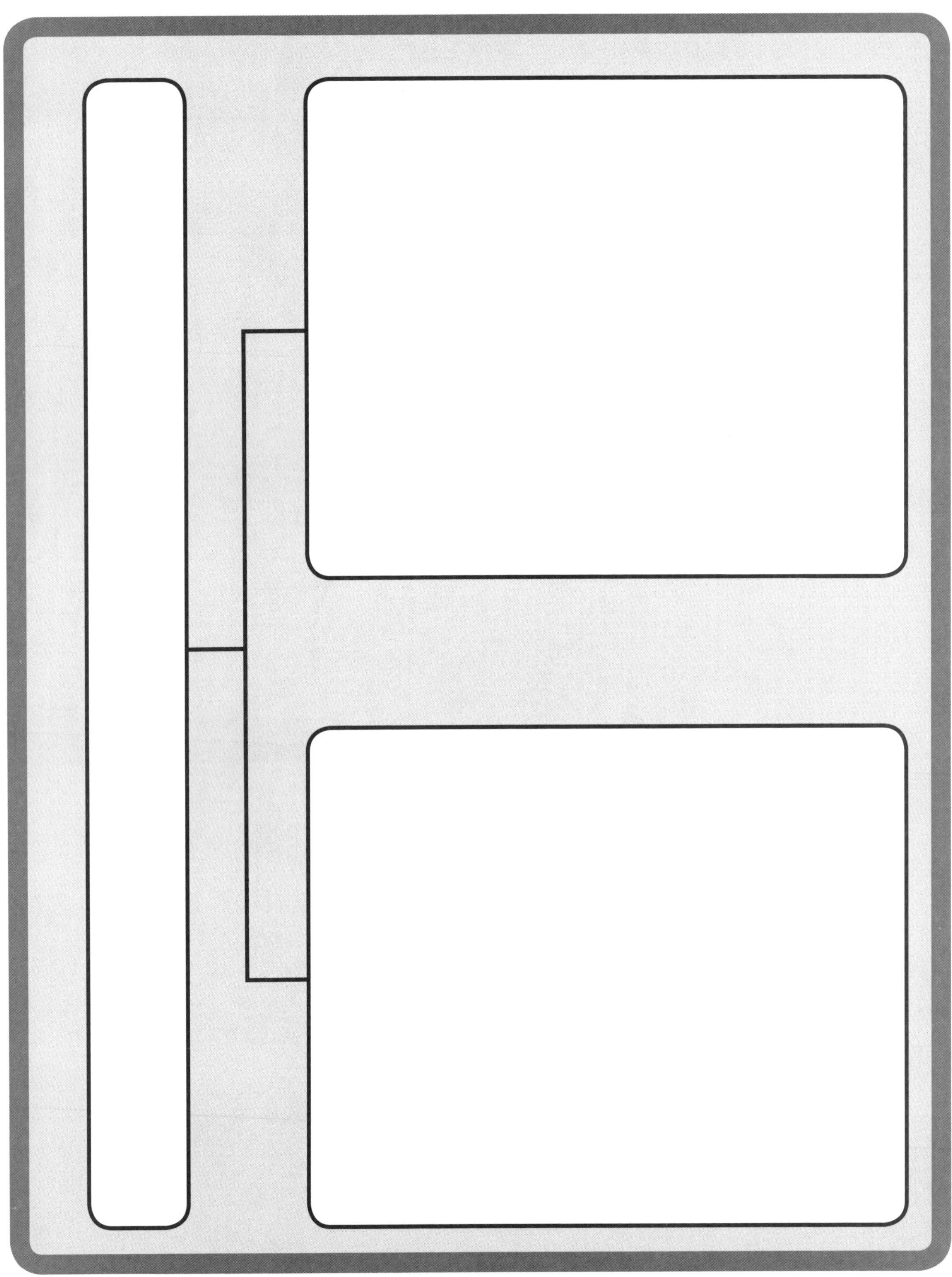

© 2016 The Critical Thinking Co.™ • www.CriticalThinking.com • 800-458-4849

GRAPHIC MASTER 11 - Branching Diagram
Use to sort a group into three classes.

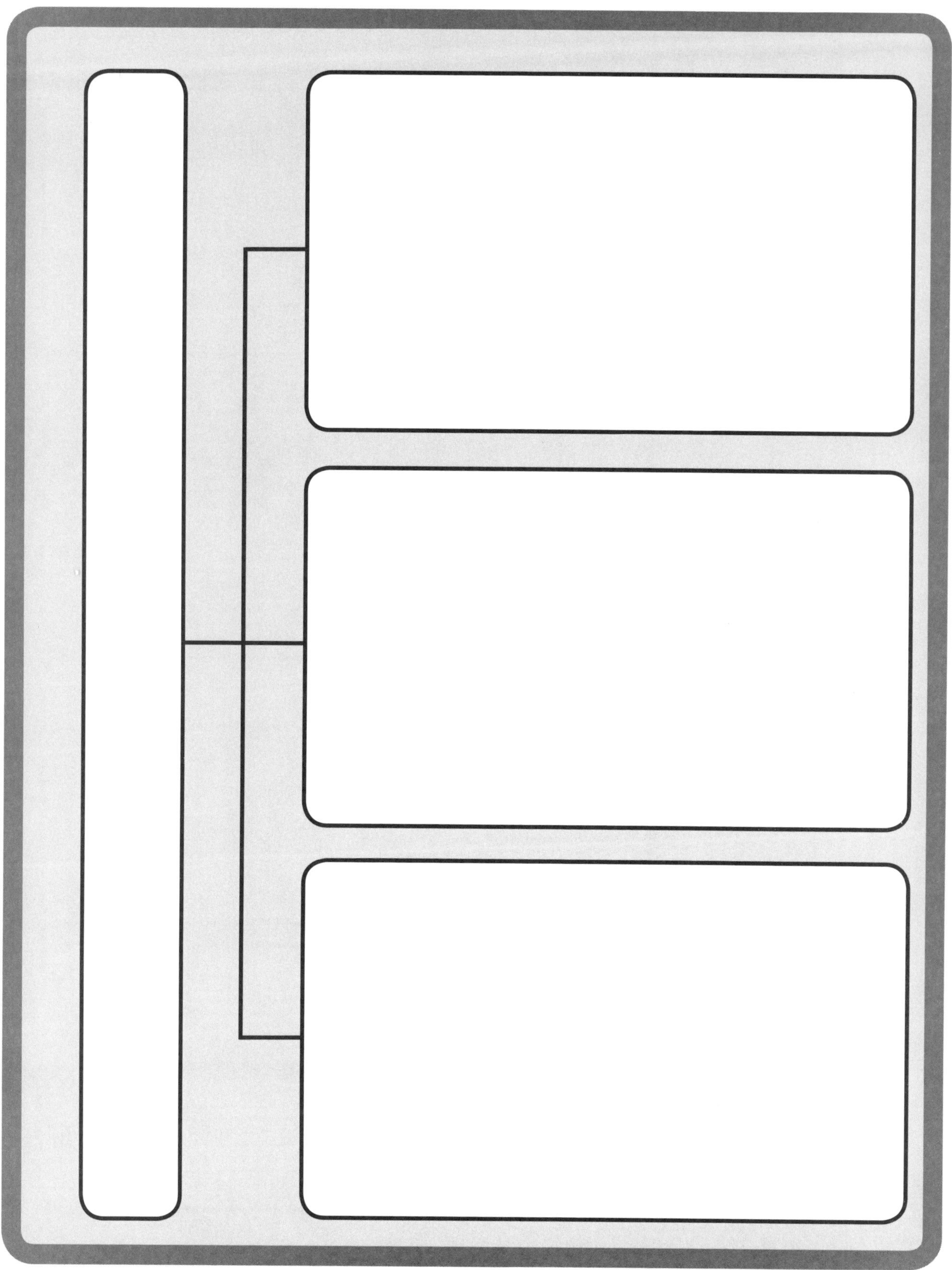

GRAPHIC MASTER 12 - Branching Diagram
Use to sort a group into four classes.

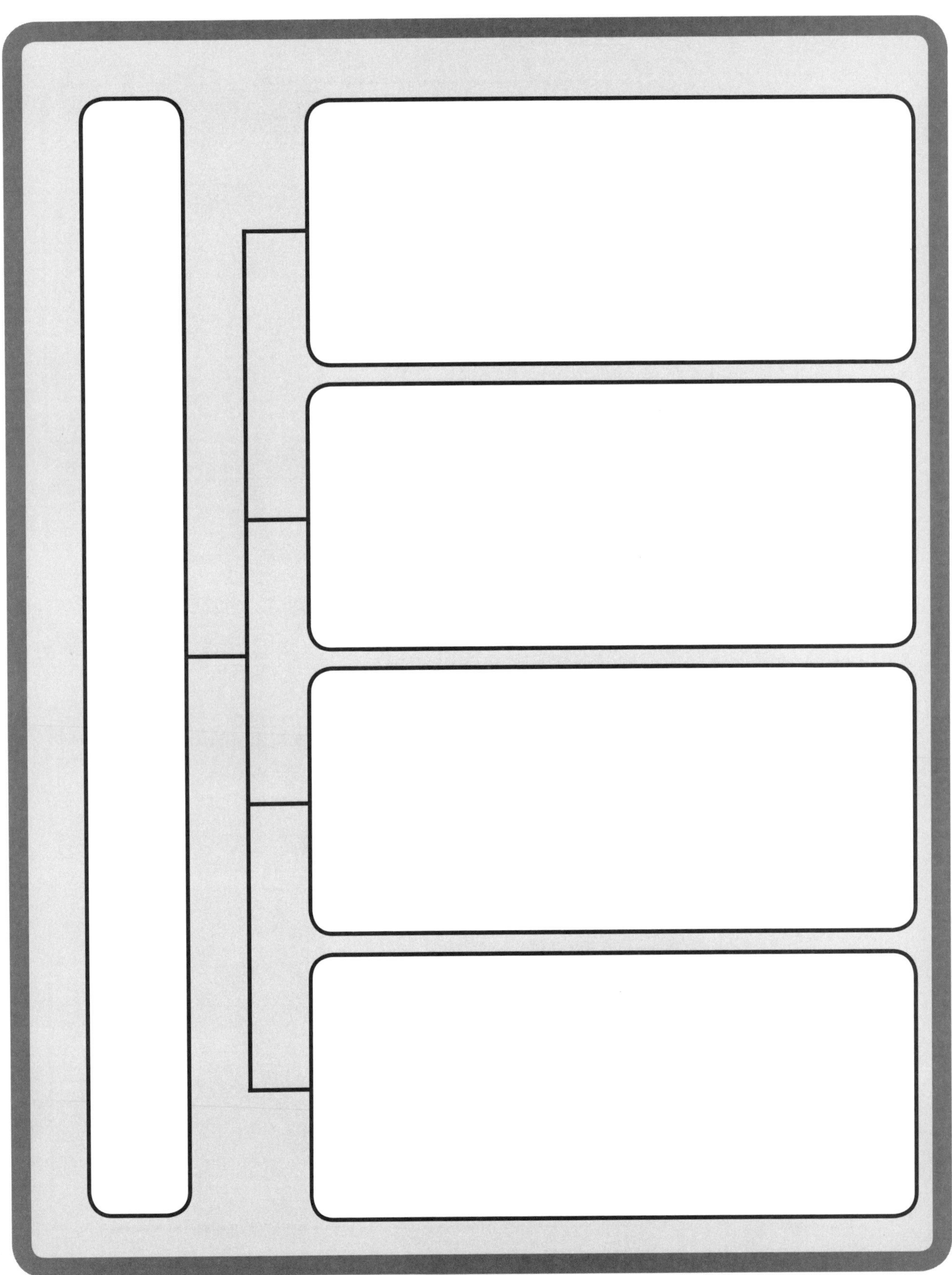

© 2016 The Critical Thinking Co.™ • www.CriticalThinking.com • 800-458-4849

GRAPHIC MASTER 13 - Sequencing Diagram

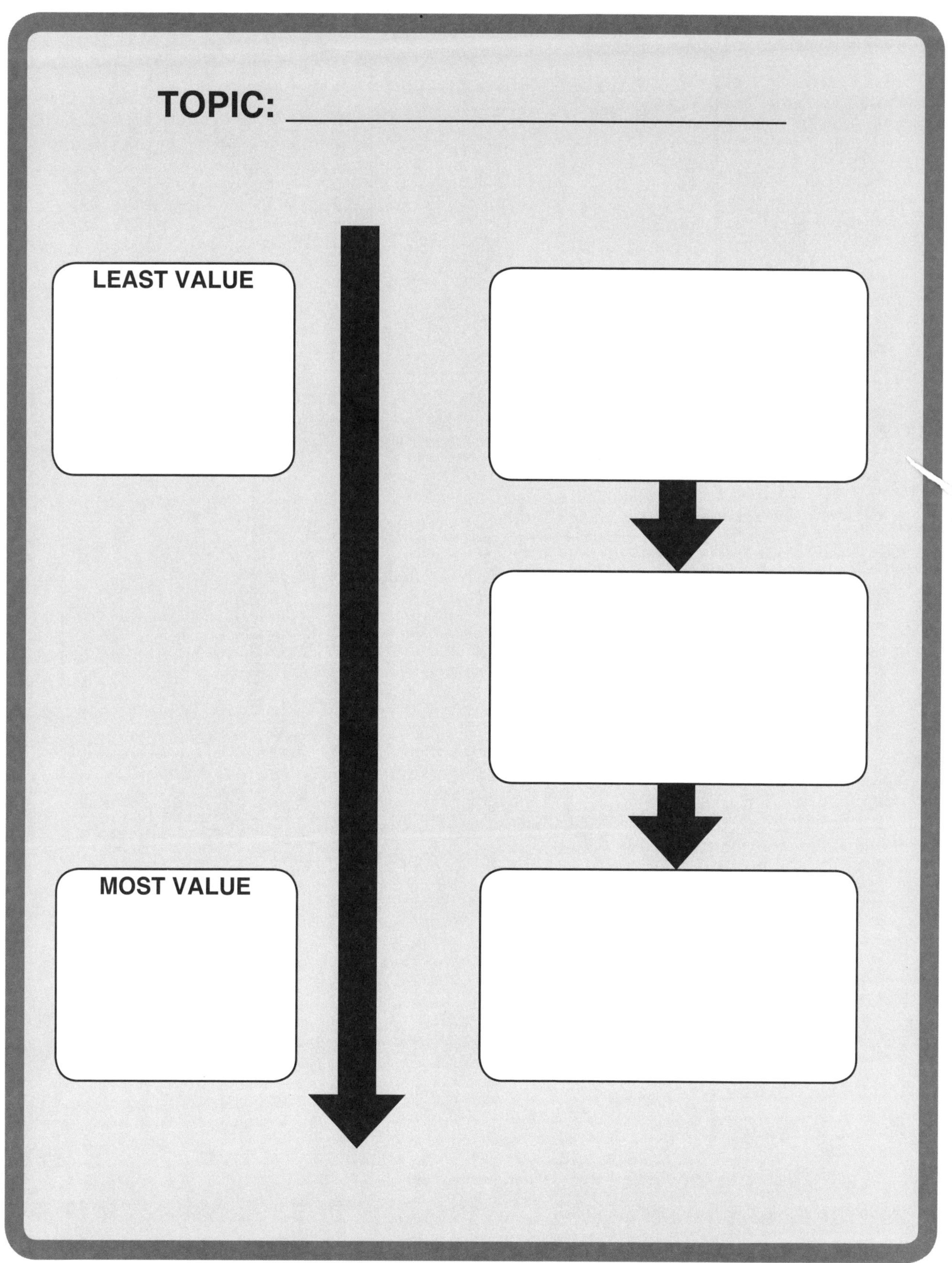

© 2016 The Critical Thinking Co.™ • www.CriticalThinking.com • 800-458-4849

GRAPHIC MASTER 14 - Mental Model of an Animal

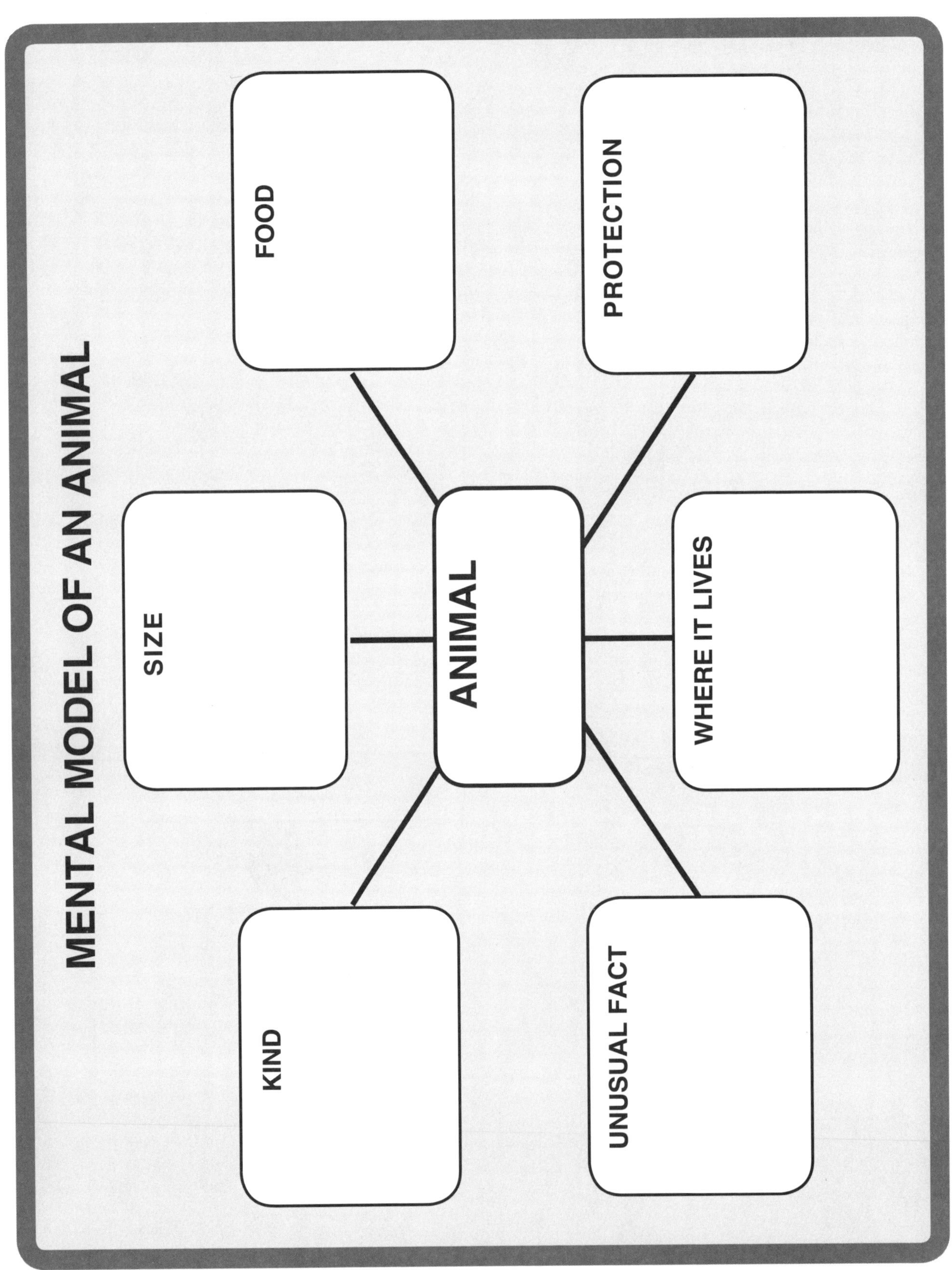

© 2016 The Critical Thinking Co.™ • www.CriticalThinking.com • 800-458-4849

GRAPHIC MASTER 15 - Mental Model of a Job

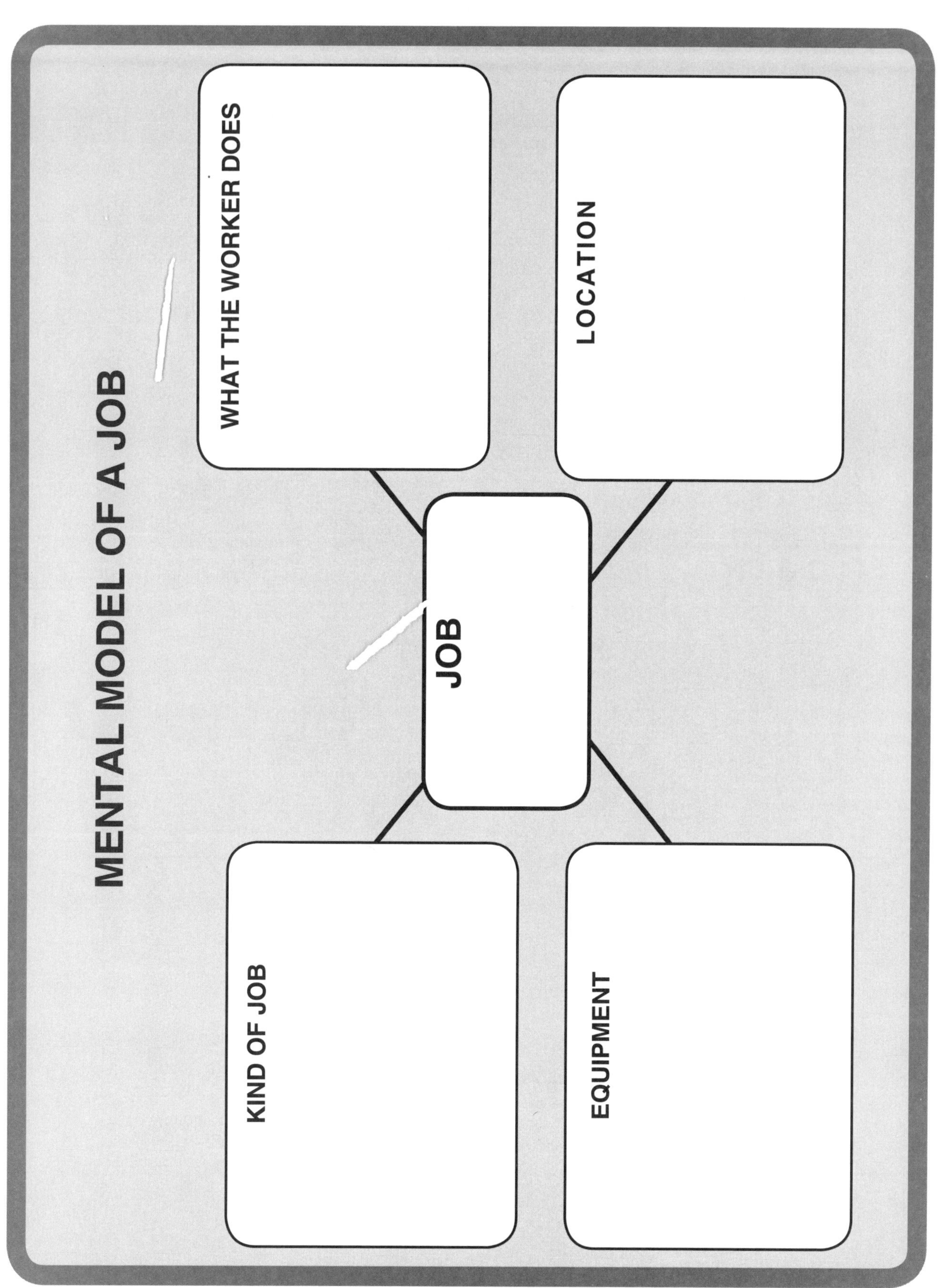

GRAPHIC MASTER 16 - Mental Model of What a Family Needs

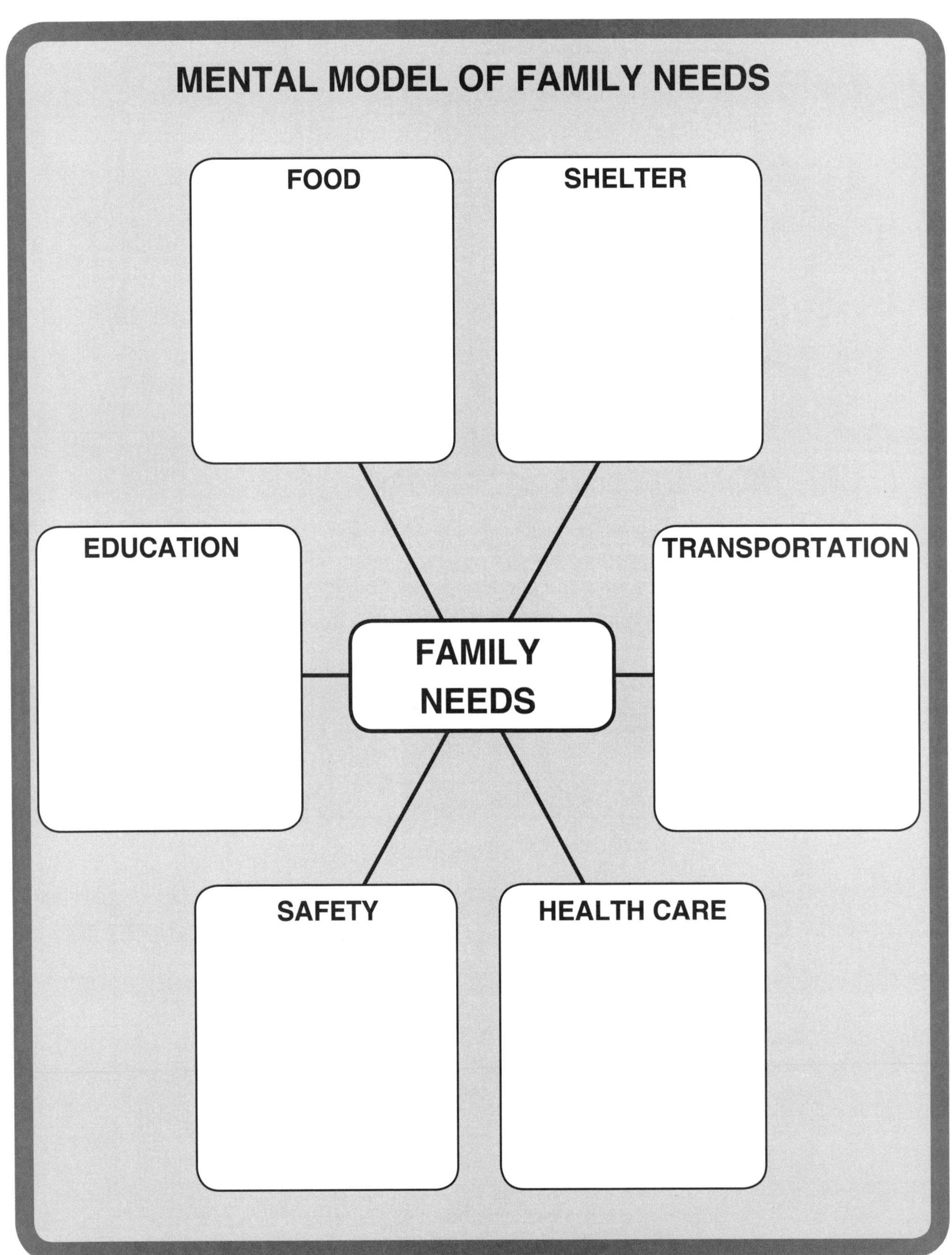

 © 2016 The Critical Thinking Co.™ • www.CriticalThinking.com • 800-458-4849

GRAPHIC MASTER 17 - Mental Model of a Community

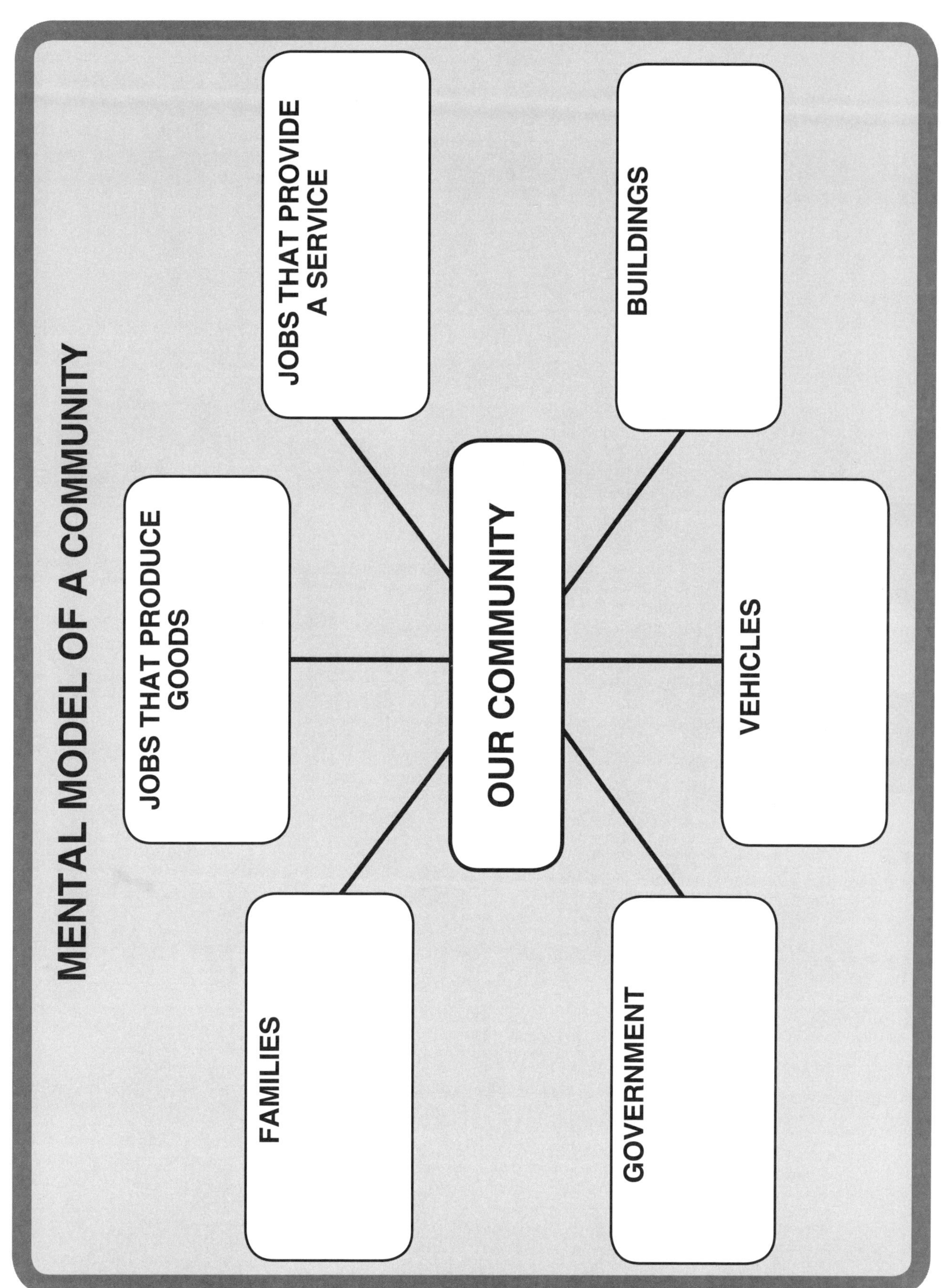

© 2016 The Critical Thinking Co.™ • www.CriticalThinking.com • 800-458-4849